BRITISH POETRY FROM THE 1950s TO THE 1990s

British Poetry from the 1950s to the 1990s

Politics and Art

Edited by

Gary Day

and

Brian Docherty

First published in Great Britain 1997 by
MACMILLAN PRESS LTD
Houndmills, Basingstoke, Hampshire RG21 6XS and London
Companies and representatives throughout the world

A catalogue record for this book is available from the British Library.

ISBN 0–333–53280–5 hardcover
ISBN 0–333–53281–3 paperback

 First published in the United States of America 1997 by
ST. MARTIN'S PRESS, INC.,
Scholarly and Reference Division,
175 Fifth Avenue, New York, N.Y. 10010

ISBN 0–312–17250–8

Library of Congress Cataloging-in-Publication Data
British poetry from the 1950s to the 1990s : politics and art / edited
by Gary Day and Brian Docherty.
p. cm.
Includes bibliographical references and index.
ISBN 0–312–17250–8 (cloth)
1. English poetry—20th century—History and criticism.
2. Literature and society—Great Britain—History—20th century.
3. Politics and literature—Great Britain—History—20th century.
4. Criticism—Great Britain—History—20th century. 5. Influence
(Literary, artistic, etc.) I. Day, Gary, 1956– . II. Docherty,
Brian.
PR603.B75   1997
821'.91409—dc21   96–44311
                                                        CIP

This book is printed on paper suitable for recycling and made from fully managed and sustained forest sources.

10   9   8   7   6   5   4   3   2   1
06   05   04   03   02   01   00   99   98   97

Printed and bound in Great Britain by
Antony Rowe Ltd, Chippenham, Wiltshire

For Charlotte
who likes to 'swing in the pie'

Contents

Acknowledgements   ix

Notes on the Contributors   x

1   Introduction: Poetry, Politics and Tradition
    Gary Day   1

2   Basil Bunting: *Briggflatts*
    Dennis Brown   23

3   'Never Such Innocence Again': the Poetry of Philip
    Larkin
    Gary Day   33

4   Poetic Subjects: Tony Harrison and Peter Reading
    Neil Roberts   48

5   Salvaged from the Ruins: Ken Smith's Constellations
    Stan Smith   63

6   Dance of Being: the Poetry of Peter Redgrove
    Neil Roberts   87

7   Seamus Heaney: From Revivalism to Postmodernism
    Alistair Davies   103

8   'Some Sweet Disorder' – the Poetry of Subversion:
    Paul Muldoon, Tom Paulin and Medbh McGuckian
    Elmer Andrews   118

9   The Gaelic Renaissance: Sorley MacLean and Derick
    Thomson
    Christopher Whyte   143

10 Edwin Morgan: Messages and Transformations
    Roderick Watson   170

11 'Half of My Seeing': the English Poetry of Iain
   Crichton Smith
   Colin Milton   193

12 Vernon Watkins and R.S. Thomas
   Dennis Brown   221

13 Anthologies of Women's Poetry: Canon-Breakers;
   Canon-Makers
   Jane Dowson   237

14 Women Poets and 'Women's Poetry': Fleur Adcock,
   Gillian Clarke and Carol Rumens
   Lyn Pykett   253

15 They Say, They Say, They Say: Some New Voices of the
   Nineties
   Michael Faherty   268

   Index   280

Acknowledgements

The editors and publishers wish to thank Anvil Press Poetry for permission to reproduce the extract from *Mean Time* by Carol Ann Duffy; Bloodaxe Books for permission to reproduce the extract from *Out of the Rain* by Glynn Maxwell; Carcanet Press for permission to reproduce extracts from *Edwin Morgan: Collected Poems*; Faber & Faber for permission to reproduce the extract from *The Dead Sea Poems* by Simon Armitage; Oxford University Press for permission to reproduce the extract from *Phrase Book* by Jo Shapcott.

We would also like to acknowledge Charmian Hearne for her help in guiding this book to publication and Deborah Day for preparing the index.

Notes on the Contributors

Elmer Andrews is a Lecturer in English at the University of Ulster, Coleraine. He has written widely on Irish poetry and his latest book is a study of the playwright Brian Friel.

Dennis Brown is a Professor of English at the University of Hertfordshire. He has written widely on modern poetry including *The Poetry of Postmodernity* (1994).

Alistair Davies is a Lecturer in English at the University of Sussex.

Gary Day is a Senior Lecturer in English and Cultural Studies at De Montfort University, Bedford. He is the author of *F.R. Leavis: 'Culture' and Literary Criticism* (1996).

Jane Dowson is a Senior Lecturer in English and Cultural Studies at De Montfort University, Bedford. She has written widely on the subject of women's poetry and is the editor of *Women's Poetry of the 1930s: A Critical Anthology* (1995).

Michael Faherty is a Senior Lecturer in English and Cultural Studies at De Montfort University, Bedford. He has organised numerous readings by contemporary poets and has written widely on Ezra Pound.

Colin Milton is a Lecturer in English at the University of Aberdeen. He is a deputy associate director of the Elphenstone Institute and has written widely on Scottish literature.

Lyn Pykett is a Lecturer in English at the University College of Wales, Aberystwyth.

Neil Roberts is a Senior Lecturer at the University of Sheffield. He has written widely on modern poetry including *The Lover, The Dreamer and The World: The Poetry of Peter Redgrove* (1994).

Stan Smith is Professor of English at the University of Dundee. He has written widely on modern poetry including *The Origins of Modernism: Eliot, Pound, Yeats and the Rhetoric of Renewal* (1994).

Roderick Watson is a Professor of English at the University of Stirling. He has edited *The Poetry of Scotland* (1995) and the second edition of his book *The Literature of Scotland* is forthcoming.

Christopher Whyte is a Lecturer in the Scottish Literature Department at the University of Glasgow and has published widely in the field of Scottish literature.

1

Introduction:
Poetry, Politics and Tradition

Gary Day

The aim of this introduction is to place the following essays into a polemical context. My basic argument is that an exclusive concern with politics is threatening to impoverish our understanding of poetry. It has led to an ignorance of tradition and a corresponding blankness in the face of poetry as art. And, if criticism is so desensitised that it cannot recognise or respond to a poem as a poem, then what possible credence can be given to its political pronouncements? It is only by reconsidering what is meant by tradition that we can revitalise our sense of poetry which will, in turn, make us demand more of our politics than that it confuse posture with action or achievement.

There are two recognisable strands to twentieth-century British poetry. For John Powell Ward they are the 'English line' and Modernism.[1] The former runs from William Wordsworth to Philip Larkin and is characterised by 'verbal reserve and the pragmatic and laconic suspicion of the visionary or the extravagant'.[2] Ward argues that the dominant mood of this tradition is melancholy. It yearns for a lost past which it identifies with the natural world. The modernist tradition, by contrast, savours words for their own sake and prefers classical and mythological subjects to pastoral ones. It is less interested in nature than in 'how humans civilise nature with buildings, works of art...ideas and forms of law and institutions.'[3] Generally, where the 'English line' is diffident, pessimistic and reserved, the modernist one is robust, optimistic and outgoing.

Ward argues that the Movement[4] represents the last of the 'English line'. Mainly written in the 1950s, Movement poetry was a reaction to the innovations and formalistic concerns of modernism and the visions, mangled syntax and runaway rhetoric of 1940s verse. The first anthology of Movement poetry was Robert Conquest's *New Lines* (1956), and this was followed by A. Alvarez's *The New Poetry* (1962).[5] Its restricted subject matter, empirical character, disciplined construction and chaste diction represented a poetic timidity, inviting charges of philistinism and provincialism. It hardly seemed possible that such a myopic and exhausted poetry could adapt to the upheavals of the 1960s and 1970s. It therefore came as no surprise when Blake Morrison and Andrew Motion in *Contemporary British Poetry* (1982)[6] claimed that their choice of poets signalled an imaginative freedom and linguistic daring wholly absent from Movement verse. Morrison and Motion also argued that the poets in their collection were aware of how language was implicated in politics, history and locality, giving it a significance beyond the circumscribed 'blokeishness' of Movement poets.

Michael Hulse, David Kennedy and David Morley distance themselves even further from the nostalgia and conservatism of the Movement in their anthology, *The New Poetry*.[7] Their title is a typical postmodernist tactic – a literal quotation from the past in order to re-evaluate and give it a new meaning in the present. Their new poetry, unlike that of the Movement, really is open, accessible and democratic. It casts off, the editors confidently announce, the negative inheritance of British poetry, 'its ironies, understatements and dissipated energies',[8] what Morrison calls the Movement's 'failure of nerve'.[9] Moreover, where Movement writers saw themselves as writing for a small, academic audience, the poets in *The New Poetry* 'reaffirm art's significance as public utterance.'[10] If Hulse and his fellow editors are to be believed, Movement poetry is dead indeed.

Eric Mottram, however, would disagree. His argument is that, even now, in the mid 1990s, it is only Movement type poetry which is anthologised and reviewed.[11] *Contemporary British Poetry* and *The New Poetry* do not so much abandon Movement poetics as develop them. Both, for example, are as wary of the romantic self as were Movement poets and, in their desire to restore value to the 'debased currency'[12] of language, they betray the influence of F.R. Leavis, the Movement's 'most important authority'.[13] Movement dominance, argues Mottram, has meant that other types of poetry, particularly that found in the small presses between 1960 and 1975, has not received the critical attention it deserves.

This body of poetry, continues Mottram, encouraged a wide readership by its emphasis on performance. It gave a voice to the regions and was also open to influences from Europe and America. It continued the experiments of Dada and Surrealism as well as producing new forms such as 'concrete' and 'visual' poetry.[14] It also drew on popular music, particularly that of The Beatles and Bob Dylan, thereby expanding the lyric form 'beyond the confines of traditional logic and grammar usage'.[15] In sum, this poetry was experimental, risk-taking and performance orientated. However, as Norman Nicholson has observed of some of the other characteristics of this verse, '[d]irectness, spontaneity, informality, the lively image, the quick, arresting phrase, wit and humour, can all help to make a poem enjoyable and effective – but they don't make a poem in themselves.'[16]

This raises the awkward but unavoidable question of what we mean by a poem. But trying to answer that pales into insignificance when we consider what we mean by a 'good' poem. For Martin Booth, it is one which 'emotively uses words to express intelligent or emotional thought from one human being to another'.[17] while for A.E. Housman the test of a good poem was whether it lifted the hairs on the back of his neck. What I mean by a 'good' poem, and also by the related terms of 'art' and 'literature' will, I hope, become clearer in the course of this introduction.

One of the reasons why it is difficult to discuss what is meant by 'good' poetry is, ironically, poetry criticism itself. Its dominant idiom is political. Thus Robert Hampson and Peter Barry see the poetry of the 1960s and 1970s as constituting a 'pattern of resistance to the hegemonic culture'[18] while Morrison and Motion favour verse that is 'aware of economic and class differences' and so has something to say 'about the relationship between art and politics'.[19] Aesthetic considerations have been replaced by political ones to such an extent that Booth feels able to declare that the only true poetry is that which 'is understood by all', and which 'relat[es] directly to the mood of the masses'.[20] The test of good poetry is whether or not it is 'for the people'.[21]

The political character of poetry criticism means that the poetry of the present is always seen as progressive, that of the past as reactionary. Hence Mottram is able to dismiss the Movement for its 'woolly, reactionary rhetoric'.[22] This tendency is complemented by another: that of seeing the past as old and the present as new. The word 'new', for example, appears in two of the anthology titles while the term 'contemporary' occurs in the third. This emphasis on the 'new' partly reflects the influence of Foucault's view of history as a series of discontinuities but it also bears the marks of the ideology of the new in consumer culture. Consumerism constantly reinvents itself through the 'new' understood as an improvement on the past. The past is thereby devalued, a process enhanced by the presentation of the 'new' as glitzy, glamorous and enticing.

Poetry criticism, then, seems to suffer from the imperatives of consumerism as well as from a desire to appear politically respectable. The effect of this has been to sever its connections with tradition. This is a fiercely contested term but, broadly speaking, tradition can be described as a way of organising poems from different periods so as to make them a force in the present without losing a sense of their pastness. The addition of new works to a tradition renews perception of its existing ones and the relations between them. Such an understanding of tradition helps to develop a sensitive and discriminating critical vocabulary that is far more alert to the values of difference than are some forms of political criticism which uncritically promote it as a virtue.

Hulse, Kennedy and Morley, for instance, link poetry to the politics of cultural identity arguing that those on the periphery have to define themselves against a repressive centre. This centre is identified with 'Standard English' which cannot render the experience of those on the margin. James Berry argues that it 'does not contain those idiosyncratic resources that allow particular textures of Caribbean experience to be expressed accurately.'[23] Hence Linton Kwesi Johnson, 'a major figure in Black British writing',[24] chooses to write in a non-standard dialect because that better captures 'the everyday bitterness of black suffering'.[25] The Scottish poet Tom Leonard also sets himself at an angle to the English language in order to recover a distinctive dialect and rhythm of speech. His work, according to Colin Nicholson, 'explores the gaps and fissures between the cultural claims and procedures of [English] and the everyday voices of Scotland.'[26]

The argument that writers should abandon 'Standard English' in favour of their own dialect is a powerful one. But its power comes from its simplicity. It assumes that one idiom is expressive while another is not. It forgets language must be made to yield its expressive capabilities. They are not spontaneously there. If they were, there would be no need for poetry. Poetry, as T.S. Eliot noted, is the 'intolerable wrestle with words', a 'raid on the inarticulate'.[27] It is an incessant guerrilla warfare conducted against the blandishments of language whether it be at the centre or the periphery. All languages have to be worked to produce poetry but this elementary insight is suppressed if criticism operates with a binary view of expressive versus non-expressive languages. In short, political imperatives dull awareness of language as a material to be worked, thereby rendering us insensitive to its protean possibilities.

This is not to suggest that Creole or Gaelic may not contain greater expressive possibilities for a West Indian or a Scottish writer than for an English one. The idea that literature must speak of a particular place, evolve out of the necessities of its history, past and present, and the aspirations of its people, is a perfectly sound one. It was, for example, advanced by F.R. Leavis in respect of English literature, a thought which ought to give us pause before that heritage is completely dismantled by theory.

A poetic practice which cultivates its own idiom in opposition to all others not only deprives itself of the opportunity to subvert the dominant tongue, to do what Chinua Achebe called 'unheard of things with [English]'[28] it also raises the question of how different groups are to communicate with one another. Literature, after all, is a mirror in which we see the other as well as ourselves. By nature it is more likely to link identities than present them in splendid isolation. Literature aims to build a community, not Babel. It is a way of speaking to one another, in a peculiarly charged and formal manner, about the great issues of life: love, desire, passion, parenthood, ageing and death. That these are all class, culture and gender specific should not be regarded as a barrier to our understanding but as a means of enriching it. No one can avoid an existential encounter with one or more of these issues and literature is a resource that helps us live them. It does so by providing us with an ever increasing vocabulary that enables us to confront our common fate, and we forget that at our peril.

In confronting these issues literature is not so much expressing as exploring them. This requires a certain sincerity, a state that, as Umberto Eco has pointed out, is almost impossible to achieve in our postmodern culture. The 'game of irony'[29] is intrinsically involved in seriousness of purpose and theme. Indeed, as Linda Hutcheon observes, 'irony may be the only way we *can* be serious today.'[30] This, however, is just another aspect of the difficulty of language, the way it constantly pulls the writer towards what is already known and what has already been said. But that is the creative writer's starting point. Sincerity is a precarious condition, hard to achieve and even harder to maintain. It consists of venturing beyond the horizon of predetermined meanings in the effort to articulate something uniquely personal. It is, furthermore, a seriousness that permeates conduct rather than an attitude to be displayed. The effort involved in trying to attain sincerity partly explains Cocteau's remark that if the poet has a dream, it is not to be famous but to be believed.

Similarly, I.A. Richards believed that the value of poetry lay in the difficult exercise of sincerity it demanded of readers even more than of poets. What he meant by that was that the reader should accept the challenge of literature to discover what his or her real beliefs and values are. Just as the writer has to resist the gravitational pull of language toward cliché and commonplace if he or she is to make it speak or even sing, so the reader has to stop sheltering behind a critical terminology that deadens each unique creation, stamping every work as the same. It is by pushing beyond conventional meanings and by being open to the challenge of literature that poetry, both for readers and writers, shows itself to be more concerned with exploration than expression.

Poetry explores issues by enacting them. Its peculiar alchemy is that it can turn words into the experience they describe. Poetry galvanises words giving them a charge and vitality they lack in ordinary usage. It rouse them from the sloth of habit to shine in use. In doing so, poetry foregrounds the intimate connection between words and experience, showing how the world is processed by language. Of course it is there in a brute sense, but it is only through the structuring operations of language that it becomes meaningful.

This tends to be forgotten in the commonsense view of things which states that, on the one hand, there is the world and, on the other, there is language and language describes the world. Poetry is an intense reminder that language, in fact, creates the world. It therefore has the potential to surprise us with something that we did not know or, as Dennis Potter remarked in his last televised interview, something that we did not know we knew. In this sense, poetry is more about epiphanies than issues.

As well as creating a new world, poetry also revives our sense of the existing one. It puts the dew back on things. It thickens what familiarity has thinned and makes palpable the unconsidered trifles of our lives. Its characteristic concern is with the concrete and so it is scrupulous and precise in its evocation of the world, favouring sensuous particularity over abstract instance.

Poetry is about the power of language, politics about the language of power. This is not to say that either poetry or the criticism of poetry have no bearing on political understanding. For example, because poetry has a special care for the relation between words and the concrete it has the potential to offer a more focused view of the world than can be found in the speciousness that characterises much political debate. The role that literary criticism can play here has been well expressed by Ezra Pound:

> It has to do with the clarity and vigour of 'any and every' thought and opinion...When...the application of word to thing goes rotten, i.e. becomes slushy and inexact, or excessive and bloated, the whole machinery of social and individual thought goes to pot. [Literary criticism] maintains the precision and clarity of thought, not merely for the benefit of a few dilettantes and 'lovers of literature' but maintains the health of thought outside literary circles and in non literary existence, in general and communal life.[31]

Poetry is on the side of what is individual, politics of what is general. Politics is interested in the individual only if it is an instance of the general, whereas poetry, unless it is in the speculative mode of a Wordsworth or an Eliot, is the advocate of '[a]ll things counter, original, spare [and] strange'.[32] Poetry makes time for things, it encourages a certain patience and quality of attention to what is particular. In so doing it offers some relief from the postmodern condition of being overwhelmed by information without the means to organise it. Poetry, it might be argued, becomes part of a politics of resistance by developing the power of concentration in a culture of distraction.

Political discourse has to be general since it seeks to address the largest possible audience in order to persuade it to a particular point of view. Its tone is therefore resolutely public. That of poetry is private, almost intimate. The reader has the sense of being singled out, of being taken into the poet's confidence to help determine whether what he or she presents is significant or not. And, accompanying this is an awareness that fundamental issues may be at stake, an awareness stimulated by the way poetry causes words to vibrate, echo and resonate.

Both in itself and in the demands it makes on the reader poetry displays a quality of sensibility that removes it from the characteristic forms of communication in consumer society. These are regulated by a regime of representations governing practically every aspect of human activity from the workplace to the bedroom: professional codes of conduct, administrative procedures, romance fiction, marriage guidance and sexual therapy. Nothing, it seems escapes being scrutinised and scripted in the public domain.

The fact that poetry also exists in this sphere – it is, after all, performed and published – does not mean that it functions as just another disciplinary discourse. Instead, it should be seen as a partial reformation of that sphere. Its whole endeavour is to engage the depth, complexity and music of language characteristics which, where they exist in the mass media, are subordinated either to selling or the promotion of conformity. Unlike the rigidities of headline culture, poetry aims to soften language to receive the impress of the personal which is otherwise lost in the opinion poll and market sample.

But the personal is public to the extent that shared experiences are expressed in a shared language. The uniquely individual element, however, adds a new dimension to both for while it assumes a community, it also seeks to extend what can be understood by that term. Here is another example of how poetry can be viewed as a form of resistance. It extends the range of language and experience whereas the institutions of mass culture, on the whole, limit them. More than that, poetry in its manner of loading and weighting words, its rootedness in tradition, its constellations of meaning and its forging of connections goes part way to answering the need for significance in human affairs, a need ignored by a society devoted to economic rather than human ends.

The political aspect of poetry's concern for the relation between words and the concrete is, then, fourfold. First it displays a sounder grasp of experience than does political rhetoric; second it helps to preserve what is individual from being subsumed under the general; third it develops a form of sustained attention in opposition to the endlessly proliferating jingles, slogans and soundbites of consumer culture; and fourth, poetry's attachment to the particular communicates a sense of 'felt significance', a sense that there is something more to life than materialism or a mere 'succession of days'. Looked at in this way, poetry can be seen as enrichment of politics whereas the imposition of politics on poetry too often results in an impoverishment of the latter.

The concern for the relation between words and the concrete is one aspect of poetry's association with politics. Another comes from poetry being the creation of a world. Ideally, in the world of the poem, each part is fulfilled in relation to the whole and this acts as an analogy for utopian society. Furthermore, in contrast to the divisions and exclusions of class society and the atomisations of consumerism, poetry enacts the principles of unity, inclusion and relation. These are not merely formal considerations for, although it is an entity in its own right, the coordinates of a poem still correspond to those of the world. Hence the sense that our experience is impenetrable can be countered by the poet's imagining some equivalent of it that makes our own more manageable. This constitutes, as Seamus Heaney argues, the pressure of imagination pushing back against reality to reveal alternative orders and more promising potentials for growth.[33] In this respect, poetry illustrates I.A. Richards's remark that the arts are an appraisal of existence, an appraisal that is far more detailed and extensive than can be found in any political manifesto.

From a political point of view, poetry is neither a matter of saying the right – or left – thing nor a means of making it rhyme. Instead, it is an exploration of experience making its political effects difficult to calculate except with hindsight. Poetry can, of course, subtilise political awareness in the ways I have indicated but it is not my intention to bring poetry and politics into a closer alliance by showing that the relationship between them is more complex than some commentators imagine. My concern is not with poetry as applied art but with poetry as art.

To view poetry as art is not an easy undertaking. The arts in England have always been treated with suspicion and therefore critics have been anxious to justify them. Most commonly this has led to their being tied, as we have seen in the case of poetry, to a programme of political resistance. Certainly poetry can be the voice of protest, as a glance at the work of Blake, Shelley and the early Wordsworth will show. But poetry is also art and art cannot be justified in any readily demonstrable way because it is hard to say what art is.

The difficulty of the question, involving, as it does, the explosive issue of value judgements, has led to it being evaded. Nowhere is this more apparent than in the case of theory – by which I mean the

British appropriations of French thought, particularly that of Althusser, Barthes, Derrida, Foucault and Lacan. Catherine Belsey speaks for many when she urges that the quest for value be replaced by an 'analysis of the social contestation of value'.[34] This has led to a denial that there is any difference between literary and other types of writing. According to Antony Easthope there are only texts which 'must be discussed' in terms of '[i]nstitution, sign system, ideology, gender, identification and subject positions [and] the other'.[35]

But this does not remove the problem of value; it simply assumes that those texts which most easily accommodate themselves to the preoccupations of theory are to be preferred to those which do not. Instead of being discussed, value is imposed. What is distinctive about a work is ignored. What it has to say is discounted in favour of what the critic makes it say about 'institution', 'sign system' and so on. A poem's worth is measured by how closely it conforms to the agenda of theory.

Theory has therefore no means of registering the power of poetry, its thrillingly unsettling effects, its ability to make the skin tingle and the spirit dilate. Poetry can be dangerous but theory makes it safe by dissipating its effects through neologism and abstraction. '[T]hinking', writes F.R. Leavis, when it is 'released from the testing and energising contact [with the concrete] is debilitated and betrayed to the academic [and] the abstract.'[36] Theorists will protest that their vocabulary is an integral part of the process of resistance to the dominant order. I would argue that this 'resistance' is rather a resistance to the beautiful. Although James Bone believed that the English desired beauty in art there was something in their national character which made them settle for prettiness.[37] Perhaps because, as Tom Paulin has suggested, the beautiful always makes the English 'angry and embarrassed'.[38]

The fact that English theorists cannot cope with their desire for beauty suggests that their oppositional stance is no more than 'a fantasy construction masking the real of [their] desire'.[39] Resistance is a fantasy because it is more rhetoric than reality. Theory, in fact, supports more than it opposes the dominant order. For example, it finds the idea of organised wholes abhorrent. At best 'they are the remnants of bourgeois liberalism' and at worst 'the images of totalitarian repression'.[40] Theory therefore deconstructs the whole to liberate the parts. This seems a reasonable undertaking until it is remembered that theory came to prominence under Mrs Thatcher's government, and she was the one who famously declared that 'there is no such thing as society.' Theory, in its attack on unity, seems to collude with a political practice committed to privatisation and the dismantling of the welfare state. Its desire is to dominate, not to set free. Such connections make it difficult to accept theory's assertion that it is a form of resistance. So too does the fact that it is now the dominant paradigm of literary and cultural studies. As a respectable part of the academic establishment, theory is not so much a politics of resistance as a good career move. If you cannot define *différance* – which, says Derrida, is 'neither a word nor a concept'[41] – you cannot, in many American universities, get tenure. Theory's integration into the middle-class career structure and its consonance with certain aspects of conservative ideology demonstrate the truth of Brecht's observation that innovations are not acceptable if they are going to change existing society, only if they are going to rejuvenate it. The essentially conservative nature of theory explains why it defuses art. Art disturbs, it is a commotion of mind and body because it is 'a challenge to discover what one's real beliefs and values are.'[42] Theory, as part of the establishment, wants no such challenge.

There is also the question of how appropriate terms like 'intervention', 'resistance' and 'opposition' are in describing our response to works of art. As an integral part of the vocabulary of theory, they assume first that art is about resistance and second that art needs theory to make that resistance effective. For reasons already given, theory's characterisation of itself as oppositional is dubious to say the least. More generally, the narrowness and inflexibility of these terms means that they are incapable of discriminating between the different levels and complexities of response which art invites. To remain sensitive to these and to account for why we should go on reading, viewing or listening to art we need to maximise our critical vocabulary. Theory, by restricting that vocabulary to a politics of resistance, empties art of its human significance. If it opposes anything, theory opposes art whose concern is precisely this significance.

In broad terms this significance is to do with human ends. To be concerned with significance is to recognise that these ends cannot be met either by the endless pursuit of a higher standard of living or by an attachment to a political or religious dogma. A preoccupation with significance is a concern with ultimate questions without being able to answer them. Art, great art, is an attempt to endow fundamental existential issues with a sense of 'felt significance' in contrast to the institutions of Western capitalism which systematically exclude them from consideration.

It is difficult to be precise about what constitutes significance. It would be too easy to say that it is either a matter of individual preference or else is the effect of certain cultural narratives such as progress or the pursuit of individual fulfilment. Too easy because both these reactions ignore the fact that we have got out of the habit of thinking, really thinking, about issues of value and significance. And yet they cannot be avoided; innumerable value judgements haunt our simplest decisions hence it is imperative that we try to be as conscious of our grounds for making them as possible. Being articulate about art is one means of doing this. However, there is little encouragement for this undertaking in a society whose paramount concerns are economic efficiency, the control of inflation and the relentless extension of the consumerist mentality. Theory offers no exit from this impoverished state of existence since its characteristic gesture, most evident in its contempt for humanism, is to distance us from all that profoundly concerns and moves us.

Since the culture is general is hostile to the issue of significance, it is not easy to discuss its particular manifestations. In the case of poetry this is compounded by its being, as Paul Valery somewhere remarked, 'a hesitation between sound and sense'. Its sweet echoes and felicities of cadence threaten to ravish the ear. Such visceral stirrings dim poetry's cerebral radiance. But even if poetry appealed to the intellect alone, as some indeed does, it would still be difficult to be precise about its significance. This is because, as William Empson so brilliantly demonstrated, the machinations of ambiguity lie at the very heart of poetry.[43] Where meaning is undecided, significance is always going to be indeterminate.

Another reason why it is hard to pronounce categorically upon a work's significance is because it would be in the nature of such a work to transform our perceptions and transcend our expectations. The poem, Heidegger argues, 'transports us out of the realm of the ordinary'[44] and this problematises the process of valuation. That is to say, critical activity is not about measuring a work by a norm brought to it from the outside, it is about coping with its impact on established modes of valuation and readjusting them accordingly. This readjustment needs to take into account not just how a poem breaks with 'the ordinary' but also how it reacts back upon it. Here, questions about the nature of society become important. What light, for example, does the poem throw on human rather than merely economic possibilities for growth envisaged by business and politicians?

The poem can raise these questions in an urgent way only if it performs the paradoxical feat of evoking the texture of lived experience while at the same time offering a critical perspective on it. Poetic form, in transfiguring empirical being, 'represents freedom where empirical life represents repression.'[45] Further, the tension between part and whole in the internal organisation of the poem gives it a certain volatility that disrupts the smooth operation of technological rationality which views people as resources or statistics. Moreover, poetic form, by endeavouring to forge a unity between senses, intellect, emotion and imagination, also strives to be sensuous. In so doing, it critiques the reduction of experience to sensation which is its characteristic form in consumer culture.

Because poetic significance is first of all a matter of transcending conventional expressions of experience, it cannot readily be put into words. However, it also reacts back upon that experience, raising all kinds of questions about freedom, development and fulfilment. And, since these questions can only be determined in the future, significance is something which awaits articulation. But significance is also a function of the sensuousness of poetic form, giving it a more concrete and immediate character. In its engagement with questions concerning the deepest purpose of life as configured in artistic form, significance can be understood as the effect of a relation between aesthetics and ethics. And, though this gives significance a certain weight, it does not necessarily clarify it because of the different and conflicting considerations introduced by those terms.

Since it is hard to maintain a clear focus when discussing poetic significance in general terms it is perhaps better to concentrate on how, if at all, it is manifested in individual poems. Heidegger claims that the poem is 'the bringing forth a being such as never was before and will never come to be again.'[46] Criticism should therefore endeavour to establish why the poem is what it is and no other thing. However, in order to grasp the poem's uniqueness it is necessary to have a knowledge and understanding of tradition. For some, tradition represents elitism, hierarchy and exclusion; for others, like Stephen Eric Bronner, it is a resource against the drastic simplifications of experience by the mass media or what he calls, using Adorno's phrase, 'the culture industry':

> Tradition provides history with coherence. With the new power of the culture industry... the past is ever more surely becoming a buffet from which the gourmet can select a bit of this and a touch of that. The culture industry celebrates the fad, immediacy, cynicism and the 'happy consciousness;' it loosens the bonds of tradition and, in keeping with the claims of postmodern thinkers, creates juxtapositions whose arbitrariness is limited only by the dictates of profit. Liquidation of the past, or the inability to give it coherence, is a principal effect of the culture industry.[47]

Criticism, in order to enable a perception of the poem's uniqueness as well as to combat the effects described above, needs to cultivate a sense of tradition. In addition to what I said earlier, tradition can be viewed as a series of complex articulations concerning peculiarly intense and focused moments of existence, which, like love, most people have experienced. There is therefore something inclusive in the very nature of tradition. It contains the possibility of common experience which is yet never the same for everyone. Tradition is, as it were, an image of the ideal community where sameness and difference are not mutually exclusive but mutually enhancing. Each, comprehending itself through the other, is in a state of continuous development. Tradition is thus dynamic, not static.

It does, however, have a certain consistency deriving from the recurrence of certain experiences. The substance of love poetry through the ages would again seem to be the obvious example here. Each generation is faced with the challenge of saying afresh what has been said before. The poetry that comes from that will eventually be surpassed as the work of previous generations has been surpassed. In those 'well wrought urns' we see how others have faced the things we face and therein lies their power to move. Their achievements inspire respect – perhaps even humility – and they remind us how important it is that, as we fade into history, we leave behind for others' use a record of our being here.

This record is a response to the problems of being alive now. It draws on past work but remains distinct from it. In coming to our own conclusions about our deepest allegiances and determinations, our own sense of what lends significance to life, we contribute to that storehouse of perceptions, apprehensions, analyses, valuations and judgements that constitutes tradition. Permanent yet provisional, tradition is a resource, not a rule book, for envisaging the manifold relations of art and life.

It is the job of criticism 'not only to give the oppressed access to tradition, but also to create it.'[48] The first part of Walter Benjamin's remark is important because it recognises that there are works – 'the canon' – which have a certain intrinsic worth. The worth of a work of art lies in its replacing a world of things with a world of values and at the heart of this process is the way art poses the problem of its own value.

Sadly, a class-divided education system has meant that for too long too many people have been prevented from reading 'the canon'. The creation of an alternative tradition that excludes 'the canon' merely perpetuates this lack of access. It is true that 'the canon' has been used more to intimate than enlighten, more to shore up than to sweep away class barriers, but that is a function of the system rather than of the works themselves. A more sympathetic attention to tradition can open up 'the canon', exploiting its unrealised 'surplus value' for emancipatory purposes. The poetry of Milton, for example, has the potential to connect with our lives in meaningful though unpredictable ways.

'The canon', in fact, provides vocabularies, syntaxes, grammars, conventions, beliefs, imaginings and modes of thought very different from our own which, in their departure from our habitual representations, make explicit *one* of the functions of literature: to make us realise that other people act on moral convictions quite unlike our own. Viewed in this way, tradition can help to develop powers of discrimination and to give a positive value to difference. Both these advantages, together with those mentioned above, are lost if tradition is constructed *only* in terms of our particular identity or politics, if it is viewed as a mirror, not a prism.

Benjamin's other point is that tradition needs to be recreated in every age if it is not to be taken over by the forces of oppression. This recreation involves making explicit – and judging – the social and political norms and interests that were and are constitutive of tradition. That way, tradition can be prevented from being appropriated by an organicist ideology that makes it the expression of a 'natural' order. This recreation of tradition also acknowledges the need to expand it to accommodate those voices which have hitherto been unrepresented in it.

But the recreation of tradition is also about conservation for it is the case that the critical meaning of a work only becomes apparent by being placed in the context of other works. Without tradition, the poem does not speak, it stutters. The poem only becomes articulate through being compared and contrasted with others. This process not only gives a sense of how tradition develops, it also encourages the habit of making connections, of experimenting with different combinations. Far from suppressing difference, as some theorists might claim, the aligning of dissimilar works relies on it to reveal unsuspected links. Thus, a lively perception of difference leads to the possibility of relation and a view of tradition as a constantly shifting pattern of constellations.

Such an understanding prompts the reader to consider the many ways of correlating literature and life. In this respect tradition is more useful than theory whose hieratic jargon severs the connection between the two terms. Indeed theory, with its rejection of notions such as purposive agency, can be seen to assist in the spread of depersonalising discourses which are so prominent a feature of our society. The increasingly pervasive language of personnel management, for example, conceives of human beings not as people, but as resources.

Tradition, by contrast, keeps alive the idea of the human being as a person. It is able to do this because, at its most intense and concentrated, it is composed of works of art which challenge the reader, 'at the profoundest level, with the question, "In what does the significance of life reside?" '[49] This question is inextricably bound up with matters of artistic form which determine the level and intensity at which it is asked. The diversity of these forms means that the question is asked in different ways and an attention to this diversity means the creation of a cumulative and finely tuned critical vocabulary that itself reacts back on the writing of literature.

For these reasons it is important to revisit the idea of tradition. This does not involve, at least not in any simplistic sense, the establishment of a 'canon'; rather it is a question of recovering and building upon a tradition of thinking about literature, particularly poetry, that theory has not dealt with but disparaged. This thinking will dwell on literature as something more than a discourse to be unmasked, it will be sensitive to its 'soaring orchestrations', its 'marvellous aspirations'[50] and its powers of enlargement.

British criticism falls into two broad but no means clearly distinct categories, the moral and the aesthetic. The moral tradition is represented by figures such as Dr Johnson and, to a lesser extent, by F.R. Leavis. This tradition, whose criterion was truth to nature, endeavoured to sustain itself by appealing to the 'common reader' who, argues Frank Kermode, was a being of 'no refinement [but] a certain moral purity'.[51] Kermode attributes the decline of this tradition first to the 'relatively uneducated hav[ing] found amusements they prefer to reading' and second to the fact 'the universities have taken over both the production and the criticism of literature'.[52]

Unlike the moral tradition the aesthetic one is fascinated by novelty and artifice and presupposes no community of 'common readers'. Its interest is in the individual alone and the pleasure afforded by his or her response to art. Walter Pater may be taken as representative of this tradition. In his view, experience is nothing more than a series of impressions, 'unstable, flickering and inconsistent, which burn and are extinguished with our consciousness of them.'[53] The job of art is to shape these impressions by lending them a form which must be ceaselessly perfected. Art, writes Pater, 'comes to you proposing to give nothing but the highest quality to your moments as they pass.'[54]

Samuel Taylor Coleridge bestrides both traditions in that, for him, a poem should faithfully adhere to 'the truth of nature' while, at the same time, giving 'the interest of novelty'.[55] Specifically, Coleridge is allied with the moral tradition in as much as he believed that there was an objective quality to poetic form that was recognisable by the 'common reader'. This form was 'a balance or reconciliation of opposites or discordant qualities'.[56] Such a view anticipates Matthew Arnold's remark that the task of criticism was 'to see the object as in itself it really is'.[57] Coleridge also believed that this form contained truth which was again something on which a common readership could agree. More subtly, Coleridge's account of the nature of this form as a balancing of opposites looks forward to I.A. Richards's point that the reading of poetry enables individuals to reconcile conflicting impulses in their psyche. The work of Arnold and Richards makes explicit what is only implicit in Coleridge, namely that poetry is an agent of social stability. In doing so, they bring out another feature of the moral tradition, its concern with order.

But Coleridge also goes beyond this tradition by his discussion of how poetry excites pleasure in the reader. This allies him with the aesthetic tradition though his notion of pleasure is more intellectual than sensuous since it depends on an appreciation of structure, 'the delight [obtained] from the whole [being] compatible with the distinct gratification of each part.'[58] Nevertheless, like its aesthetic counterpart, Coleridge's conception of pleasure arises from a perception of form. Similarly both Coleridge and the artists of the aesthetic movement placed a high value on the sensuous properties of art. Poetry, wrote Coleridge, should be 'simple, sensuous and passionate'.[59] And though he tried to subordinate these effects to truth, 'the ultimate end'[60] of poetry, he never quite succeeded; hence they continued to send seismic ripples through the poetic structure.

What Coleridge offers is a possible synthesis between the two traditions of thinking about literature. His analysis of poetic structure also revives the principle of aesthetic autonomy in an age which witnesses the dissolution of art into the prevailing form of commodity production. Where there is no difference between art and life, where, in other words, art is continuous with ideology, then there are no creative tensions or transactions whereby each can complement or critique the other.

Crucial to Coleridge's idea of poetic form is his account of the imagination. He argues that there is a primary and a secondary imagination. The primary one is essentially creative whereas the secondary one 'dissolves, diffuses and dissipates in order to recreate ... It is essentially vital.'[61] The term imagination is in danger of being consigned to the archives of criticism. But I believe there is an urgent need for it to counteract the sterility of theory. The imagination presents the power of creativity in an age where art, 'incapable of achieving aesthetic representations of our own current experience',[62] has been reduced to borrowing from the past. It aspires to nothing higher than pastiche. Imagination, by contrast, looks to the future by building on the past. To use Coleridge's terms it dissolves in order to create something new. Furthermore, as a vital principle, imagination animates our sense of form so that we use terms like 'mutuality', 'proportion', 'harmony' and 'purpose', not just of poetry, also as a means of breaking down calcified social structures whose characteristic relations are those of domination and repression.

The vitality of imagination is a feature of its contact with experience, hence its creations are more likely to react back upon it, rendering, extending and illuminating it. Unlike theory whose language is remote from and untainted by the pressures of life, the imagination dwells in the concrete and inheres in details, the better to transform – perhaps even redeem – them through its characteristic act of relation.

The point of revisiting tradition is not to apply it to our understanding of poetry from 1950 to the 1990s. Rather it is a way of recovering a vocabulary and a mode of apprehension that allows us to find out the reason why a particular poem 'is so and not otherwise'[63] and, at the same time, to make a comparison between poems.

> In comparing different poems with each other we should inquire which have brought into the fullest play our imagination and our reason or have created the greatest excitement and produced the greatest harmony.[64]

Tradition is also a source for finding links between art and life. It is therefore a means of widening access to it in contrast to theory which has made art a matter for initiates. By acting as a sort of connective tissue, tradition marries the language of criticism with the experience of art. It is important to stress that in this relationship neither term takes precedence, again unlike theory which seeks only to master art. Claiming to demystify it, theory only cloaks art in obscurity. The value of Coleridge's work is that it encourages us to think about these issues and, in so doing, acts as a thread which, if it does not lead us out of the labyrinth, at least makes us aware of how its walls screen off the limitless horizon.

No selection of poets can be regarded as representative until we have a better understanding of tradition. My argument has been that the traditions described by the editors of the three anthologies discussed earlier are based on *political* rather than aesthetic considerations and this has resulted in a simplification of both poetry and literary history. Such simplifications are of no use either to an understanding of poetry or to a politics of real change. The first task, therefore, is to undo the neat opposition between an 'elitist' and democratic tradition of poetry. This can be achieved by presenting the poets from the two traditions in one volume without trying to label them. The second task is to focus on the artistic qualities of these poets in such a way as to raise some of the issues covered in this introduction. Hopefully, the reader will thereby be stimulated to a fresh consideration of poetry in the latter half of the twentieth century, to its relationship to tradition and to where it might be going in the future.

Notes

1. John Powell Ward, *The English Line: Poetry of the Unpoetic from Wordsworth to Larkin* (London: Macmillan, 1991).
2. Ibid., p. 7.
3. Ibid., p. 16.
4. For a full account of the Movement see Blake Morrison, *The Movement: English Poetry and Fiction of the 1950s* (London and New York: Methuen, 1980).
5. Robert Conquest (ed.), *New Lines* (London: Macmillan, 1956) and A. Alvarez (ed.), *The New Poetry* (Harmondsworth: Penguin, 1962).
6. Blake Morrison and Andrew Motion (eds), *Contemporary British Poetry* (Harmondsworth: Penguin, 1982).
7. Michael Hulse, David Kennedy and David Morley (eds), *The New Poetry* (Newcastle: Bloodaxe Books, 1993).
8. Hulse, Kennedy and Morley, 'Introduction' to *The New Poetry*, op. cit., p. 22.
9. Morrison, *The Movement: English Poetry and Fiction of the 1950s*, op. cit., p. 84.
10. Hulse et al., 'Introduction' to *The New Poetry*, op. cit., p. 16.
11. Eric Mottram, 'The British Poetry Revival, 1960–1975', in Peter Barry and Robert Hampson (eds), *New British Poetries: The Scope of the Possible* (Manchester: Manchester University Press, 1993), pp. 15–50.
12. Hulse et al., 'Introduction' to *The New Poetry*, op. cit., p. 22.
13. Morrison, *The Movement: English Poetry and Fiction of the 1950s*, op. cit., p. 63.
14. Concrete poetry uses words as sounds. Its exponents 'gave recitals with tape recorders, sound effects and their own mouths'. Visual poetry 'consisted of collages made of pictures, news cuttings, instant lettering sets, duplication machine smudges and blanked out text.' See Martin Booth, *British Poetry 1964–1984: Driving Through the Barricades* (London: Routledge & Kegan Paul, 1985), pp. 230–1.
15. Mottram, 'The British Poetry Revival 1960–75', op. cit., p. 27.
16. Norman Nicholson, 'Introduction' to F.E.S. Finn, *Poems of the Sixties* (London: John Murray, 1970), p. vii.
17. Martin Booth, *British Poetry 1964–84: Driving Through the Barricades*, op. cit., p. 20.
18. Peter Barry and Robert Hampson, 'Introduction: The Scope of the Possible', in Barry and Hampson (eds), *New British Poetries: The Scope of the Possible*, op. cit., pp. 1–11, p. 9.
19. Morrison and Motion, 'Introduction' to *Contemporary British Poetry*, op. cit., p. 17 and 16.

20. Booth, *British Poetry 1964–84: Driving Through the Barricades*, op. cit., pp. 34 and 12.
21. Ibid., p. 12.
22. Mottram, 'The British Poetry Revival, 1960–75', op. cit., p. 21.
23. James Berry, 'Introduction' to *News For Babylon*, ed. James Berry (London: Chatto & Windus, 1984), pp. i–xxvii, p. xxv.
24. Hulse, Kennedy and Morley, 'Introduction' to *The New Poetry*, op. cit., p. 19.
25. Ibid.
26. Colin Nicholson, *Poem, Purpose and Place: Shaping Identity in Contemporary Scottish Verse* (Edinburgh: Polygon, 1992), p. xvii.
27. T.S. Eliot, 'East Coker', in *The Complete Poems and Plays of T.S. Eliot* (London: Faber & Faber, 1969), pp. 182 and 179.
28. Chinua Achebe, 'Colonialist Criticism', in Chinua Achebe, *Hopes and Impediments: Selected Essays 1965–87* (London: Heinemann, 1988), pp. 46–58, p. 49.
29. Umberto Eco, 'Reflections on The Name of the Rose', in Mark Currie, *Metafiction* (Harlow: Longman, 1995), pp. 172–8, p. 174.
30. Linda Hutcheon, *A Poetics of Postmodernism: History, Theory, Practice* (New York and London: Routledge, 1988), p. 39.
31. Ezra Pound, 'How to Read', in T.S. Eliot (ed.), *Literary Essays of Ezra Pound* (London: Faber & Faber, 1954), pp. 15–40, p. 21.
32. Gerard Manley Hopkins, 'Pied Beauty', in Gerard Manley Hopkins, *Poems and Prose*, ed. W.H. Gardner (Harmondsworth: Penguin, 1953), p. 31.
33. For a full account of Heaney's views see Seamus Heaney, *The Redress of Poetry* (London: Faber, 1995).
34. Catherine Belsey, 'Literature, History, Politics', in David Lodge, *Modern Criticism and Theory* (Harlow: Longman, 1988), pp. 400–10, p. 406.
35. Antony Easthope, *Literary into Cultural Studies* (London and New York: Routledge, 1991), p. 71.
36. F.R. Leavis, 'Towards Standards of Criticism', in F.R. Leavis, *Anna Karenina and Other Essays* (London: Chatto & Windus, 1967), pp. 219–34, p. 224.
37. James Bone, 'The Tendencies of Modern Art', in Judy Giles and Tim Middleton, *Writing Englishness 1900–1950: An Introductory Sourcebook on National Identity* (London and New York: Routledge, 1995), pp. 160–1, p. 160.
38. Tom Paulin quoted by Sian Griffiths, 'Battle for the Standard', in *The Times Higher Educational Supplement*, 11 June 1993, pp. 17–18, p. 17.
39. Slavoj Zizek, *The Sublime Object of Ideology* (London and New York: Verso, 1989), p. 45.
40. Frank Kermode, *History and Value* (Oxford: Clarendon Press, 1988), p. 133 See also Jean-François Lyotard, *The Postmodern Condition: A Report on Knowledge*, trans. Geoff Bennington and Brian Massumi (Manchester: Manchester University Press, 1984), particularly the section 'Answering the Question: What is Postmodernism?', pp. 71–82.

41. Jacques Derrida, 'Différance', in Jacques Derrida, *Margins of Philosophy*, trans. and with notes by Alan Bass (New York and London: Harvester Wheatsheaf, 1982), pp. 3–27, p. 3.
42. F.R. Leavis, 'Valuation in Criticism', in *Valuation in Criticism and Other Essays*, ed. G. Singh (Cambridge: Cambridge University Press, 1986), pp. 276–84, p. 282.
43. See William Empson, *Seven Types of Ambiguity* (Harmondsworth: Penguin, 1961).
44. Martin Heidegger, 'The Origin of the Work of Art', in Martin Heidegger, *Basic Writings*, ed. David Farrell Krell (London and New York: Routledge, 1978), pp. 143–212, p. 191.
45. Stephen Eric Bronner, *Of Critical Theory and its Theorists* (Oxford, UK and Cambridge, Mass.: Blackwell, 1994), p. 191.
46. Heidegger, 'The Origin of the Work of Art', op. cit., p. 187.
47. Bronner, *Of Critical Theory and its Theorists*, op. cit., p. 330.
48. Walter Benjamin, quoted in ibid., p. 135. The source of the quotation is not given.
49. F.R. Leavis, 'Tragedy and the Medium', in F.R. Leavis, *The Common Pursuit* (Harmondsworth: Penguin, 1993), pp. 121–35, p. 132.
50. Seamus Heaney, *The Redress Of Poetry*, op. cit., p. 17.
51. Frank Kermode, 'The Common Reader', in Frank Kermode, *An Appetite for Poetry: Essays in Literary Interpretation* (London: Fontana, 1990), pp. 47–58, p. 54.
52. Ibid., p. 53.
53. Walter Pater, *The Renaissance* (Oxford and New York: Oxford University Press, 1986), p. 151.
54. Ibid., p. 152.
55. Samuel Taylor Coleridge, *Biographia Literaria*, ed. George Watson (London: Dent, 1991), p. 168.
56. Ibid., p. 174.
57. Matthew Arnold, 'The Function of Criticism at the Present Time', in Peter Keating (ed.), *The Victorian Prophets* (London: Fontana, 1981), pp. 186–213, p. 186.
58. Coleridge, *Biographia Literaria*, op.cit., p. 172.
59. John Milton, quoted by Coleridge in 'Definition of Poetry', in *Coleridge: Poems and Prose*, selected by Kathleen Raine (Harmondsworth: Penguin, 1957), pp. 225–7, p. 226.
60. Coleridge, *Biographia Literaria*, op. cit., p. 171.
61. Ibid., p. 167.
62. Frederic Jameson, 'Postmodernism and Consumer Society', in Hal Foster (ed.), *The Anti-Aesthetic: Essays in Postmodern Culture* (Port Townsend: Bay Press, 1983), pp. 111–25, p. 117.
63. Coleridge, *Biographia Literaria*, op. cit., p. 172.
64. Coleridge, 'The Essence of Poetry', in *Coleridge: Poems and Prose*, op. cit., pp. 227–8, p. 217.

2

Basil Bunting:
Briggflatts

Dennis Brown

Basil Bunting's major poem *Briggflatts* (1966)[1] was published in a cultural world still dominated by the Movement poets, despite A. Alvarez's challenging anthology *The New Poets* of 1962. Quite apart from its prioritisation of verbal music over positivistic sentiment and its 'Lindisfarne'[2] intricacy of patterning, the poem broke away from the consensus that the short lyric was the vehicle of contemporary poetics. *Briggflatts* is, like *The Waste Land*, a shrunken epic – though one as personalised as *The Prelude*. Influenced by Ezra Pound in particular,[3] the poem could be characterised as neo-modernist – resistant to the current recycling of Georgian tropes and Augustan empiricism[4] alike, while not attracted to the exciting excesses of postmodern verse as would be exemplified in Ted Hughes's *Crow* (1970). The poem exemplifies the quality verse can achieve if group-fashion is eschewed and the craftsman sticks to his toil. Though in thrall to a mythologised history, it also speaks to the environmental concern of the 1990s: its preoccupation with the spirit of place also communicates what Mikhail Bakhtin has called 'Great Time', where the 'chronotope' of many centuries finds particular articulation and 'every meaning' has its 'homecoming festival'.[5] In this, it has one particular precedent in David Jones's *The Anathemata* (1952)[6] which, even more than his war-epic *In Parenthesis* (1937), combines affective musicality with 'Celtic' principles of serendipitous interweaving to construct a neo-modernist verse-saga.

The aim of evoking *The Anathemata* here is not to demonstrate an imputed influence but to stress a shared continuity from poetic modernism – and in this, to suggest the inherent oddity, insularity and short-mindedness of what generally passed for poetry in the decade when *Briggflatts* was published. Briefly, Jones's poem is an extended, visionary construct where spiritual vision and environ-

23

mental feel combine to express relations between human history and nature as a continuous dialectic mediated by signs:

> The adaptations, the fusions
> the transmogrifications
> > but always
> the inward continuities
> > of the site
> > of place ...

(p. 90)

Such moments emerge out of a complex design where Graeco-Roman narrative is replaced by an elaboration of structure-as-web, much as in *Briggflatts*. David Blamires's description of Jones's poem works equally well for Bunting's, if Augustine can be diffused into Columba, Aidan, Cuthbert and Quakerism:

> There is no clearly conceived centre to the work, or rather, to adapt St Augustine's definition of the nature of God, the poem is a circle whose centre is everywhere and whose circumference is nowhere. For the important substance of the poem is to be found at every point in it. The direction and intention of the words are apparent from the start. The transmutations, the transference of significance from one thing to another, the transparency of things – all these are hymned in the very first words.[7]

The first words of *The Anathemata* are: 'We already and first of all discern him making this thing other' (49); the first words of *Briggflatts* are: 'Brag, sweet tenor bull,/Descant on Rawthey's madrigal' (51); thereafter both poems elaborate neo-modernist pioneering through arabesque patterning – both environmentally sensitive, both in search of the Holy as it reveals itself in natural and incarnational life.

Yet while *Briggflatts* is also a poem of local site and historical depth, its uneven overall grittiness makes it rather different in affect to Jones's fluid polyphony. As a young man, Bunting spent some years near the Pounds in Rapallo and W.B. Yeats felt he was one of 'Ezra's more savage disciples'.[8] Bunting was particularly an admirer of Pound's quasi-translation 'Homage to Sextus Propertius' and something of that poem's assertive virility and contempt for the socio-political order, as well as its use of lyrical free verse, appears in Bunting's own work. His 'Villon' (1925) plays off the mediaeval French poet as Pound had played off Propertius, at times achieving the stark epigrammatic flavour of the Scottish Chaucerians:

> Abelard and Eloise,
> Henry the Fowler, Charlemagne,
> Genée, Lopokova, all these
> die, die in pain.

> (p. 14)

Like *The Anathemata*, 'Villon' contains its own form of ecological message: 'They have melted the snows from Erebus, weighed the clouds/hunted down the white bear...the seal the kangaroo.' It also exploits Poundian scenarios from Cathay – a colouring that will recur in the specifically Orientalist 'Chomei at Toyama' (1932). These poems, together with 'The Spoils' (1951) and a variety of (misnamed?) 'Odes' develop Pound's notion of 'translation' – 'the past should be a light for the future'[9] – as a central poetic mission. Bunting's work typically foregrounds that diachronic intertextuality which characterises the poetic tradition – and adds to it with exotic material. This remains the case even in his 'Autobiography'[10] which is the key achievement of his career.

Like *The Anathemata*, *Briggflatts* initially appeals to the reader in discrete passages of sudden revelation. Rooted in the Northumberland coast line and west Yorkshire countryside, the poem hymns exact particularities of natural feature as forged by climate. Its ecological feel is rugged and robust and is characteristically couched in terms as Saxon-Viking hard-edged as Jones's diction is sweetly mediaeval:

> Who sang, sea takes,
> brawn brine, bone grit.
> Keener the kittiwake.
> Fells forget him.

> (p. 56)

Such a passage grounds all personal and historical allusions (where fantasy and memory seem to mingle) in a landscape, beautiful in its very bleakness, which is everywhere highly specific. The poem is exact of colour and tone and celebrates the primal interrelation between climate, coastline and animal life:

> Winter wrings pigment
> from petal and slough
> but thin light lays
> white next red on sea-crow wing...

> (p. 68)

Such sharp natural evocation is perhaps the poem's key contribution to Modernist verse in general. *Briggflatts* is first and primarily a lyric of incisive description.

Like David Jones, Bunting was always concerned with the sound of his verse.[11] The short, consonantal, staccato line is his norm but this can be cunningly contrasted with neo-Baroque mellifluousness:

> It is time to consider how Domenico Scarlatti
> condensed so much music so few bars
> with never a crabbed turn or congested cadence...

> (p. 66)

A one-time music critic, Bunting adapted Pound's free-verse 'musical phrase'[12] to his own purposes – 'laying the tune on the air.' It is a distinctly Modernist music – sharing an ear with jazz-men, and with early Stravinsky, or Antheil, or Bartok. It is irregularly rhythmic, syllabically percussive and ostinato in effect. If, as Edgar Varèse believed, music is the intelligence of sound, then Bunting is an orchestrator of specifically twentieth-century sounds – their randomness, contrasts and fortuitous chimings. His lines share a world with the *Rite of Spring* or Messaien's *Turangalila*: this is a truly modernised lyricism.

It is as hard to demonstrate conventional narrative design in *Briggflatts* as in *The Anathemata* – a characteristic of all longer Modernist poems. The work is divided into five numbered sections, with a 'Coda' at the end. Section I apostrophises the 'tenor bull' and evokes love-making in May-time; II begins with a London 'Fall' and betrayal ('He lies with one to long for another') and concludes with Parsiphae and the bull; III combines excremental satire with an invocation of 'Macedonia' and dissolves into the ambiguous 'slow-worm's song'; IV summons Aneurin and Taliesin (bardic figures shared with Jones), re-evokes love but concludes in vagrancy; V describes winter, looks toward spring, remembers the woman and concludes with the 'Coda' as the poet departs with his imaginary 'kings'. *Briggflatts*, Bunting tells us, is autobiographical but not 'chronicle' – 'the truth of the poem is of another kind.'[13] For all its third-person voice, the poem is inherently personal – yet as self-projection not a self-registration: a fantasia, in depth, of a varied experience. Edward Lucie-Smith compares it to 'Lycidas'. '*Briggflatts*, too,' he writes, 'is an elegy – but for the poet's own life.'[14]

In personal terms, the woman seems central: there is celebration of joyous love yet hints of lost Paradise – of 'the road not taken':

> What can he, changed, tell
> her, changed, perhaps dead?

> (p. 54)

Unlike Jones's heavenly Muse, Bunting's is of the earth, earthy: her genitals are 'thatch'ed' (p. 53), her girdle 'greased with lard' (p. 66). Here woman is local, natural, wholesome and simple. She is 'home'. And however far she was 'real', she stands as embodiment and epiphany of all the poet seems to have lost of his youth itself. But woman does not suffice for the dreamer of Bloodaxe, Scarlatti, Macedonia or 'Schoenberg's maze', as Northumberland and York-shire were not enough in the life of the Villonesque poet of transi-tion – Paris, Rapallo, the Canaries, Persia and North America. Like the Pound of 'The Seafarer', 'Exile's Letter' or the *Cantos*, Bunting's vision and life were exploratory, his poetry Modernist-Interna-tional where 'all ages are contemporaneous'.[15] *Briggflatts* celebrates local continuities but it also evokes Italy and Greece, and its gaze looks beyond: 'we follow/... to fields we do not know'; 'Who/ ... guesses/where we go?' Thus the 'Coda' (like Tennyson's 'Ulysses') constitutes elegy as aspiration: the poem rejects woman for the open road: 'rat, roommate, unreconciled' (p. 67). It is the song of a Modernist 'Viking', plunderer of experience, who chooses freedom instead of 'hearth' ('Offshore wind, shout', p. 71). A Julia Kristeva might construe this as a masculinist choice of Thanatos over Eros – a 'strong song' composed from 'a letter unanswered' (p. 70).

Yet this is the poet's choice: the 'maker' is, like the reiterated 'mason', a grammatologist of the graven mark. 'The tune' comes first and the poet's concern is with language itself – even though he uses it to celebrate his lost love. The attempt is to create a permanent 'trace' of the life as adamantine text: 'Pens are too light./Take a chisel to write' (p. 53). Bunting's method is to work at the very unitary level of language, ringing sly changes and chimes within the subtleties of difference.

> Painful lark, labouring to rise!
> The solemn mallet says:
> In the grave's slot
> he lies. We rot.

(p 51)

The first line, alliterative and caesuraed as in Old English verse, concludes with the rich monosyllabic word 'rise' which sets up a series of sound-similarities – 'says', 'slot', 'lies' and 'rot'. Half-rhymes ('rise', 'says'), alliteration ('rise', 'rot'; 'slot' and 'lies') and full rhymes ('rise', 'lies'; 'slot', 'rot' – and, indeed, the crucial 'he', 'we') jangle the more resonantly because of the primary similarities in the vital differentiality in 'says', 'rise', 'lies' and 'slot', 'rot'. The technique can effect a gnomic resonance quite beyond explanation: 'ears err/for fear ...' (p. 51); 'crust and crumb' (p. 53); onomatopoeia, itself, is here frequently created by shuffling the right monosyllabic differences: 'rut thud the rim,/crushed grit' (p. 52) or 'Rain rinses the road' (p. 53). Bunting's reputation of being a poet's poet has much to do with this ability to foreground and activate the primal sound units from which meaning itself is created. Language here operates awarely, within the magical field of echoes and half-echoes which separates the 'semiotic chora'[16] of the mother–child unit ('infans' – unable to speak) from the symbolic order of the speaking subject. The method of *Briggflatts*, then, is fully authentic – establishing its meanings by performing the conditions of meaning creation itself.

However, Bunting is not only the enactor of synchronic *difference* but also a connoisseur of etymological depth. His fundamental word-hoard is composed of historically rooted terms which have survived debasement or semantic drift and hence constitute a

particular refinement of 'the dialect of the tribe'. Here is a typical
'verse' from within *Briggflatts*:

> Heat and hammer
>   draw out a bar.
> Wheel and water
>   grind an edge.

(p. 58)

Beyond pronunciation, there is nothing here that would puzzle
Langland – or perhaps even Caedmon. Bunting's language comprises a kind of basic English in etymological good faith. His
transitions of thought and scenario may be puzzling but his diction
constitutes plain honesty itself: even when we may not initially
understand it ('becks', 'grommets', 'gabbro', etc.), that is because
we are not acquainted with the local specificities they denote. The
world of *Briggflatts* is a place of historical continuities and to express it Bunting has collated timelessly valid words. His linguistic
craft builds up a textual site where words, as thoughts, constitute
one transhistorical continuum:

> Bloodaxe, king of York,
> king of Dublin, king of Orkney.
> Take no notice of tears;
> letter the stone to stand...

(p. 54)

'Great Time', here, is resonated in words hard as stones, washed
endlessly in the seas of history.

One way of placing Bunting's unique contribution would be to
evoke the 'Orality' of such as Walter J. Ong and Ruth Finnegan.[17]
Bunting's own formulation is crucial here: 'I have never said that
music is the only thing in poetry. I have said that it is the only
indispensable thing'.[18] The primacy of sound is what makes the
scenarios of *Briggflatts* so compelling, so haunting. Orality here is
interfused everywhere in the unrevisable (hence 'literary') authority of elaborately chosen writing – by a Gutenberg professional[19]
who worked in a newspaper office for years. The result is a wonderful hybrid. Pure Orality (Eric Clapton's 'Tears in Heaven' as

much as Croatian epic) is mnemonic, formulaic and open to variation; Bunting is very much a writer in that memorability in his
work is achieved as invented pattern (not formula but formational)
and steady accumulation of exact (and unvarying) words in specific order. *Briggflatts* combines the differing virtues of oral culture,
manuscript labour and print exactitude:

> Dung will not soil the slowworm's
> mosaic. Breathless lark
> drops to nest in sodden trash...

(p. 54)

The solidifying medium of print here immortalises (beyond fear of
some copyist's slip) an inscriptional labour for those with ears to
hear. Peter Makin has described Bunting's initial attraction to poetry as 'a need to respond aurally to aural stimuli'.[20] In terms of
cultural studies, Bunting can perhaps be seen as connoisseur of
Northumberland dialect, in the radio era, utilising printed words to
achieve uniquely resonant effect. Such a description by no means
explains the quality of Bunting's major poem, but it suggests the
specific situation of its achievement.

Bunting then (like Jones) has created a historically allusive and
linguistically canny long poem in the era of the short, idiosyncra-
tically (or 'personally') voiced lyric. In Hugh Kenner's astringent
and amusing diatribe *A Sinking Island*,[21] Bunting is held out as the
last of the 'makers' amid a metropolitanised welter of versifying
superficiality. It is engaging to find F.R. Leavis resurrected in a
Californian drawl, but there is room in both life and letters for a
multifarious 'poeticity'.[22]

There are those who have backed Bunting's achievement out of
what appears to be regional loyalty – this is limiting to his achievement even if the poet's craggy Northern partisanship encouraged
it. *Briggflatts* helped extend a modernist poetic into the years of
post-structuralism and postmodernism with admirable particularity. It has connected the remote past ('historiographic metafiction')[23] and the near present in an expressed field of awareness
which can survive into the third millennium with little transitory or
parochial contamination. It represents one of the finest contributions to British poetry of the latter half of the twentieth century. It
constitutes a 'light for the future'.

Notes

1. All quotations from Basil Bunting, *Collected Poems* (London: Fulcrum Press, 1970).
2. Much is made of the influence of the Lindisfarne Gospels in Peter Makin, *Bunting: The Shaping of His Verse* (Oxford: Clarendon Press, 1992).
3. However, he was influenced by other modern poets too. See Michael Schmidt, *A Reader's Guide to Fifty Modern British Poets* (London: Heinemann, 1979), p. 194. In the early 1970s Bunting recounted to myself and some colleagues from the University of Victoria, Canada, how he once applied for a Guggenheim Fellowship with W. B. Yeats, Ezra Pound and T. S. Eliot as referees: he did not attain one. Diana Collecott, Co-director of the Basil Bunting Poetry Centre at Durham University, has confirmed the anecdote – apparently Pound did not send a reference.
4. As in the Movement. See Blake Morrison, *The Movement* (Oxford: Oxford University Press, 1980).
5. See M. M. Bakhtin, *Speech Genres and Other Late Essays*, translated by Vern W. McGee, eds Caryl Emerson and Michael Holquist (Austin, Tex.: University of Texas Press, 1986), p. 170.
6. David Jones, *The Anathemata: Fragments of an Attempted Writing* (London: Faber, 1972).
7. David Blamires, *David Jones: Artist and Writer* (Manchester: Manchester University Press, 1978), p. 431.
8. Quoted in Humphrey Carpenter, *A Serious Character: The Life of Ezra Pound* (London: Faber, 1988), p. 431. For a highly informative account of Bunting's earlier poems see Eric Mottram's essay ' "An Acknowledged Land": Love and Poetry in Bunting's Sonatas' in the Basil Bunting Special Issue, *Poetry Information*, Vol. 19, Autumn 1978, pp. 11–29.
9. See Ezra Pound, *Selected Prose 1909–1965*, ed. William Cookson (London: Faber, 1978), p. 236.
10. See Bunting's note about *Briggflatts*, in *Collected Poems*, op. cit., p. 156.
11. *Briggflatts* tended to take pride of place in Bunting's many readings. I myself recall the resonance he could give to such an unfortunate compound as 'turd-bakers'.
12. 'As regarding rhythm: to compose in the sequence of the musical phrase, not in the sequence of a metronone', from 'A Retrospect', Ezra Pound, *Literary Essays*, ed. T.S. Eliot (London: Faber, 1968), p. 3.
13. From the Notes, *Collected Poems*, op. cit., p. 156.
14. Edward Lucie-Smith, *Contemporary Poets of the English Language* (London: Saint James Press, 1970), p. 162.
15. Ezra Pound, *The Spirit of Romance*, quoted in Humphrey Carpenter, *A Serious Character*, op. cit., p. 126.
16. 'The mother's body is therefore what mediates the symbolic law organizing social relations and becomes the ordering principle of the semiotic *chora* ...' The whole essay 'Revolution in Poetic Language' should be read for a full understanding of this

term. *The Kristeva Reader*, ed. Toril Moi (Oxford: Basil Blackwell, 1986) p. 95.

17.   See Walter J. Ong, *Orality and Literacy: The Technologizing of the Word* (London: Methuen, 1982) and Ruth Finnegan, *Oral Poetry: Its Nature, Significance and Social Context* (Oxford: Oxford University Press, 1977).

18.   Quoted in Hugh Kenner, *A Sinking Island: The Modern English Writers* (London: Barrie & Jenkins, 1986), p. 257.

19.   I mean that in the sense of Marshall McLuhan in *The Gutenberg Galaxy* (London: Routledge & Kegan Paul, 1967).

20.   Peter Makin, *Bunting*, op. cit., p. 3.

21.   See note 18 above.

22.   I mean this also in the expanded sense of Richard Rorty in *Contingency, Irony, and Solidarity* (Cambridge: Cambridge University Press, 1989).

23.   Linda Hutcheon's somewhat ungainly, if well worked-out, phrase in *A Poetics of Postmodernism: History, Theory, Fiction* (London, Routledge, 1988).

3

'Never Such Innocence Again'[1]:
The Poetry of Philip Larkin

Gary Day

Larkin once remarked that 'First and foremost, writing poems should be a pleasure. So should reading them by God.'[2] At first sight it is hard to see how poems about 'unhappiness, loss [and] a sense of missing out'[3] can be a pleasure either to read or write but, as Larkin said on another occasion, '[t]he impulse for producing a poem is never negative; the most negative poem in the world is a very positive thing to have done.'[4] Larkin enters into more detail about the writing of poetry in his essay 'The Pleasure Principle' where he says that it consists of three stages:

> The first is when a man becomes obsessed with an emotional concept to such a degree that he is compelled to do something about it. What he does is the second stage, namely, construct a verbal device that will reproduce this emotional concept in anyone who cares to read it, anywhere, anytime. The third stage is the recurrent situation of people in different times and places setting off the device and re-creating in themselves what the poet felt when he wrote it.[5]

This conveys a somewhat simplistic notion of poetic composition. Leaving on one side the fact that Larkin refers only to males he asserts that a poem can only have one meaning to which he gives the rather cumbersome term 'emotional concept'. He also assumes a division between form and content which cannot really be sustained, since form and content are locked together in a mutually determining relationship. Larkin sees form as secondary to content. It is almost like a freezer keeping the emotional concept fresh until the appearance of the reader. There is some ambiguity here because it is not clear how far the poem reproduces the emotional concept, nor how far the reader sets it off. Clearly the poem needs the reader and the reader needs the poem, but Larkin writes as if they are somehow independent.

Larkin's view of the reader is equally problematic, even naive, for he sees no difficulty in the reader experiencing the same emotional concept that he did before enclosing it in the poem. What Larkin of course ignores is the reader's historical and class position and the literary codes and conventions which he or she brings to the work. Larkin takes an authoritarian attitude towards the reader, circumscribing his or her experience of the work by insisting on its one meaning which, moreover, never changes. Indeed, the reader is envisaged as someone incapable of seeing things as the poet sees them for he or she lacks the poet's 'experience [and] education'.[6] In this scenario, the reader is someone to be educated and the question of pleasure disappears into the background. However, the idea that the reader needs educating would make it impossible for him or her to experience the emotional concept in the same way that the poet does, thus collapsing Larkin's case even further.

Indeed, Larkin's view of the reader is highly confused. He disparages the academic reader and exalts the common reader who simply enjoys poetry, yet in the poem 'Fiction and the Reading Public' he reviles this same reader for his or her vulgarity and ignorance. Who, then, does Larkin imagine the common reader to be? It is unlikely that it is any of the characters who inhabit his poetry though they with their blighted lives, like Mr Bleaney, are common enough. The answer, quite simply, is Larkin himself. Andrew Motion has pointed out how Larkin's poems characteristically take the form of a debate between the two sides of his personality[7] and, I would add, one of these sides functions as a reader whom Larkin addresses and argues with.

In 'Dockery & Son' he asks where the assumptions discussed derive from and answers:

> ... They're more a style
> Our lives bring with them: habit for a while
> Suddenly they harden into all we've got ...

> (*CP*, p. 165)

Here he assumes a reader with whom he is on familiar terms, and the use of 'we' suggests shared experience and values. The reader is there to bounce ideas off, and through this process the poem takes shape. In this instance, the reader is not someone who receives the poet's emotional concept but rather someone who is constitutive of the poem. The same is true of 'Self's the Man' whose opening lines contrasting Arnold and the narrator suggest that Larkin has been provoked into that statement by a reader's moral questioning.

Larkin's engagement with an implied reader not only undermines his view of the poem as a one-way message but it also suggests that his poetry is not as self-contained as he seems to think. If it does indeed take the form of a debate then that debate is never quite resolved, questions are raised which continue to reverberate making a mockery of the poem's apparent closure. This 'closure' is often achieved by an image or a highly charged phrase which far from reconciling the poem's tensions seems to increase them before abandoning them to the reader. At the end of 'Home is so Sad' the phrase 'That vase', seems to direct a jet of bile at the 'Home' which elsewhere is described sympathetically. The image at the end of 'Aubade' again calls in doubt what has previously been said. The poem is unremitting in the way it confronts death which is 'always there' and the last line perhaps reinforces this by the comparison of postmen with doctors. However, doctors are also people who cure and this introduces a positive note which is sustained by the general sense of day beginning again. This sense of an enduring continuity contrasts with the stark fact of death and the poem hesitates between these two positions which are in such stark opposition that there can be no reconciliation between them.

Clearly then, Larkin's pronouncements on poetry are not borne out by his practice of it. The openness of his poems, their lack of fixity or closure suggest that views of Larkin as 'a hopeless and inflexible pessimist'[8] need to be revised. Andrew Motion points out 'the mitigating function of his language...his hope of deriving comfort from social and natural rituals [and] his symbolist devices [through which he manages] to transcend the flow of contingent time altogether.'[9] This view, while slightly redressing the balance, does not radically extend our understanding of Larkin for it keeps within the tradition of the poet as creator. This tradition views poetry as the lyrical outpouring of a unified consciousness. What I would wish to argue is that Larkin's poetry is not an expression of that consciousness; on the contrary, it is an attempt to establish it.

In this respect, Larkin's 'borrowings' from psychoanalysis may be quite instructive if only because, at some level, psychoanalysis is concerned with the creation and history of a consciousness that we inadequately refer to as the self. Larkin talks of being 'obsessed' prior to writing and obsession is one of the neuroses investigated in psychoanalysis, from which Larkin also takes the phrase 'the pleasure principle'. Larkin's use of psychoanalytic terminology inevitably invites a different view of his poetry to the one he purposes. Psychoanalysis, with its emphasis on the importance of the unconscious, posits a divided view of the human psyche which Larkin unwittingly endorses by his use of psychoanalytic vocabulary. For example, the term 'obsession' suggests a distorted view of reality and this undermines the poet's authority which is thus transferred to the reader as he or she tries to discover what the source of Larkin's obsession or unhappiness is. Could it be, as he himself suggests, 'Something to do with violence/A long way back,...' ('Love Again', *CP*, p. 215). The point is not whether it would be profitable to conduct a psychoanalytic investigation of Philip Larkin, but to show, firstly, that Larkin talks about poetry using a language so haunted by its original meanings that it disrupts the ones he intends and, secondly, that there is a basis for a thoroughgoing psychoanalytic account of Larkin's work but one concentrating on psychoanalysis and language rather than psychoanalysis and character.

Larkin uses the term 'pleasure principle' to discourage discussion not just of his work but that of other poets too, and yet his own work is highly discursive, inviting therefore a discursive response. However, although the poetry is allowed to be discursive, no one is allowed to be discursive about the poetry. Larkin's remarks about poetry are defensive (perhaps suggestive of the relationship between the analyst and the analysand?). He excludes the reader from any experience of the poem other than the one sanctioned by himself, though this resurrects the old debate about intention. As far as Larkin is concerned, he has done the reader's work and so he or she is not to worry about ambiguities, complexities or contradictions since Larkin has shown that he is able to balance all these. True, this may not always work but, if the poems do remain open, this can be overridden by Larkin's assertion that they should be enjoyed.

More important than Larkin's use of the phrase 'the pleasure principle' as a defence against legitimate criticism is its root in psychoanalysis. In Freud's writings, the pleasure principle is opposed to the reality principle which, unlike the former, does not take the most direct route to satisfaction, but instead makes detours, postponing the attainment of its goal according to the constraints of the outside world. It could be said that Larkin adheres strongly to the reality principle in his verse which would further undermine his view of poetry as pleasure. In 'Poetry of Departures' he juxtaposes the dullness of his own life with the excitement of the adventurer, but that only helps him to stay 'Sober and industrious' since to act on these fantasies would only be '...a deliberate step backwards/To create.../...a life/Reprehensibly perfect'. The same view is apparent in 'Toads' and 'Toads Revisited' where, in the latter, 'Walking around in the park/Should feel better than work' (CP, p. 147). but, inevitably, it doesn't; far better to have the 'in-tray' with all its paper work instead.

The acceptance of the reality principle points to the conservatism at the heart of Larkin's verse and his revulsion at the hedonism of mass culture. More importantly, however, the acceptance of the reality principle is one stage in the construction of the self, particularly in relation to work which can be one of the prime ways of gaining self-definition. The acceptance of the reality principle also involves an act of repression, although we need to be careful here for there is a case for saying that the debate in Larkin's verse, at least as it affects the reality/pleasure principles, may be something of an illusion. The very choice of pleasures in 'Toads Revisited', for instance, together with the way they are presented strongly suggests that they are not equal competitors in the debate with 'reality'. This implies that Larkin's mind is already made up; more, it indicates that he is not truly examining the nature, the *reality* of the pleasure he represses and so the establishment of the reality principle is founded, in part, on a flight from reality. Whatever the truth of the matter the repression of pleasure ensures its return; it is something with which Larkin never ceases to struggle.

It is a puzzle to him why he can derive little pleasure from things, and he wonders '...why it never worked for me' ('Love Again'). The pleasures of jazz and sex are tinged with the sadness. In 'Reference Back' King Oliver's *Riverside Blues* triggers unhappy memories while 'Talking In Bed' gives a bleak picture of post-coital depression. As for the pleasures of others, Larkin is given to denigrating them, though this is more complex than it at first seems. He describes the women who shop in 'The Large Cool Store' as 'synthetic' and 'natureless' (*CP*, p. 135). This suggests that Larkin distinguishes between natural and artificial pleasure. It is at this point that one of the major differences between Larkin's early and later verse becomes relevant. In early poems such as 'Deep Analysis' and 'Thaw' Larkin uses natural imagery for a variety of purposes, including the registering and recording of pleasure but, as this imagery slowly disappears from his verse, so too do the capacities it gave him for exploring and representing pleasure. What this shows is that pleasure is, at least in part, a function of a particular type of poetic diction rather than simply an event or sensation.

The use of natural imagery in the early verse is also responsible for some of that verse's obscurity and this is particularly true of 'Many famous feet have trod'. This 'natural' imagery seems to be implicated in the exploration of inwardness, an idea supported by there being few references to the 'real world' in the early verse. This dense, florid diction which makes copious use of natural imagery reflects the Symbolist influence in Larkin's work which came to him via Yeats. The symbolists stressed the priority of suggestion over direct description and the function of the symbol was to convey a private mood or emotion or suggest affinities between the material and spiritual world. Larkin slowly sifted out this rich diction from his poetry, inclining to a more empirical idiom that he saw as one of the virtues of Hardy, another influence. Larkin's poetry is thus, in part, the shifting relationship between two types of poetic discourse, though it is important to remember that their differences should not obscure their similarities – both, for example, are grounded in the notion of individual expression. Larkin may have cut out the obvious influences of the symbolists from his work but their assumption of a unique and private consciousness is partly what sustains that sense of isolation which pervades his poetry and prevents him from exploiting the more integrative possibilities of his more characteristic plain and empirical language: the ghost of the old self prevents the creation of a new.

Larkin, then, seems to be torn between two different types of language, which might perhaps correspond to the division between the pleasure and reality principles. For the sake of expediency I will call these languages the natural and the empirical. The former is orientated inwards, is symbolic and only weakly referential. The latter is orientated outwards, is referential and only weakly symbolic. Despite Larkin's move towards the empirical language he still has a vision of himself as natural, 'One of those old type *natural fouled up guys*' (original italics), he says in 'Posterity', a poem which incidentally continues the theme of 'The Pleasure Principle' in its attack on researchers and would-be biographers. The difference between the early and late styles and the consequence this has for the perception and expression of pleasure is not without irony in that the language of the early poems is highly conventional and so cannot provide an authentic experience of pleasure any more than can large cool stores. This irony escapes Larkin who can only inveigh against manufactured pleasure. What he is objecting to here is a false representation and, in so doing, he reveals his poetic ethic that the word should correspond to the thing. In this context, poems like 'Sunny Prestatyn' make a great deal of sense. This describes the defacement of an advertisement but, more importantly, it dramatises at some level Larkin's poetic development. Put simply, the poster offers an unrealistic view of life which corresponds to the sort of ideas found in Larkin's early verse. His later work corrects that view and this is reflected in the spifflication of the poster. However, this vandalising of the poster shows that the move towards the empirical has achieved nothing but a spectacle of destruction. On the other hand, tearing the poster and ripping away the dream reveals, if the poem is to be believed, only another text, 'Fight Cancer', which belongs to the same signifying chain as the poster itself. There is, in other words, no reality behind the text except another text and this calls into question the accepted view of Larkin as a poet of the real. Finally it is worth commenting that the woman in the poster is humiliated and degraded and the violence inflicted on her does, to some extent, mirror the occasional violence of Larkin's language when he's writing about love or sex. An example is the comparison of women to game birds in ('Letter to a Friend about Girls') and in 'The Life with a Hole in it' (itself a sexually ambiguous title) he is quite vicious about women whom he brands as 'ratbags'.

The bitterness that boils up from what should be a source of pleasure is yet another reminder of the instability of that word, its original context and connotations urging the reader to view Larkin's work from an angle different to the one he suggests. I have already looked at the relationship between the pleasure principle and the reality principle but there is still another aspect of the former, again drawing from psychoanalysis, which may have some bearing on Larkin's work. Freud's basic idea of the pleasure principle is that it is aimed at procuring pleasure through a reduction of tension. It is linked to the compulsion to repeat. Freud developed two views of this phenomenon, the first concerned repetition of needs and the second the need for repetition. It was this second view which made Freud doubt the dominance of the pleasure principle for he found something daemonic in a repetition which seemed to go beyond the simple satisfaction of the instincts or the attempt to come to terms with an unpleasant experience. He eventually interpreted the daemonic character of repetition as the death instinct and, since death is the ultimate reduction of tension, it could be linked with the pleasure principle which Freud eventually came to believe served the death instinct.

Repetition, daemonic or not, occurs in a number of ways in Larkin. The first relates to imagery – 'sheep', 'rain', 'trees' and 'snow', to mention but a few, all occur throughout his work. What is noticeable is that these are all images to do with nature and they therefore belong to that natural language which Larkin 'abandoned'. The significance of the images is hard to define. The sheep in 'To a Very Slow Air' are a symbol of joy and contentment which is the very opposite of the women in 'Faith Healing' who are biblical sheep, distressed and disorientated. The meaning depends on the context. Another kind of repetition is the poetic tradition which Larkin inherited and a third is his constant use of regular patterns of rhyme and rhythm. These repetitions offer some reassurance against the instability of meaning in the poems, and they also help to shore up the sense of self which is so loosely and vulnerably established in them. The movement of these repetitions is minimal compared with the riotous motion of meaning but it would perhaps be going too far to suggest this relative stasis functioned as a sort of textual death wish.

On another level, however, it is tempting to see Larkin's pessimism as a kind of death instinct though this view is contradicted by the fear of death which runs through Larkin's work. Andrew Motion rejects the idea of a death wish in Larkin on the basis that only one poem, 'Wants', contains a desire for oblivion. What Motion does not explain, however, even though he notices it, is Larkin's desire for release from the ordinary, contingent world which can be found in poems such as 'High Windows'. In the first four verses Larkin wonders whether anyone looked as enviously at him as he looks at the young lovers, though, as always, he is sceptical about pleasure and this comes through in his brutal diction, 'when I see a couple of Kids/And guess he's fucking her' (*CP*, p. 165). As he contemplates this scenario and tries to relate it to his past he apparently experiences a feeling of transcendence in the last stanza. In actual fact, this represents an escape from trying to reconcile past and present and from the words used to do that. The lines reveal a desire for nothingness which is also a tacit admission of the failure of empirical language to relate past and present in a meaningful way which, incidentally, is the aim psychoanalysis achieved, despite the claims made for its empirical scientific status, through a basically literary language. One thinks, for example, of its reliance on the Oedipus complex. In this context, one wonders what the significance is of finding psychoanalytic terms in Larkin's criticism and empiricism in his poetry.

Empiricism is the language of democracy, the welfare state and mass culture and yet it somehow fails to accommodate the experiences of twentieth-century life. Its rational, realistic character gives it a kind of anonymity which makes it difficult to use as a medium of personal expression, this despite the fact that the accent of modern life since the 1950s has been on the personal. However, this 'personal' is invariably linked to public interest, though public here means the state or big business. In the language of politics, consumerism and the media the personal is subtly identified with the public. This is one bar to developing an individual voice. Another is the generally inclusive nature of this language. By cleverly conflating public and private it makes it difficult for anyone, poet or railway worker, to distance themselves from what that language directs them to – a definition of themselves which helps to reproduce the society of which they are a part. This language constructs everyone as citizens at the very moment it addresses them. Larkin's problem is how to construct his own sense of self using a language which has already constructed a self for him. This process can be seen in a very schematic way in 'Self's The Man'. Larkin compares himself to Arnold saying that the latter is less selfish than he. By the end of the poem though, Larkin is unsure who is the 'better person', Arnold or himself. Arnold represents the 'average citizen' from whom Larkin is constantly trying to differentiate himself in his own quest for selfhood but, by the penultimate verse, he recognises that he and Arnold are more alike than he at first thought. Larkin says that he's '. . . a better hand/At knowing what [he] can stand' thus differentiating himself from

Arnold, but the final line, 'Or I suppose I can', introduces doubt and uncertaintity. Maybe he and Arnold are the same. The inclusive nature of the empirical language consistently inhibits any attempt to establish a unique self.

Another poem which endeavours to generate a sense of self is 'Reasons for Attendance'. Here, Larkin appears to define himself against the dancers whom he watches through the window but the poem is a little more complicated than that. In the first place he depends on the trumpet, not on himself, to tell him that he is individual, '... that lifted, rough tongued bell/ ... whose individual sound/Insists I too am individual' (*CP*, p. 80). That 'insists' is significant, suggesting as it does the poet's deprecation as well as a sense of force – one *has* to be individual. Even more important is the way the poem breaks down the distinction between inside and outside on which the poet depends for his sense of self. Both he and the dancers '... are satisfied/If no-one has misjudged himself. Or lied'. The same considerations apply to both observer and observed and so the barrier separating them breaks down. The language of the poem militates against its attempt to establish a sense of self which collapses back into what it tried to differentiate itself from.

A sense of self involves a perception or experiences of continuity and this is achieved by being able to relate past to present. The empirical, rational, realistic language that Larkin uses is not one which readily makes connections. It is a language primarily of the present, the here and now. It is a language designed to smooth over the contradictions of capitalism, not underline them. In some profound sense it is a language that abolishes history and it is the more effective in this because of the way it combines with the rhythms of work, leisure and technology to generate a sense of sameness. Familiar ways of seeing the world appear regularly in the media complementing the largely unchanging routine of everyday life. This suppresses any sense of break, discontinuity or even development, anything new being so quickly absorbed into the existing structures that it appears as if it has always been part of them. The empirical language is a language of taxonomy, not relation. It is hardly surprising therefore that Larkin should have difficulty in connecting past and present and this is an issue not just in 'High Windows' as we have seen, but also, in different ways, in 'Going, Going', 'The Old Fools' and 'I Remember, I Remember'.

The qualities of empirical language then, its anonymity, its conflation of the public and the private, its inclusiveness and its taxonomies all obstruct the effort to establish a sense of self, not the least because this is a language which provides people with a standardised self by interpellating them as consumers and citizens. Larkin tries to establish a sense of self by differentiating himself from the modern world but the nature of the language he is compelled to use propels him back into it. If the poems do sometime give a sense of a transcendent consciousness that is due to empirical language requiring one. It is a language that depends on the distinction between observer and observed and so it could be argued that it actually positions people as outsiders despite its otherwise inclusive nature. Larkin the observer, the outsider, is positioned as such by his language; his isolation, therefore, is as linguistic as his pleasure. However, if empirical language positions Larkin as the observer looking in, his poems, as in 'Reasons For Attendance', collapse distinctions between outside and inside, observer and observed, and so constitute an assault on the hierarchies of empiricism which is the first step to creating a sense of self. This is a more positive interpretation of Larkin's failure to differentiate himself from the modern world and its inhabitants. Whether it is more true is another matter. What is certain is that the pressures Larkin faces in trying to construct a sense of self prove intolerable, forcing him, as at the end of 'High Windows', to seek a wordless region, a nothingness.

The collapse of distinctions in Larkin's later poetry recalls that mingled, non-differentiated state typical of some of his early work; '...that peacock fan/The future [...] in which [is] temptingly spread/All that elaborative nature can' ('To My Wife', *CP*, p. 54). The question arises as to why Larkin cannot go beyond this state and the answer seems to lie in the innate conservatism of his empirical language. It pays a great deal of respect to things as they are and this helps to secure them even though there is a strong sense that they are unsatisfactory and need to be changed. Larkin may find no satisfaction in the world he describes but the logic of his language compels him to render it faithfully rather than conceive ways of changing it. However, this strong link between word and thing is disrupted by Larkin's characteristic irony, hesitation and doubt, as he put it in 'Ignorance': 'Strange to know nothing, never to be sure/of what is true or right or real? (*CP*, p. 107). These same qualities may also be said to prevent his being pulled back into the society from which he tries to differentiate himself. They also constitute the beginnings of the postmodern consciousness.

To return to the 'death wish', it is not a psychological problem so much as a solution to the failure of language to realise a coherent self: where words generate so many contradictions there is 'Nothing to be Said' and so it is better to escape words altogether. But this 'death wish' is also implicated in the notion of form. For example, death is a crucial part of the significance of 'An Arundel Tomb'. The form of the effigies, particularly the grace imported by the sculptor, both expresses and guarantees their meaning. However, it is in the early verse that the link between death and form is most apparent but before that can be demonstrated it is necessary to give a brief description of the character of the early verse.

One of its chief features is an awareness of multiplicity, of a plethora of choice, and of a wide range of identities. There is also a strong sense of movement in the early verse of things criss–crossing, cutting into and articulating with each other in a perpetual process of becoming that never quite settles into being. 'We are born each morning...' Larkin declares in 'Many famous feet have trod', and, in the same poem, he writes that 'Nothing's to reach, but something's to become' (CP, pp. 17–18). In 'And the wave sings because it is moving' the symbolic waves work 'To break with beating all our false devices' (CP, p. 6). The early verse brims with possibilities and meaning has not yet acquired the repressive force it comes to have in Larkin's empirical language for reality is expressed in language containing its own rebuttal as in 'If, My Darling'. The qualities found in these and other poems bear a striking resemblance to the characteristics of postmodernism with its emphasis on the relativity of meaning. Larkin embraces this condition and endeavours to learn 'The difficult triple sanity/of being water, stone and flower in turn' ('Many famous feet have trod'). This sense of possibility, of freedom, may be related to the historic election of the Labour government in 1945 on a radical programme that constituted a fundamental assault on the old hierarchies and orthodoxies of British society. The poems I have mentioned were mostly written in 1946 and their mood, if not their language, reflects a belief in change and progress, a belief in the ability to abandon old ways and try new ones.

Although this condition of freedom and possibility is welcomed there is an anxiety about whether it can be sustained, 'Can it be borne, this bodying-forth by wind/of joy my actions turn on...?'

('Wedding-Wind'), *CP*, p. 11). This is linked to a perception of death in that movement of being which was to transcend it, '...For in the word death/There is nothing to grasp; nothing to catch or claim' (*CP*, p. 6). Death thus becomes synonymous with what was previously a pleasurable formlessness and a perpetual becoming. Form, which before was perceived as a limitation, is now something which focuses and animates. 'I am suddenly charged with their language, these six strings/suddenly made to see they can declare/Nothing but harmony' ('Two Guitar Pieces', *CP*, p. 8).

Formlessness implies a surrender to what is. Form is a matter of will or choice, an idea that is very important to Larkin and, of course, to consumer capitalism generally. One of the terrible things about getting old for Larkin is that the adult power of choice disappears as shown in ('The Old Fools'). To choose form is also to choose a self but this involves the repression of other choices so form is oppressive at the same time that it is enabling, 'No Road' being one of the poems where this struggle is dramatised.

The self comes into being through an act of will and a withdrawal from plenitude in a movement that parallels the passage from the imaginary to the symbolic. Also, just as the possibilities of Larkin's early verse mirrored the hopes for the future of British society so does his withdrawal reflect, in a sense, the decline of Britain as a world power, to wit the pulling back of her troops from around the globe and the development of a comparative insularity as the government tried to reorganise the currency after its near collapse in 1947. A new subjectivity is constituted as a new England emerges. Larkin may object in 'Homage to a Government' to the withdrawal of troops from around the world yet it is a movement he himself has enacted.

The creation of form, of a sense of self, involves choice and a kind of death. However, the emphasis on choice is contradicted by Larkin saying that 'Most things are never meant' ('Going, Going', *CP*, p. 190). This relates to the detail in 'An Arundel Tomb' of the earl and countess holding hands. This, unintended by either earl or countess, is a gratuitous addition by the sculptor, nevertheless it comes to be their emblem. The most accidental part of the work comes to be its most revealing aspect, an idea that is, of course, common in psychoanalysis. Deliberate choice then cannot create an authentic sense of self firstly because 'most things aren't meant' and secondly because the importance of the unintended detail undermines any notion of choice. Formlessness was a threat to self because it came to resemble death, but form also involves a kind of death and, furthermore, it does not help to establish a sense of self. The more strongly defined form of the later poetry does not resolve the problem of merging and mingling of identifies in the earlier work which came to seem like death; what it may offer, however, in its clever use of rhyme and rhythm, is some sort of order which acts as a relief from the instability of sense and identity. In this way perhaps form comes to take on the burden of establishing a sense of self which is somehow always elsewhere or already created. If this is the case then self becomes a rhythm which depends on words for its beat but not for meaning and this perhaps is the nearest Larkin can come to that state of nothing and wordlessness desired not just in 'High Windows' but in poems like 'The Winter Palace', 'Then there will be nothing I know/My mind will fold into itself, like fields, like snow'. It would be interesting to see whether this inter-pretation of rhythm has any bearing on technology. Eliot said that the internal combustion engine altered people's perception of rhythm and there would seem to be good grounds for considering the relationship between the rhythms of poetry and those of tech-nology. Is Larkin popular not because of the accessibility of his verse but because his rhythms correspond to the rhythms of mod-ern life, both imposing a kind of order on otherwise unmanageable reality?

The discussion of form has come a long way from Larkin's 'verbal device'. In 'The Pleasure Principle' he assumed a division between form and content but in the last verse of 'Toads', when he talks about one bodying the other's spiritual truth, they seem indistinguishable; work and pleasure, form and content somehow seem to blend together. Pleasure is not what Larkin imagined it to be. He saw it as relating to the reading and writing of poetry but it is also the opposite of work and his verse often deals with having to choose between them. This pleasure is squeezed out, frustrated and eventually relocated in that wordless realm which is also a refuge from the contradictions involved in trying to establish the self. That wordless realm is ultimately the rhymes and rhythms of the verse, their repetitions a sign of reassuring order. Contained within these rhymes and rhythms are the traditional English metres ensuring that Larkin is at last integrated into some sort of community. But frustrated pleasure can also be turned into bitter-ness and this is its other face, as can be seen in the vicious diction of

'Love Again' or the crazed recognition of 'The secret, bestial peace', in 'The Card Players' This too is a wordless realm, but it has an oppressive intensity about it that focuses the self rather than dispersing it across a variety of rhythmic patterns.

This essay has glimpsed at the buried psychoanalytic dimension of Larkin's views on poetry and suggested how that might affect our understanding of his work. It has also looked at how Larkin's language hinders his project of establishing a sense of self. Larkin's views on poetry are quite aggressively expressed, which itself is suggestive. His criterion of pleasure is too simple to account for either the reading or writing of poetry. The last verse of 'Toads', which brings work and pleasure together, should be the new starting point for readers of his work who, freed from his strictures, can begin 'afresh, afresh, afresh' ('The Trees'. *CP*, p. 166).

Notes

1. MCMXIV. All quotations from the poems are taken from Anthony Thwaite (ed.) *Philip Larkin Collected Poems* (London and Boston: Faber & Faber, 1988). Page references to *CP* henceforth are given after the quote.
2. 'An Interview with Paris Review', in Philip Larkin, *Required Writing Miscellaneous Pieces 1955–1982* (London and Boston: Faber & Faber, 1983), p. 68.
3. 'An Interview with the Observer', ibid., p. 47.
4. 'A Conversation with Philip Larkin', *Tracks*, Vol. I, Summer, 1967.
5. 'The Pleasure Principle', in Philip Larkin, *Required Writing*, op. cit., pp. 80–2, p. 80.
6. Ibid., p. 82.
7. Andrew Motion, *Philip Larkin* (London and New York: Routledge, 1982), p. 66.
8. Ibid., p. 59.
9. Ibid.

4

Poetic Subjects:
Tony Harrison and Peter Reading

Neil Roberts

The apparent parallels between the poetry of Tony Harrison and Peter Reading are numerous. They are, of contemporary British poets, among the most preoccupied with and drawn to 'traditional' forms, and yet they are both vehemently hostile to poetry as a 'special preserve' (Harrison) or 'Ovaltine' (Reading). Contemporary social reality, often in ugly manifestations, finds its way into the work of both, and they make deliberately shocking and foregrounded use of obscene language – Harrison's *v.* caused an uproar when it was televised, and there is no doubt that either of Reading's last two volumes would have provoked a similar response. This is related to a more extensive and significant attempt on the part of both to integrate vernacular working-class speech into poetry – not only into poetry but, explicitly and self-consciously, into verse-forms that by custom belong to the educated classes.

> *You're supposed to be the bright boy at description*
> *and you can't tell them what the fuck to put!*[1]

> *Who would have thought it Sir, actually putting ME in a WRITING!*
> *me and the Capting and ALL. What a turn up for the books.*[2]

In Harrison's case the filling of the iambic pentameter with the words his father (or mother or, in *v.*, skinhead) might speak is a literal representation of the desire stated in 'Them and [uz]' to 'occupy' the 'lousy leasehold' (*SP*, p. 123) of literature. The speaker in the extract I have quoted from Reading's *Ukulele Music* is Viv, the 'poet''s daily help, whose voice has hitherto been heard in ungrammatical prose. Tom Paulin has claimed, though with a

48

sympathetically sceptical note, that this transition is a similar kind of 'occupation':

> This suggests that by some miraculous movement of the spirit the British working class might suddenly take power from those who divide and manipulate it. This is the pastoral poet's dream of stealing a march on his exploitative urban readership and seizing real power.[3]

These similarities are all quite real, and almost compel the reader who admires both poets to make the comparison, but it reveals very marked contrasts.

Harrison is routinely praised for his metrical craftsmanship, and yet his handling of the iambic pentameter is actually quite loose. Although, unlike such formal practitioners as Larkin and Hill, he invariably uses full rhyme, he often leaves the reader uncertain how many stresses there are in a line – to take a typical example, the first line of *v.*:

> Next millenium you'll have to search quite hard ...

> (*SP*, p. 236)

This method is interestingly illuminated by the two kinds of comment that Harrison makes about metre. He makes them conveniently together in his interview with John Haffenden:

> Originally I was drawn to metrical verse because I wanted to 'occupy' literature ... Now that I've occupied it in the sense that I can do it ... I still instinctively feel that it's associated with the heart beat, with the sexual instinct, with all those physical rhythms which go on despite the moments when you feel suicidal.[4]

On the one hand a concern with culture and tradition, the project of appropriating these; on the other, the rhythms of the body. These might be seen as manifestations of two different and (at least in the arena of poetry) conflicting kinds of humanism: the kind associated with 'humane letters', which draws the poet to imitate established forms, and the kind invoked by D.H. Lawrence when he instructed Edward Marsh to read his poetry with the 'sensitive soul', not with

the 'mechanical' ear.[5] Another, more obvious, conflict at work in
the poetry is between the granting to the reader by the 'occupier' of
what Harrison calls 'that literary frisson' and the exacting of the
price in 'the consciousness of social gaps and divisions' (Haffenden, p. 21).

Of prominent contemporary poets in our language, Harrison is
perhaps the one whom the description 'humanist' most suits. In the
most traditional of senses, his classical education and his activity as
translator of the great works of antiquity, French neoclassicism and
mediaeval English, and his preoccupation with the contemporary
relevance of the classics, put him in a line that stretches back to the
Renaissance. And, more importantly, his poetry is affirmatively
humanist in a sense that has lately been brought into question.
Since I do not want to make this point in a negative way, let me
say that it is part of Harrison's distinction that his poetry speaks
with a unitary voice, and although it inevitably speaks of conflicts
and divisions, these are situated within a unified subject. Apart
from obvious dramatic monologues such as 'The Nuptial Torches'
and 'The White Queen' or translations such as the Palladas poems,
there is no overt distinction between the speaker, the poet and the
biographical Tony Harrison. The biography of course is a construct
– heavily weighted towards his childhood, and to a lesser degree
his life in Florida with Teresa Stratas, and almost nothing of the
breakdown of his first marriage – but only to the extent that
biography in literature is invariably so.

The most obvious strength that the poetry derives from this is
that, at least since the beginning of the 'School of Eloquence',
everything forms part of an interrelating *oeuvre*, and poems derive
meaning from each other in an unusually direct way. To take a
simple example, the gibe of the skinhead in *v.* about the poet's
mother:

> *She didn't understand yer fucking 'art'!*
> *She thought yer fucking poetry obscene!*

(*SP*, p. 241)

is for the reader of the *Selected Poems* informed by 'Bringing Up' in
which the poet recollects his mother's distress about *The Loiners* –
'*You weren't brought up to write such mucky books!*' (*SP*, p. 166) – and
this in turn is informed by having read the *Loiners* poems them-

selves. Moreover, we are enabled to see retrospectively that one of the meanings of the earlier sexually liberated poems is a defiance of the puritanism in Harrison's working-class upbringing, and this defiance is part of what has to be paid for in the elegies for his parents. A final point about this set of connections (which I shall return to) is that the shadow-voice of the skinhead in *v.* doesn't tell Harrison the poet anything that he doesn't know already.

'The School of Eloquence' contains some of the most moving poems writen in recent years. In 'Timer' the poet receives, at the crematorium, the clothes his mother died in and the wedding ring that survived the cremation.

> It's on my warm palm now, your burnished ring!
> I feel your ashes, head, arms, breasts, womb, legs,
> sift through its circle slowly, like that thing
> you used to let me watch to time the eggs.

> *(SP*, p. 167)

To say that this is more moving than 'A Slumber Did My Spirit Seal' or 'Break! Break! Break!' is not to assert that it is a better poem than Wordsworth's or Tennyson's, but to focus sharply the fact that the emotional exposure is not just of the speaker but of the poet as poet and as biographical individual. Perhaps a nearer comparison would be with Hardy's elegies for his first wife, but even there the language of the poems is not so permeated with an intimacy violated by both death and exposure.

There is a violation, or transgression, in the son's coming into possession of the intimate garments of the mother, and in his imagining the intimate parts of her body passing through the ring in his hand. This is appeased by the ritualistic reversed birth of the trope by which the mother's womb passes through the ring in the son's hand (the poet stepping slightly out of his biographical self) but this ceremoniousness does not take over the poem completely. There is still a resonating intimacy from the word 'cardy', coming straight from the world of the poet's childhood and so identifying him *as* the child and *with* his family's class. With similar effect, the final evocation of his dependence on the mother's permission, and his not naming the object that was familiar but perhaps unnamed in his childhood, reasserts the identity of speaker, poet and biographical individual. It is the strong sense of *presence* achieved in this way that makes the poem so moving.

A poem that achieves a very different effect, equally dependent on the unified subject, is 'Them and [uz]' (*SP*, pp. 122–3), which recalls an English teacher's mockery of the young Harrison's Leeds accent and refusal to allow him to recite Keats or play any part in *Macbeth* other than the drunken porter: ' 'You're one of those/ Shakespeare gives the comic bits to: prose!' ' A large swathe of English cultural history passes through this short poem: the parallel between social and literary hierarchies in the Elizabethan period; the imposition of RP and its stultifying association with the reading aloud of poetry; the stresses and deformations exacted by educational opportunity and social mobility via the grammar schools after the war; how the alienating divisions of the past still live and reinforce those of the present. But the poem owes much of its strength to convincing us that this history has also passed through the experience of the individual at its centre, who is both the humiliated schoolboy and the sophisticated poet, able to punningly parallel ancient Greek and the patter of a Northern comedian ($\alpha\grave{\imath}$ $\alpha\grave{\imath}$, ay. ay!'), to distance the tyrannical RP by representing it phonetically, to parody the speech of the schoolmaster by inserting into it a ludicrous rhyme and a satirical pun (' ''please believe [Λs]/your speech is in the hands of the Receivers'' '), and to point out that he knows better than the master how the great English poets actually spoke (Keats was a cockney and Wordsworth's 'matter' and 'water' were full rhymes); who is, moreover, still sufficiently hurt to *want* to take this revenge on the now probably dead old snob – the element of spite in the poem does not deform it but brings it even more alive. The poem evokes 'stutterer Demosthenes', who owes much of his significance to stammering Uncle Joe of 'Heredity', 'Study' and 'Fire-eater', a powerful representative of Harrison's concern for the 'tongueless' whom, ironically, he credits as the progenitor of his own poetic talent.

The 'School of Eloquence' sonnets (or *Continuous* as Harrison alternatively titles them, indicating his sense that they are 'a continual enterprise', Haffenden, p. 18) are obviously an interlocking sequence, but they are also, as it were, the backbone of Harrison's non-dramatic work over the period in which they have been written. Although he has said that he came to feel 'a little trapped in the sequence', and going to America 'helped [him] to write different poems' (Haffenden, p. 19), and though it is true that his poems outside the sequence are thematically different and burst the constraints of 16 lines, their method is predominantly autobiographical, and they invite cross-reference. For example, the gloomy writing-room in Newcastle that is the focus of 'Facing North' will be in our minds when we read of the wooden writing-hut in Florida in 'The Fire-Gap'; the woman for whom he leaves the writing-room in 'Facing North' is the one from whom he parts to return to England in 'Following Pine'. These later poems depend as much as the 'School of Eloquence' sonnets on a cumulative sense of the poet's life, often suggested marginally in the individual poem.

How can my claim that Harrison's poetry speaks with a unitary voice be reconciled with the fact that he is concerned to incorporate vernacular working-class English into poetry – especially since he makes a point of setting off the words attributed to his parents or other speakers by using italics? 'Book Ends', for example, narrates a quarrel between the poet and his father on his mother's death; however, the poetic relationship between the two voices in it is not confrontational or even dialectical, but strongly cooperative. Both times the father speaks he completes rhymes proposed by the voice of the poet, and without any jarring shift of register:

> The stone's too full. The wording must be terse.
> There's scarcely room to carve the FLORENCE on it –
>
> *Come on, it's not as if we're wanting verse.*
> *It's not as if we're wanting a whole sonnet!*

(SP p. 127)

Interestingly, Harrison never exploits the obvious possibilities offered by rhyme for pointing up the contrasts between educated and vernacular speech, or for parodying the verse form. In this poem, in fact, there is very little difference between the two voices. The poet's voice (and this is typical of the whole sequence) is as it were chastened by the proximity of the other voice and the role, explicit or implicit, of the parents as audience. ('The shock of my parents' deaths made me finally find a language I could address to them': Haffenden, p. 19.) This enables him to achieve the monosyllabic sombre simplicity of 'I've got to find the right words on my own' and the daringly successful flirtation with mawkishness and inverted cliché in 'but I can't squeeze more love into their stone.' In other poems the voice of the poet itself slips into vernacular:

Now mi dad's the only one keeps up his front.

('Next Door', *SP*, p. 130)

At the same time the father's voice is appropriated or, to use a less harsh word, assimilated. If, as the poet claims in 'Confessional Poetry', 'Mi dad's did scan, like yours do, many times!' (*SP*, p. 128), the 'occupation' of poetry is so much the smoother. There is a strong case for arguing that the 'literary frisson' is enhanced, rather than paid for, by this incorporation of the vernacular. Harrison has said about these voices:

> It seemed as if the *italic* could somehow take over from the *roman* – I mean a pun on *roman*, since what I designate in roman type is me as the poet – so in the end I could become a mouthpiece. In the end, that is to say, there could be poems which are all italic.

(Haffenden, p. 19)

This implies a supplanting of the 'roman' voice of the poet by the 'italic' vernacular speech. But this, as I have tried to show, exaggerates and misrepresents the relation between the two. What the poems move towards – what they achieve – is the discourse of a unified subject who is the poet and to whom the italic voice belongs.

These sonnets in the second part of 'The School of Eloquence' are poems of love: the unifying of their voices is an act of love. It is this that made me replace the harsh word 'appropriated' with 'assimilated'. This is unfortunately not true of Harrison's other major experiment with vernacular, *v*. In this poem Harrison confronts a ghostly skinhead who has sprayed UNITED in red on his parents' grave in Leeds. The skinhead begins by jeering at the poet for using the phrase *cri-de-coeur* (which he calls Greek); then gives him the reminder about his mother's reaction to *The Loiners*. Harrison has just been wondering

> What is it that these crude words are revealing?
> What is it that this aggro act implies?

(*SP*, p. 241)

(The poem, notoriously, lavishly reproduces the CUNTs, FUCKs and SHITs with which less favoured graves than his parents' are desecrated.) The skinhead gives him his answer:

> *Ah'll tell yer then what really riles a bloke.*
> *It's reading on their graves the jobs they did –*
> *butcher, publican and baker. Me, I'll croak*
> *doing t'same nowt ah do now as a kid.*

(*SP*, p. 217)

Harrison tells him that 'the reason why I want this in a book/'s to give ungrateful cunts like you a hearing!' to which the skinhead replies, '*A book, yer stupid cunt, 's not worth a fuck!*' (*SP*. p. 222) Harrison tries to ingratiate himself with the skinhead by recalling what he considers a piece of 'mindless aggro' from his own youth, beginning, 'No, shut yer gob a while. Ah'll tell yer 'ow...' (*SP*, p. 242). Finally he challenges him to sign his graffiti with his name, which turns out to be the poet's own.

A poet cannot of course invent a character who can tell him something that he as a biographical individual does not already know, and in that sense it is quite appropriate that the skinhead should bear the poet's name. But in this case the shadow self does not tell him anything that the *poetry* does not already know, has not already articulated. 'Bringing Up' has told us the story of his mother's reaction to *The Loiners*; the sentiment about books is close to that expressed in 'Book Ends' and 'A Good Read'. The skinhead's explanation of vandalism suits the poet's ideology, as does his use of the phrase 'class war'. The poet, moreover, has no difficulty in adopting the skinhead's language. The rhetorical structure of this poem and of 'The School of Eloquence' is in a sense the same: an ostensibly 'other' voice is actually assimilated to the unitary voice of the poet. But the results are very different. The assimilation in 'The School of Eloquence' signifies intimacy, love, the processes of memory, the healing of emotional scars, reconciliation. Pacts are made by the poet not only with the memory of his parents but also with his childhood self, between the language of his education and what he calls 'the *mother* tongue, the early speech' (Haffenden, p. 21). None of this is true of *v.*, where the poet uses the vernacular as a kind of shibboleth by which the famous writer with his name in Broadway lights who grew up

poor but in a full-employment economy tries to gain privileged
access to the world of the unemployed and alienated youth of the
early 1980s. The result is something that can properly be called
'appropriation'.

Although Harrison's 'occupation' of the traditional forms of
English poetry could be described as an act of radicalism, his
use of form is in another sense conservative. Having occupied the
metre, he does something new with it – his poetry could not be
described as merely imitative – but having found a metre that suits
him he stays with it and does not question it. There is very little
formal experiment in his work; he is inventive in the ways he
divides up the Meredithian 16-line sonnet, and he sometimes varies
his rhyme schemes, but rhymed iambic pentameters form the sta-
ple of almost all his poetry. (This applies, of course, only to his non-
dramatic verse. In the theatre he has been more experimental.)

Peter Reading's relation to poetic form is very different. Early in
his career he shifted from English pentameters to a variety of
accentual approximations to classical quantitative metres, for
which the only significant precedent in English poetry is Clough.
Clough used classical hexameters in *The Bothie* and *Amours de
Voyage* to achieve a colloquial effect and narrative momentum for
what are in effect versified epistolary novels. Reading's use encom-
passes these effects and others. He uses hexameters, elegiac distiches, Alcaic and Alcmanic stanzas, and possibly other metres that
I have been unable to identify. Unlike Clough – and unlike Harrison in his use of traditional English metres – Reading cannot
assume the reader's familiarity with the classical models. For
most of us no ghosts haunt the Alcaic stanza in the way that, say,
Gray's *Elegy* haunts Harrison's quatrains. Reading's use of these
metres therefore is self-consciously gratuitous and ludic:

> [Bit of a habit, the feigned indignation,
> various metres, Alcmanics and so forth,
> ludic responses to global debacles.
> Just Going On remains possible through the
> slick prestidigital art of Not Caring/Hopelessly Caring.]

> ('Going On', *UM*, p. 92)

The slash in the last line quoted is just one example – one of the
most poignant but not the most violent – of ruptures in Reading's

texts. Here the alternative words complete the metre; else-where (particularly in *Final Demands*) different words compete to occupy the same metrical space. The voice of the poet which, un-like Harrison's, is only tenuously linked to Peter Reading as a biographical individual, shares the text with other voices – fictive ones such as Viv and the Captain in *Ukulele Music*, reviews of Reading's poetry, graffiti, newspaper headlines, 'found' Victorian letters and verses etc., any of which may be more or less invented or doctored:

Efforts are now being made to encase the damaged reactor[6]

is a newspaper report/classical hexameter (but journalism often *does* scan, just like Harrison's father). Metrical space may be usurped by the meaningless 'plinkety-plonk' of a ukulele or be left unoccupied, represented merely by a metrical skeleton. (At the end of *Final Demands*, a book that broods on death, Harrison's idea that metre is associated with the 'physical rhythms that go on despite...' becomes a poignant conceit when the line is reduced to its metrical skeleton, which is then deleted.) In *Final Demands* and *Perduta Gente* the textual surface is invaded by newspaper clippings, typescripts of a military report and a 'secret' report on nuclear safety, various typefaces, and 'manuscript' ranging from the letters of a Victorian lady to the diary of a derelict alcoholic.

The spirit in which Reading uses form, and the severity of the slash in 'Not Caring/Hopelessly Caring', are perhaps most obvious in *C*, a volume whose title epitomises Reading's grim conception of the ludic, since it stands both for cancer and for the grotesque formal decision to compose a hundred hundred-word units. There are some intensely poignant moments in this sequence, perhaps none more so than the conclusion: 'My wife patiently washes my faece-besmirched pyjamas, for *prosaic* love.'[7] But they are only moments, punctuating a text whose dominant mode is one of anguished and bitterly sardonic self-reference. One frequently gets from Reading's work a sense that, the note of pathos, tragedy or sympathy once struck, to prolong or repeat it would be a dishonest indulgence.

C ends with *prosaic* italicised, and begins with and is continually punctuated by snide remarks about verse. But typically the open-ing section asks,

What do you expect me to do – break into bloody haiku?
Verse is for healthy
arty-farties. The dying
and surgeons use prose.

(C, p. 9)

(Even the 'prose' question is actually a classical pentameter, one of Reading's favourite metres.) Nothing could better epitomise the fragmentation of the poetic subject in Reading's work. Again and again C breaks into verse, including a '13-line sonnet for unlucky people (100 words, inc. title)' (C, p. 24) and a '17-liner, 100-word, pentameter acrostic, first letters forming CARCINOMATOPHOBIA' (C, p. 33). Both typically are announced beforehand in the text. The 'author' of the text is sardonically called the 'Master of the 100 100-Word Units' and included with various more obviously fictional personae in an '*Ubi sunt*' section that concludes, 'Poor frail dear frightened little vulnerable creatures' (C, p. 55). Language such as this is frequently tagged as 'mawkish drivel', but the voice that makes this judgement has no more authority than the 'mawkish' voice itself. That, or 'Oh, my darling, if only I could stay here not go not go not die!' (C, p. 51) is, it is implied, how human beings express feeling, and if one of the poem's voices finds it mawkish, this is not because this voice has anything more adequate to offer. The poem does not belong to any of its constituent voices, or even to the 'author' of the whole, the 'Master of the 100 100-word units'. C is typical of Reading's more recent work, in that the fictional representation of 'unliterary' language is placed in a dialectical tension with a heavily foregrounded pursuit of literary form. The result is, paradoxically, that both the 'mawkish' language and the 'unvindicable' poetic form are vindicated – not that we as readers are disarmed, but that we are forced to look at them more carefully because of their mutual quarrel.

Reading is probably at his most compelling in *Ukulele Music* (1985) and *Final Demands* (1988). *Ukulele Music* plays off the voices of the poet ('Peter Reading', whose work appears to attract critical responses similar to Peter Reading's), his daily help Viv, the mad 'Captain' for whom she also works, and an increasingly demented-sounding ukulele instruction manual. Viv, as we have seen, 'occupies' the elegiac distiches that have hitherto belonged to the poet, and the Captain has a wonderful section in which he narrates various maritime adventures which he imagines to have been his own, a narrative that is as persuasive as it is mad, and as immediate as it is pastiche. By the conclusion of the poem, all these other voices are occupying the poet's metrical territory, in a marvellous cacophony that is like an uproarious version of the conclusion of *The Waste Land*.

For the remainder of this chapter, however, I want to focus on *Final Demands*, and first take a passage that in some respects could have come from any of Reading's recent volumes.

> Season of dangerous nincompoops daubing cul-de-sac stark
>   walls
>   prettily bright tangerine: MURDER THE FUCKING SHITE
>   POPE.
> 25 yards away, there is a bleak brick aerosolled dead-end –
> LONG LIVE THE POPE/ORANGE SHIT lividly sprayed
>   emerald.
> (Similar sentiments stimulate crazed trog footy fans' scrawlings–
>
> LCFC KILL THE REST –baying for mashed flesh and gore.)
> Mad, atavistic –REMEMBER SIXTEEN NINETY in orange;
> squirted in green, SMASH THE PRODS. 12th of July, '86:
> ludicrous faithfuls in camouflaged shirts and black Balaclavas
> romp in each other's spilt guts; Prods, internecines, RCs ...
> Season and geography fecund of microcephalic idiots –
> clad in absurd fancy dress, sect, in good faith, *purees* sect
>
>   gratuitous scrivenings
>   gratuitous lunacies
>   [Strike out the old obsessional nastiness][8]

It might seem odd that I have chosen to begin discussing what I claim to be one of Reading's best books with such an obviously bad piece of writing. This is partly because it is characteristic of one vein of his writing – not only in this volume but also in *Diplopic*, *Ukulele Music* and *Stet*. The classical metres of the poet are often occupied by insults – not only 'trog' and 'microcephalic' but also 'simian', 'pongoid' etc., which are not only crude but inaccurate, since apes certainly do not behave like soccer hooligans or sectarian bigots, and there is no evidence that Early Man did. The inaccuracy spreads to simple description – how can a colour be both green and livid? – as if the poet's command of language has broken down

under the stress of his rage. In startling contrast to *v.*, this language
signifies an angry, reactionary populist refusal to 'understand'. An
understanding of the passage, and its place in the whole text, must
begin with critical observations such as these. Then of course we
notice that the passage has been crossed out, and the poet supplies
his own criticism. Yet it remains in the text; once again the fragmentation of the poetic subject is illustrated: the passage both is
and is not authorised. Its function is further complicated when we
notice that on the facing page is part of a Victorian letter, represented in 'manuscript', that includes a patriotic song, the work of
its 'author':

> Britons once more strike home
> Tell the proud Church of Rome
> That we despise
> All her idolatries
> Masses and mummeries,
> And pray that she may fall
> Never to rise.

The tune, of course, is the National Anthem. This juxtaposition
makes the effect of the accompanying passage incomparably
more subtle, and the whole is a more penetrating piece of political
writing than Harrison's appropriation of the skinhead's voice in *v.*

This is, however, marginal to the main effect of *Final Demands*,
which is centrally concerned with death, and with the poignant
strangeness of texts that have become detached from their dead
authors, and fictional fragments that do not tell us the whole story.
The author of the patriotic song, a Victorian lady, writes several
letters to her daughters. One of these, evidently her favourite, dies,
with devastating effect on the mother. The other is constantly asked
to visit but never does, though she seems about to at the end. One
of the letters is interrupted by an operation for breast cancer.[9] This
family situation is eerily refracted in the supposed last chapter of a
novel, written in pastiche plush late Victorian style. Two other
mothers, apparently descendants of people mentioned in the Victorian letters, write unsuccessfully to ask for their sons to be sent
home from active service in the Second World War; the deaths of
both sons are narrated in a report by their commanding officer
(who is, incidentally, one of the madmen in the earlier volume
Tom o'Bedlam's Beauties). This is counterpointed by the Alcaics,
hexameters and elegiacs of the poet, in the grip of 'crapulous

death-fright', which include some of Reading's best writing in
these forms, such as the opening passage in which he compares
himself to Odysseus, storm-wrecked in Phaeacia, who:

dreamingly crawls and his hands have now raked a litter together,
spacious and deep, for the leafage is lying in plentiful downfall,
lays him to rest in the midst of the leaves and piles them around
    him,
just as a man might cover a brand with char-blacked ashes,
guarding the seed of the fire for his tribe to use in the future,
so does he deeply immerse in the fall of past generations,
litter of leaves, not from olives, but the sepia, brittle
leaves of the letters of lost correspondents, infinite, death-frail
(Croxley, papyrus and bond), sinks in the lines of the dead.

The transposition of the passage in Homer (for once the classical
metre does have echoes) is a brilliant conceit.[10] The poet 'sinks' like
Odysseus in the comfort of 'analgesics', and the book does conclude, as I mentioned earlier, with his 'death' in the form of a
deleted metrical skeleton. He also 'sinks in the lines of the dead'
in the sense that he disappears behind texts of which he is only
dubiously the author, both this version of Homer and the letters
which Peter Reading may or may not have written or rewritten:
whatever his hand in the writing neither the poet of the classical
metres nor the author of *Final Demands* can give us any answers to
the enigmas of the text. And, most importantly, the effect is not
merely of a fashionable postmodernist trick. Reading may be coming to be seen as a definitively postmodern poet, but one feels that
he arrives at these devices because of the pressure of his material
more than literary fashion. The unresolved enigmas and incomplete narratives of *Final Demands* leave us with voices – especially
the voice of the Victorian mother – in one sense ghostly but nevertheless compelling, impaled by moments of anguish, loss and help-
lessness from which no narrative will rescue them.

Emily I do not know how I write I have written to most of her
cousins this morning God be with us I want someone to hold my
distressed trembling heart this is the greatest sorrow I have ever
felt – pray – pray for me – your Aunt is here and I have Jane
Benson but Oh! I have not my delight my Sophy Mary my Jesus
has taken my beautiful blossom at 4 and twenty Oh my Saviour

keep me in the hollow of thine hand...
I will not attempt to tell you my feelings for it is in vain

In this very different way, Reading achieves an effect nearly as moving as that of Harrison's sonnet.

Notes

1. T. Harrison, 'Book Ends II', *Selected Poems*, new expanded edition (Harmondsworth: Penguin, 1987), p. 127; hereafter referred to as *SP* with page references given in the text.
2. P. Reading, *Ukulele Music* (London: Secker, 1985), p. 36; reprinted in *3 in 1* (London: Cape, 1992); hereafter referred to as *UM* with page references given in the text.
3. T. Paulin, 'Peter Reading', *Grand Street*, Summer 1988, p. 210.
4. J. Haffenden, 'Tony Harrison, An Interview', *Poetry Review*, Vol. 73, No. 4, January 1984, p. 23; hereafter referred to as Haffenden with page references given in the text.
5. D.H. Lawrence, *The Letters of D.H. Lawrence*, Vol. II (Cambridge University Press, 1981), p. 104.
6. This line occurs in both *Final Demands* (London: Secker, 1988) and *Perduta Gente* (London: Secker, 1989). Both volumes are unpaginated.
7. Peter Reading, *C* (London: Secker, 1984), p. 61; reprinted in *3 in 1*; page references hereafter given in text.
8. P. Reading, *Final Demands*, unpaginated. All remaining quotations are from this text.
9. Reviewing *Final Demands* in the *TLS* (15–21 April 1988, p. 419) Eric Korn claims that the Victorian letters are 'much reworked' versions of actual letters that he had found and sent to Reading. He also says that he can 'vouch' for the 'genuineness' of the verse in the letters.
10. Pope translates the passage (the conclusion of Book V of the *Odyssey*) as follows:

> Of gather'd leaves an ample bed he made
> (Thick strewn by tempest through the bowery shade);
> Where three at least might winter's cold defy,
> Though Boreas raged along the inclement sky.
> This store with joy the patient hero found,
> And, sunk amidst them, heap'd the leaves around.
> As some poor peasant, fated to reside
> Remote from neighbours in a forest wide,
> Studious to save what human wants require,
> In embers heap'd, preserves the seeds of fire:
> Hid in dry foliage thus Ulysses lies,
> Till Pallas pour'd soft slumbers on his eyes;
> And golden dreams (the gift of sweet repose)
> Lull'd all his cares, and banish'd all his woes.

5

Salvaged from the Ruins:
Ken Smith's Constellations

Stan Smith

BEGINNING FROM WHAT'S BROKEN

Walter Benjamin's 'Theses on the Philosophy of History'[1] observe, famously, that bourgeois historians 'who wish to relive an era... blot out everything they know about the later course of history' in 'a process of empathy whose origin is the indolence of the heart, *acedia*, which despairs of grasping and holding the genuine historical image as it flares up briefly'. Such a historiography, he says, is 'the root cause of sadness':

> The nature of this sadness stands out more clearly if one asks with whom the adherents of historicism actually empathize. The answer is inevitable: with the victor.

Empathy leads them to join 'the triumphal procession in which the present rulers step over those who are lying prostrate', elevating 'great minds and talents' at the expense of 'the anonymous toil of their contemporaries' on which such triumphs were founded. 'There is no document of civilisation which is not at the same time a document of barbarism', and 'barbarism taints also the manner in which it was transmitted from one owner to another.' A historical materialist therefore 'dissociates himself from it as far as possible. He regards it as his task to brush history against the grain.'

Ken Smith's writing is charged with a deep historical sadness, but this arises neither from acedia nor nostalgia. His poem 'Against the grain', in one of his most recent volumes, *The heart, the border*, 1990, p. 20, echoes Benjamin to protest on behalf of the anonymous multitudes – the living who remain behind as much as the dead

63

whose remains they have to dispose of. 'Someone must count them, the bodies that come up/one by one out of the fire' or the North Sea, he says; 'someone must stare at the remnants of the dead' from such contemporary disasters as Zeebrugge, Kings Cross, Piper Alpha. The poet himself cannot 'tally the ongoing total'. In fact, no one individual can, and the changing 'someones' who actually do the job are as plural and anonymous as the bodies they process. In the last words of the poem, 'It goes against the grain' to perform such a task as much as it does to let the dead go without commemoration. 'Against the grain' speaks with outrage of a country literally 'dying of neglect', where such catastrophes occur because cost-cutting in the 'free enterprise disaster zone' stints on safety precautions, counts the wasted lives as expendable.

This is a characteristic position in Smith's verse, which insists on demanding who is responsible for events when the 'responsible bodies' have themselves opted out. The 'sadness' of his poetry is coupled with a fierce and lyric anger at the sense of enormous, pathetic waste, where 'Running on empty', also in *The heart, the border* (p. 24), spells out the grounds of his anger:

> So many lives are wasted and no one knows why.
> That sounds to me like a crime.

This is a volume full of elegies for lost futures, cheated lives, in a time where 'Now there's too much to be angry about,/and no one left to forgive', and all is imposture:

> On and on down the dirty decades.
> Nothing as described in the brochure,
> as promised on the party platform...
> My country is falling off the back of a lorry.

The whole volume constitutes a revolutionary protest against a spiv's culture under what the title of one poem fingers as 'The New Management' (p. 23), which renders individual lives and whole communities redundant in the interests of profit, leaving, on the 'city's/skinny peripheries' 'only departure's uncountable sadness'. The 'Management', who in the old days marched in with invading armies, are now always elsewhere, with an alibi, 'the missing witnesses to an accident' in which it is always the same people who are the victims, and (ostensibly) no one is to blame.

Smith's historical 'sadness' is more active than Benjamin's, and its anger dissociates it from the nostalgic laments of apologists for the status quo. Placed between this poem and 'Against the grain' in *The heart, the border* are 'Three Dockland Fragments' which chart how the 'enterprise zone' (here the Docklands Developments of the 1980s) erased all but the most fragmentary traces of the working-class communities whose labours created the wealth now ploughed back into property speculation and the delights of (the title of one poem, p. 22) 'Yuppy love'. Now 'the rich inherit' a zone carved from 'London's residuary body' (a pithy play on the name of the non-elective body the Tory government appointed to run down the duties of an abolished GLC) amidst 'the racket of money being made' in the shadow of tower blocks 'where pass lives sadder than yours, mine'.

'The London Poems' in *Terra* (1986) had already linked personal losses to a world where 'everything you see is up for sale' and 'all the best words have moved to Surrey' (p. 54). Telling tales of the past remains one of the few ways of resisting such cynicism and entropy, as in the last quatrain of 'The meridian at Greenwich' (p. 54) trying to get messages across a border that has been closed. The last of 'The London poems', a collection of vignettes self-parodi-cally called 'The John poems', inserts the protesting individual into the totality by declaring accountability: 'I'm the missing witness. And they never ask' (p. 70). Our relation to the past is an act of witness which voluntarily takes responsibility for what has happened. The present, an earlier poem reprinted in *The Poet Reclining* (1982) suggests, is constituted from these traces, its 'grain' a series of past events become material *presence*:

> This wood then, its grain
> recorded its own growing.
> And these stones of the cathedral,
> what do they record?

> ('Little notes', p. 38)

What they record are the small agonies of brief lives, 'men and women dancing in time', and the double-take on that phrase (as in the exploration of all the implications of the word 'time' in *Worm-wood*, 1987) speaks volumes.

There is a preoccupation throughout Smith's poetry with what remains after catastrophic loss. In a less frequently quoted passage

in the 'Theses on the Philosophy of History', Benjamin wrote that
'the sinews of its greatest strength' for the working class are a
hatred 'nourished by the image of enslaved ancestors rather than
that of liberated grandchildren'. Smith's poetry draws its nourishment from the same source, seeking what Benjamin calls 'a revolutionary chance in the fight for the oppressed past'. Smith's poems
are characterised by a kind of lyric anger which turns an abstract
idea of 'history' into the impassioned vindication of many individual lives. The title poem of one of his earliest volumes, *The Pity*,
takes its cue from a poem of Mao Tse-tung's about being forced to
witness the garrotting of his pregnant first wife in a Chinese jail.
The shift of emotions in the poem charts a lifetime's fury: 'China
was patience you said', Mao observes, but 'Patience was prised
from me'; in jail 'I wore contempt, grew hatred'. For 'compassion
had not anything to do with this / . . . Compassion cannot go forever
in the sun'. The origins of a revolution which shook the world may
lie in a little local atrocity in a far-away country, for there is no real
division between the personal life and the political abstractions:

> She was destroyed and my child ceased.
> I cut my hands on the cords at the strangling post,
> but no blood spilled from my veins;
> instead of blood I watched and saw the pity run out of me.

The present as a prison cell is a recurring motif in Smith's verse,
culminating in that powerful volume written out of his two years
as a Writer-in-Residence at Wormwood Scrubs, *Wormwood*, a title
which moves symptomatically between history and apocalypse
(in *Revelation* 8:2 it is the name of a fateful star, presiding over
poisoned waters) and the mundane and quotidian. 'Writing in
prison', one of the opening poems of *The heart, the border* (p. 13)
sums up its significance. Writing in prison, the speaker can recover
'all the lost places of my life', remaking them in the restricted space
of the poem which resembles the prison cell. In this little room
become an everywhere, there is *time* (a pun which works its way
through *Wormwood*) to reconstruct all that led up to this place of
recollection and re-collection.

Smith's image for the poet's activity is repeatedly that of Benjamin's *chiffonier* (in his study of Baudelaire), rag-picking in the
junkyard of history, or Lévi-Strauss's *bricoleur*, beachcombing on
the shores of a vast sea, in each case making new uses of the debris

recovered from the past. The self in these poems is both the collector of junk and the junk he collects. In one poem, there is a strange division of function, in which the earlier self, though he has escaped to some desert island, is still surrounded by rubbish, while the residuary survivor inherits his oppressive traces:

> Now wherever he is that I was, wrecked maybe
> on some beach with the rest of the flyblown
> plastic debris, living under a rusty tub
> with the name gone forever from its side,
> when here I am answering his letters,
> paying his bills, signing books he wrote,
> picking up his pieces...

Life is constructed, love recovered, according to 'In transit' (*The Poet Reclining*, p. 173), in 'scrap of news/from places we lived'. 'Departure's speech' (*Terra*, p. 87) admits:

> In my trade
> I'm a journeyman living the life of waste nothing,
> odds picked in skips, scraps my dead father kept,
> all the words I can steal so look out for yourself.

This is a *bricoleur's* planet, where everything is re-used, as 'The stone poems' remind us in *The Poet Reclining* (p. 24): 'Stone ballast used again/building the shipman's house,/the miller's table'. We too share in the recycling of cosmic dust,

> the hot gas
> of atoms blown back into space
> that were Socrates, chert,
> flakes of flint tool,
> touch of all lovers.

In the disturbing sequence, 'Fox Running' (*The Poet Reclining*, pp. 130ff.), the poet is, like the fox finding a new home in the exile of the city, a 'scavenger of skips, parks/and desirable period residences', and identity is constructed belatedly from a series of alienations:

> Years ago long ago late he is
> skin of his name of his legend

skin of his alias son of his alibi
son of his tale told for children.

Identity for Smith is always a matter of traces and belatedness, as
in Fox's meditation on the first moving film of a long-dead naked
man bouncing a ball, fixed until the film itself decomposes as an
'instant of the image the trace/on the retina'. But this film was not
the beginning of the traces, merely one more moment in their
endless circulation. There are no authenticating origins, and the

> Sunlight on him then
>
> is the travelled light our star
> sows in the thin electron milk
> where will be galaxies.

Human history is constructed from these recyclings and lags in
time, as the light from the sun, which takes eight minutes to reach
us, and from the stars, which may travel for millions of light years,
becomes a model of how we all relate to the messages from our
past. This moving image is still part of *us*. It is our perceiving in the
here and now which turns the successive still frames of the film
into a comprehended narrative of movement and purpose, in
which the past is perpetually reborn, in its birthday suit, in the
constellation we make with it in the present:

> our man
> in the Victorian back yard...
>
> is a ripple of overlapped slides,
> still frames of himself running silently
> up and down in his birthday suit.
> Where we see him we never would have...
> In the space we occupy. Here.
>
> Called *persistence of vision*,
> the image on the retina a space.
> Called retinal memory...

The picture of a ball bouncing 'all the years since' persists for us as
an image of the reclaimable past and of the possible future,

> Beginning again and again
> beginning from what's broken.

RESTORER OF MARGINS

A series of poems in *The heart, the border* considers an excavated Herculaneum where the dead lives, 'Caught side by side in the sudden dust' as if in a snapshot (another of Smith's motifs) 'dead as all the dead are' in their 'stopped rooms', still transmit 'Ercolano's message': *'nothing so well endures as the ruin of things'*. The penultimate poem of the sequence, 'A traveller's question', puts an almost consolatory complexion on this process of ruination, in which over the millennia, *'Not much changes'*. The last poem of the sequence, however, spells out Smith's characteristic mode of historical perception. 'Postscript: nunc pro tunc' substitutes now for then, ironically completing the unfulfilled wish of a Roman citizen who had retired to Herculaneum for peace and quiet in which to 'take/a long view of the town's doings and write', by adding a long-delayed postscript to his fate, refiguring 'all the sad wants' as the modern poet finally writes of them, in these last days. (The Latin drily plays off this modern 'postscript' against the long 'postscriptum' of history.)

A briefer span between *nunc* and *tunc*, also bridged by writing, is considered in 'Letters from a lost uncle' (*Terra*, p. 44), which recalls a postcard of Chicago streets showing a blurred figure ringed in ink, and 'written on the back *it's me now*. // Wherever he was then'. 'Back from Leah's country' (*The heart, the border*, p. 28) extends this into a general sense of *belatedness* built in to our historical self-awareness. We live in a perpetual retrospect, as if like Benjamin's angel of history (the *Angelus Novus*) we were blown backwards into the future by a wind from Paradise:

> We are what the rain sees, never
> where we are but somewhere yesterday,
> some other place we're on the way to...
>
> These events are put together backwards
> from hints, shreds of evidence and hearsay,
> restricted information, bias measured out
> into the tight little shoes of language.
>
> And it's too late to learn anything from them.

The earliest poems collected in *The Poet Reclining* fret anxiously over the erasure of past things, recalling a troubled and impover-

ished childhood which seems nevertheless the site of a lost plenitude enriched by the fact of dispossession. In 'Country: Keld to
Reeth' (p. 15), for example:

> We were a darker blur on the stubble,
> a fragment in time gone, we left
> not a mark, not a footprint;
> the cold forest, the birds of the moor
> do not recall us.

At the moment that the poem speaks of an orphaning supersession,
it inscribes longevity and survival in the brilliant image of glacial
deposits on the hillside 'as if the ice might come back for them', the
poet's taciturn and inaccessible father equated with the unyielding
stone. The note is struck early in 'The stone poems' (p. 23), in the
celebration of a planet which is itself the eroded memorial of many
presences, blurred or erased meanings which challenge the final
depredations not of nature but of men:

> In the blank faceless thing
> nothing of our meanings
> but that it outlasts us, holds up
> the names that mean nothing now
> in the wind wearing them away
> where the scripts change
> and the dialects weather
> as the words shift their meanings
> in the long war with silence
> till what's left is a finger-traced
> blur where the chisel cut
> *let vandals look upon this epitaph.*

In *Terra*, a sequence of poems about the poet's own northern
childhood recalls a strange, exaggerated world of intense focus on
small, mysteriously significant things and events, where the meaning remains always about to be revealed. The poems situate the
personal reminiscences in a whole history of small lives shaped
and overwhelmed by the Industrial Revolution:

> And all its children gone through millyards
> into stone they chiselled *Billy, Emma, Jack,*

and gave their dates and shut the ground
in work and prayer. Or they are almost here,

their short days closing in an owl's hoot.

(p. 35)

Each moment testifies to this immanence and withholding of
meaning, 'a footstep always just about to fall/and all their
voices just about to start'. This just-about-to quality of the past
links his personal memories with the remoter pasts of the dead
generations, 'almost here', as in 'Roads in the north between two
seas' (p. 36),

I am again in my own true country
that surely existed, a map in a drawer,
a postcard, a print in a seafront cafe,
a place it has always just stopped raining.

Such moments offer a kind of deferred epiphany, a place where the
retrospective narratives find their numinous origins and their resurrection, as the farm clanked 'long ago, its moment comes back
now', in a constellation of moments:

Clear again is one moment, as to detail
precise in my imprecise memory, it begins
this long tale I am telling myself
as to why and who I am on this road.

In all these evocations of the past, whether the poet's own or that of
lost generations of predecessors, the backward look of the poet here
and now becomes part of the process, as, in 'Spartan communiqué'
(*The Poet Reclining*, p. 171), the infinite perspectives created by
opposing mirrors blocked by the interposing head of the observer:

we find coming between us
ourselves and our vision
that would otherwise be
to infinity

merely our eyes
only our looking.

By reinserting the living subject, here and now, back into the process of historical recall, Smith implicitly rejects the absolutism of Benjamin's historicists. We do not inherit from the past one 'total' truth written by the victors. Rather the victors' hegemonic discourse is only one of the many partial traditions that come down to us. Everywhere dominant, it neither suppresses all the contrary moments to be deciphered from its grand narrative, nor displaces all the discourses that lie outside it. Rather the past is gapped, condensed, full of aporetic absences and half-presences. It is quite literally a bundle of documents, some mildewed and vanished, others guessed-at and inferred, surviving in fragments and hints. From this material we construct a past according to our lights, what Benjamin calls a 'constellation' of the past and the present, in which the historian

> ... stops telling the sequence of events like the beads of a rosary. Instead, he grasps the constellation which his own era has formed with a definite earlier one. Thus he establishes a conception of the present as 'the time of the now' which is shot through with chips of Messianic time.

This *Jetztzeit* is a 'Messianic time', in Arendt's words a 'mystical *nunc stans*', because it forms a constellation between *nunc* and *tunc* in which each interpenetrates the other. It affirms a 'time of the now' in which the past can still be reclaimed, won back from the victors in the name of the vanquished, by the patient and loving effort of recall.

In *Burned Books* (1981), the blurb tells us, 'is preserved all that remains of an entire culture, fragments salvaged from the ruins of the Perdu library by ex-President Perdu himself'. About this 'lost president' 'little is known'. A name which itself means 'Lost' may be no more than a fabrication inferred from a fragment of the *Recherche du Temps Perdus*, like the 'Collected Works of AZ' (p. 51), or 'the long poet' who wrote of lost wholeness and whose truncated name we can still discern in the 'Fragment: memo to Milto' (p. 39), or the saintly fiction 'San Quixote of the cinders' (p. 14), constructed from the erroneous retrospective merging of Sancho Panza and Don Quixote from the few fragments that survive.

In this volume, the history *in* books in 'Collège des beaux arts' (p. 18) depends upon the history *of* books, on the accidents of transmission and survival. Books carry material traces of their use and abuse, 'chopped at by drunks/slopping boozy cup marks'; a falling beam 'has inwardly marred/a good chapter or two, the/last uncountable pages will always be missing'. All that survives sometimes are 'some clots/of language . . . /burned black porridge'. This poem 'when we came to speak/of the future . . . / spoke of the past', forging thus constellation reiterated in the play of its last lines, 'through these vowels/that reach us, thinking/how come it's so late so early' ('late' and 'early' simultaneously because 'thinking' can refer both to 'us' and to the 'vowels that reach us', fusing *nunc* and *tunc*). It mocks the hubris of the victors' supposedly totalitarian command over history. If, in these poems, the self is 'the library/of gutted works', a survivor always 'picks up the pieces'. When even the fullest text suffers from 'occasional/lacuna, gap/ or hiatus', the true historian in 'San Quixote' is, like Smith himself, a 'restorer of margins', creating a constellation of past and present out of 'what was salvaged/& all but survived/ruin'.

CHINESE WHISPERS

A fictively distanced conversation recalled in 'Book users' note' (*The heart, the border*, p. 33) offers an archly self-subverted rationale of the constellations forged by Smith's poems:

> We agreed that 'the poem is amongst other things a way of reliving; a fine system of cross reference and recall bringing back the world and ourselves briefly in it. Memory and anticipation,' we said, 'the dreamed and the imagined and the actual are all alike in language. So there is one hole in the wall and one door at least against the onrush of time whether it passes in Los Angeles or Minoan Crete; we open the door; for us it is the poem.' This was an example of didactic statement.

Smith's poems seek to relive the past not as pastness but as presence, recreating not how it actually happened but how it can be imagined to have happened. In this reconstruction, 'the dreamed and the imagined' share a common element. The poem records a conversation beside a pond about the nature of similes. But 'that day' has given place to a 'now' in which he tries to avoid similes: 'then was different'. Difference is as important as similitude in these constellations, as, in the subsequent titleless prose-poem,

the poet sitting at his typewriter addresses a future compositor still
to set this as-yet-incomplete text. Each of them, the poem says, sits
at a keyboard, 'you in my future, I in your past... And both in
different tenses of the present'.

The blurb for Smith's prose collection, *A Book of Chinese Whispers*
(1987), provides his model of how history devolves to us through
these different tenses of the present:

> As in the game of Chinese Whispers, messages are passed, re-
> peated, misheard, misremembered, deliberately tampered with,
> fiddled with in the interests of politics, commerce and the pur-
> suit of power. Even the language is suspect. So are our percep-
> tions.

'The talk at the big house', one of the 'London poems' in *Terra* (p.
59), offers a droll reflection on this process as a necessary and even
intended tendency of history:

> the signal from the government in exile

> is opened by the wrong hands, so much lost
> in the foreign tongue, so much of meaning
> is a border always shifting in dispute.

Similarly, a line in one of the Fox poems condenses the semantic
history of a simple domestic word to make it a paradigm of the
way language evolves through a succession of Chinese whispers,
but also of how it recurrently recuperates its slippages: 'Avocado,
aguacate, ahuacatl, testicle'. The original meaning of the Aztec word
refers to the testicular shape of the fruit; the Spanish transliteration
of it shifts by popular etymology to a completely unconnected
meaning. In recovering these etymologies, however, the poet reinstates the 'original' analogy by a parallel etymological metaphor in
the Latin, for as an *advocate* speaks for and in support of so a *testicle*
originally witnessed, testified, to masculinity.

The penultimate poem in *The heart, the border*, 'Chinese whisper'
(immediately after two poems about the destruction of the Berlin
Wall in 1990), offers a different kind of witness, speaking in the
imagined persona of 'a labourer on the Chinese Wall, one of thou-
sands', indistinguishable from the other coolies to right and left
('my thought could be either of theirs'), replaced when he dies by

another identikit coolie, for 'Only the wall grows.' History itself
('when I die the line will move up in my place') is the Wall of the
victors, but it is also a series of intangible Chinese whispers, of
faulty transmissions. The fact that each of these men is indistinguishable from the next does not dismiss them from history.
Rather it underlines a common humanity to be recovered in the
act of historical imagination. The coolie's dreams glimpse an imaginary world ('far away, impossible now') he shares with his
neighbours, and with those who replace him in the line. The
poem insists on the actual continuities which extend back across
the great tracts and ruptures of prehistory, preserving a
substratum of shared experience, of a subjectivity whose utopian
moments of dream and fantasy, happiness and sorrow lay a claim,
in whispers, to a different world, which can be salvaged from the
ruin of things.

In 'Still life' (*Burned Books*, p. 28), a series of apparently discon-
nected scraps, each with their separate histories, form a still life
with a few crumbs of bread on a table, to open up a universal
history of bequests and survivals. The crumbs are only here because they are 'descendants of the cargoes despatched from Carth-
age and the wheat measured out by Jacob'; the table itself is in a
double sense 'bearer of objects and the marks of men paid off years
ago for their labour'. History leaves its traces everywhere, for the
present is constructed in its most minute particulars from the past,
and 'My life is a snail's pace amongst these things, feeling only the
strangeness of its presence'. Such illusive self-sufficiency lives,
most of the time, by repressing the past which constituted it. Yet
that past does not threaten identity, but underwrites it. In history,
we are all Chinese whispers, as the gene pools make their way
down the centuries, handing on a life always unique and always
similar to but not identical with that which preceded it. 'Things to
remember' (*The heart, the border*, p. 26), lists, along with 'Stars
remembering their places. Dust forming new rocks', a more chas-
tening memorandum: 'That I am not my name, that among fictions
I am another'. Both poem and poet speak here, aware of that
potentially disabling distance between them in which each finds
meaning only in difference and relation, in the act of communication.

The sequence 'Serbian letters' (*Wormwood*, p. 22) offers a marvellous recreation of what seems at first like a Borgesian world parallel to our own, where mediaeval caravanserai and modern

neurosurgeon coexist. But this telescoping of time zones is not anachronism or time travel. It simply reflects that balkanisation of experience within the global village familiar to all postmodern subjects, who repeatedly travel through exotic territories only to find themselves along with the poet in the final poem 'Home again in the enterprise zone'. The persistence of the forms transmitted down the generations in this sequence is confirmed in a relation of *tunc* and *nunc* figured even in the cemeteries,

> lettered in stones,
> names that never give in: *Adam,*
> *Jordan, Stepan . . .*
> your words through our mouths,
> our mouths through your words.

The *Abel Baker Charlie Delta Epic Sonnets* (1982) and 'Apocrypha from the Western Kingdom' work a similar magic on the *objets* (and *conversations*) *trouvés* of quotidian experience, which 'never give in'. The latter text (in *The Poet Reclining*, pp. 114–23) moves between archaic Anglo-Saxon past and mundane present with a rare aplomb, picking up apocryphal 'items' – discursive fragments detached from the narratives they imply, enigmatic snippets of conversation, referentless signs – like archaeological 'finds' which survive outside the canon, without the authority of an official history, in 'three locations in Leeds and Exeter'. The play in the sequence between those items 'heard' and those 'imagined' reiterates the conviction of 'Book users' note' that 'the dreamed and the imagined and the actual are all alike in language'. Smith's reclamation of the past does not subject itself to recoverable fact: the dreaming and imagining of *what it must have been like* are a crucial part of the constellations he creates.

This is made explicit in that intense vision of a possible family history in *The Eli Poems* (*The Poet Reclining*, pp. 57–69), which seek to redream the reality of an imagined ancestor whose forfeit life, dying in childbirth, haunts his own, announcing herself a few days before his father's death in a dream: 'My name is Kate, I am an Irish girl'. For 'Kate', in the opening poem, the past is already where 'rumours go back', like the bog where people have disappeared, 'mistaking/the look of firm footing – /ghosts, river vapours'. Yet there is still reciprocity between these two darks, which both have human faces:

As she leaves that place
that after will speak of her:
face peering through water
into a face, into a dark.

There is a temporal double-take in this sequence, in which the 'I' of
the poem shifts between then and now, as time is telescoped in the
'effort/to release you...give sound to your moving'. The imagining present 'I' is also distanced from the poet through the fictive
persona of Eli. Neither the present nor the past experience is 'real',
then, in any literal sense. The sexual act which begot one of the
speaker's imagined ancestors is overlaid with the act of imaginative
recreation that tries to re-enter the lost life: 'you cried out as I
entered you'. In Kate's interior monologue, reciprocally, the baby
in the womb is an invasive presence figuring forth a supplanting
future, 'this/feeding itself/on herself' which foreshadows her des-
cendant's parasitism. But these dead ancestors also invade the
present, for the speaker too feels of Kate that 'you stir in my bones
now'. He in turn is possessed by an obsession which rebukes him
for misperceiving: the slope of her shoulder as she departs in his
recurrent dream is a reproach, 'says/I have shaped you in words/
that aren't true'. But the childbirth in which Kate dies is also seen
in terms of an inscribing of traces, 'your own body's shafts/and the
driving muscle...print out/its track, the child'.

The sequence does not aim to recreate an actual lost life. Indeed,
though the speaker reports that after his father's death he learnt
that his grandmother died in childbirth, the names and dates don't
fit. This is no simple *pentimento* of a 'real' history. The 'Kate' of his
dreams lived much further back, at the beginning of the Industrial
Revolution (1790 is the date offered by the imagination). Her *imagined* life comes to constitute a whole history in miniature of that
casual and careless uprooting of populations brought about by
industrialisation. Kate's story, in another variant on Smith's image
of the present as a prison cell in which we can re-collect the past, is
'perhaps only a tale told by the prisoner to the jailer'. Perhaps 'the
patterns of separate events containing certain details in common as
to birth and death and origin, perhaps these overlie each other' in
its telling. Nevertheless, the poem insists, the place of dreams
'where this narrative happened' surely exists: 'they were alive
once; they were real fictions, the mask, the face, the voice'. In the
words of 'Book users' note', ' "the poem is amongst other things a

way of reliving; a fine system of cross reference and recall bringing back the world and ourselves briefly in it" ', standing against ' "the onrush of time" '. In Benjamin's terms these poems blast open the continuum of history to create a 'time of the now' which in its telling is compacted of all human times.

TELL ME SOMEONE REMEMBERING US

The major sequence in *Terra*, 'Hawkwood', seems like a response to the vision of late mediaeval England in Geoffrey Hill's 'Funeral Music', displaying the same plangent sense of a historical uprooting amidst the ubiquitous ruins of the past. Sir John Hawkwood's life as a freebooting mercenary in fourteenth-century Europe, immortalised by Uccello's equestrian fresco in the Florence Duomo, is a life of fragments beyond praise or blame, or rather an anthology of several incomplete lives, fighting at Crècy and Poitiers, going on to become a *condottiere* in Northern Italy for 30 years, his one point of principle that he would not renege on a contract. According to Smith, 'in an age of cruel men [he] was said to be brave, fair, merciful and honest in his dealings', though capable of massacre at Cesena, obeying the orders of his employer the Papacy, therefore 'in our terms ... a war criminal'.

Hawkwood is one who 'by day lives the life of his time', but he is also a man who makes the future in the most literal sense, turning rich cities to ash, able to 'grind out the future/between millstone and millstone', and the opening address in mock Middle English establishes the distance between his world and ours as that between two texts barely comprehensible to each other: 'I thinke this worlde a boke/and wolde rede it/turning back the pages/chapter by century/into the distant background'. In this constellation, 'all that's certain now/has already happened', but its interpretation remains problematic, shifting as history accumulates new moral perspectives – a point reinforced by the uncertainty as to whether it is Hawkwood or the poet who uses the 'I':

> Who knows what any of it was now?
> I move between the dead and the dead,
> always erudite and fractious.

This man 'Who might have been anyone' is now, in this poem, 'a man becoming an emblem,/inscribing the book of his name'. Devising a *memento mori* medallion which advises 'What I am now so you will be./ What you are now so I was once', he proleptically overlays *tunc* and *nunc*, warning the reader that very soon 'Your moment in the sunlight will be over'. For him, in fact:

> it has already happened, the flash
> winked out its message to the other stars,
> the ink burned in the engraving, such record
> as survived now in dispute.

Beneath these differentiated moments of history beats the same rhythm of rapacity and violence, 'in their different speech the same:/the same dangerous commonwealth, men/totting up loot'. He offers 'A long tale the same again sir/repeating itself', pain eating into the page. Each person in this configuration can say 'I merely disable myself/in this condotta with words', for words are 'so many flags/under conflicting allegiance,/meanings that dodge//across factions and borders'. It is for this reason that Hawkwood clings on to the idea of the contract as inviolable:

> Men's speech is all cunning...
> we must make some agreement,
>
> And honour it...
> down to the letter.

If he dies in bed, cheating a worse death in a 'ratslicked dungeon', history for him is 'a meaculpa':

> In the text known as *Where I failed*,
> in the addendum *But we tried*,
> directions to this place are fanciful,
> the map's white terra incognita. Or lost.

This textualisation of history, apparent at the start, recurs as the sequence nears its end, as if Smith, speaking through the mouthpiece of an obscure, reimagined life, acknowledges that he can only fabricate, not recover, the real moment as it flashes up on the sight. In the words he attributes to Hawkwood, both poet and persona are 'a blank slate on which is set/*menace* and *oblivion*'. If the last

poem of the sequence asserts, hopefully, 'somewhere there's an
end to it', Hawkwood himself finds egress only in becoming the
text he reads, 'And then, the last page turned . . . /the book shut and
I tell no more' – at which point the reader of Smith's book confronts
a photograph of a Florentine wall of massive stone blocks. There is,
in the end, no way out to history except through the textuality
Smith reinstates here at the very moment that he seems brilliantly
to have recreated the authentic voice of the past.

Smith's consummate achievement is to re-evoke the past through
a minute attention to detail, an archaeologist's eye for the little
significant things, the material traces that encapsulate a whole
epoch. His history is seen from below, from the point of view of
the underdog who has to carry the can for the generals and emper-
ors. In 'Caesar Caesar' (*The Poet Reclining*, p. 85), for example, he
deconstructs the whole order of Empire with a sly subversive
slave's question whose implicit premise is futility:

> Where does it go?
> All the bootleather,
> sweat, curses, orders,
> the lists
> of those to be shut of.

In 'At the Western Beacon', more positively, to imagine the history
of place is to invoke anonymous generations of toiling predecessors
reaching back to the Stone Age (*The Poet Reclining*, p. 94). The urge
of this poetry is to unearth 'the lost tale of the arrowmaker's vision'
from a soil that carries still the traces of past inhabitants ('All their
tools, bones,/legends and gods are one wash/through the peat
now'), a place now occupied by a new people with transitory
hubris 'calling themselves *people of this land*'.

A series of poems about the vanishing American in *The Poet
Reclining*, 'The Sioux cleared from Minnesota', 'From the Nahua',
'Ghost dances' and 'Ghost songs', articulates a constellation of past
and present formed by memory and recall based on mutual need:

> Only a little way the dead come with us
> wanting to live in their names spoken out.

Without such a continuum, time and space are reduced to the
vacuous abstract relations of a universe stripped of the numinous:

This is the feel of belonging to no place:
the gods come loose from their stones.

The way to overcome both this dispossession and the statute of limitations upon remembering is to transmit the reality of loss to a new generation, writing it all down on a postcard and sending it to 'someone at random'. In Smith's vision, 'someone' is not a vague evasion of personal commitment but a perpetual hope: *someone* will be there to receive it; there is always *someone* to pass on the message. We inherit a past which is at once burden and gift. In 'Song for the whites' (*The Poet Reclining*, p. 40), the tables are turned in that it is the native American, living 'among strangers/for whom words have too many shadows', with his memories of starvation and massacre, who pities the white man, offering him the chance to preserve for his own good that which he has almost wiped out for reasons of short-term gain, recalling:

> White Antelope who sang *nothing lives long*
> *only the earth and mountains.*
> You may write that in your books if you will.
> It was his death-song, his and the buffalo's.

Such a white man receives his own epitaphic recall in 'The clearing' (*The Poet Reclining*, p. 126), where, amidst Minnesota woods, a field half-reverted to forest recalls the life and labour once invested in it. The poem imagines moments from that past life so powerfully that at times the modern speaker's own subjectivity seems invaded by that of the man he imagines, in a history of hard work as abiding in its testimonies as the traces of 'Old iron implements shedding into rust, the soil faintly red'. 'He stares now//in my mind catching his breath into me, as if he were my death', the poem says, in a characteristic Smith move making it impossible for the reader to determine whether it is the dead man looking forward or the living man looking back who imagines this haunting. What both seek here is 'a space amongst others I can open in my mind to walk there, to return, all my days', in a process which turns time into a *mutual* haunting:

> Though I can't hear
> their immigrant speech, can't see
> their scowl from the house

> wanting me gone, there's some thickening
> of air I walk through.

People and trees are alike here, for the birches also record their
own stories:

> survivors
> gathered in old parchments, their skins'

> weathered alphabets, pitted bark
> of lost writing, lost marks
> a language left in the baggage trains,
> stolen from docksides.

Again, the last request of the poem is for the reassurance of mutuality between past and present experiencing subjects:

> Tell me it's so. We remember.
> Tell me someone remembering us
> sitting out in the last woods
> warms our old cheeks.

The voice of the text, the poet speaking like a shaman through the
mask of the farmer, finds itself like Rip van Winkle, 'stolen away/
waking years later among elm roots' to speak again, here, in this
act of historical recreation, as if for the first time.

TIME STOPS HERE

One of the earliest and most recurrent motifs in Smith's verse is
that of the Holocaust. 'The magic of Poland' sequence in *The heart,
the border* finds its sinister magic at Auschwitz-Birkenau. The poem
'*Work will make you free*' lists one or two personal names among
many, from Hamburg, Krakow, 'tenants from the Ghetto Nuovo',
all now reduced to 'a pond of white human ash', mingled together
in Hitler's ghastly parody of the Internationale, 'So close, far away
as the moon,/as all the lives all the dead lived'. 'The photograph'
(p. 54) tells us, 'Time stops here./And I am not in it', complicating
the voice of the poem, at the end of time, with that of an imagined
murdered speaker meeting his or her own end amidst the chipped
bowls, piles of hair clippings, spectacles outside the gas chamber.

Of both speakers it is true that 'Beyond this moment nothing ever changes'. The photograph arrests time (a theme of Benjamin's) but it is also fragile, expungeable, losing its colours, the yellow light across the fields bleaching out, a corner curling where it burns, like the brief lives of those it briefly reminds us of:

> Nothing beyond this:
> a deathless landscape
> with the heart burned out, the smile intact.

In the same way 'Sinistra' (p. 44), one of several poems about Venice, moves from the museum of prehistoric remains in the first stanza, through saints' relics rotting in their boxes, to the recently remaindered dead, the Jews of the Ghetto Nuovo taken away to the camps, whose silence and absence the poem endlessly repeats, *'our memory is your only grave'*.

An early poem about the Nazi death camps, 'To survive' (*The Poet Reclining*, p. 86), offers a powerful summation of Smith's sense of historical accountability. One of a loose sequence which includes 'Maria the thief', 'Reports from the east', 'Bowl', 'Wants' and 'The veterans', this poem opens on a world where apocalypse has already happened, and each day *is* the last day, a 'shaft/other days fall into'. Psychic dispossession, as Bruno Bettelheim has shown, manifests itself most brutally in loss of the ability to say 'I' and 'mine', to hold on to the sense of self as *my* self, rather than a mere bundle of discourses thrown together by others, by an acculturation which interpellates the subject to a merely delusory selfhood. In a sense to which Louis Althusser witnessed not only in his theory but in the catastrophic ending of his own psychic life, the concentration camps were the great deconstructors of the bourgeois subject. For Smith, self-possession is a positive value not to be confused with the delusions of private property. Rather 'my' and 'mine' are words used to describe a functional relationship between self and objects in a functioning universe, where 'Books, tables, lost objects/call back to us'. To lose a sense of this exchange between self and world is to cease to *function*, but merely to survive, so that one's own limbs are reduced to unattached presences:

> *Mine* I said *mine*, doubting now
> whether these fingers, these knees
> would answer in my name.

The speaking subject, 'A man assembled from nothings', suffers attrition of the personal pronoun and possessive adjecture, and their renders him down from 'us', through 'I' to 'he', until, prepared to 'swallow his name for nourishment', he is a mere reciprocation of the dark which 'looks out on *it*self' (my italics). In 'Reports from the east' (*The Poet Reclining*, p. 85), the days themselves are 'coming apart', and 'whether the clocks shedding/moment across moment record it or not, pain, no longer that of an experiencing 'I' but of a decentred, almost subjectless condition, still comes to be fed. These poems record that slow abolition of the personal pronouns in a world where experience seems to happen to objects, not subjects. Yet, as in 'Bowl', a simple bowl of soup can renew that experiencing self, moving from an alienated perception of 'the hands/melded together' to the rebirth of the pronoun as reflexive person ('she cups the heat into herself'), a self measuring itself in absences, who 'fill herself/in the warmth, in its lack', the imaginary fulness of self-presence restored in the very extremity of lack.

'Wants' sums up with epigrammatic force the fatuity of a whole cycle of history: 'Such effort to make ruins.' But in its conclusion it moves to a desire that the pronouns can be restored to their proper places in sentences which once again construct a human meaning, where the speaking voices and the grammatical voices of the verb coincide, in a process in which the present keeps faith with the past and the future:

> I want the voices to find each other.
> I want the parts of speech rising towards each other.

In *The heart, the border*, a moment of renewed historic hope celebrates the great liberating events in which, during 1989–90, the frozen frontiers of half a century collapsed under the pressure of human desires. 'Monument' speaks of the fraudulent heroic narratives of Hitler and Stalin inscribed in statuesque figures of 'the ego telling itself the same lie'. But the monolithic archetype of a frozen history, so daunting to Orwell, turns out to be human and vulnerable too, pointing a stony finger into a future 'which completely ignores him'. The repressed returns; nothing is ever forever and, in a moment of *Jetztzeit*, of Messianic time, the lost generations rise up in the flesh and blood of the living. In 'The Wall (Obligatory)', the ideological histories of the victors, their frontiers vigorously patrolled against truth each side of the border, finally collapse under their own weight. Ideologies like individuals are, in the words of the next poem's title, just 'Passing through', depart to leave only 'disbelief on the faces of the tyrants,/end of system without escape clause. Walls fall and men'.

The final poem of this most recent volume is 'After Brecht' in a double sense. Written by one of those 'Nachgeborene' Brecht addressed in a famous poem, it is both *influenced by* and *supersedes* him. The poem begins, ironically, 'In the end'. It offers, instead of Brecht's titanic clash of metaphysical absolutes, a history of that everyday life which somewhere somehow survives the great catastrophes ('In the end it is Joachim with his maps...'). The poet salvages what was positive and abiding in Brecht's writing – its concern with a history seen from below by men in dark times – from its (willing) co-option in a new triumphal procession of the victors. All Smith's poetry in a sense addresses the 'one single catastrophe' Benjamin's angel of history confronts:

His face is turned to the past. Where we perceive a chain of events, he sees one single catastrophe which keeps piling wreckage upon wreckage and hurls it in front of his feet. The angel would like to stay, awaken the dead, and make whole what has been smashed. But a storm is blowing from Paradise; it has got caught in his wings with such violence that the angel can no longer close them. This storm irresistibly propels him into the future to which his back is turned, while the pile of debris before him grows skyward. This storm is what we call progress.

But if 'Time stops here' this is where it also begins over again, in each moment. For Smith, no progress can ever redeem the waste of lives. But the sadness of his poems is transfigured by another mood, a kind of patient lyric anger at the waste combined with a faith in the capacity of this tale-telling creature to salvage what is salvageable from the ruins of history, to begin all over again from what was broken, in *the time of the now* 'after Brecht' which is all that remains to any of us:

> Telling our tales. We grew up on the other side
> of a long long war we all lost.
> Years have gone by. All our lives have...

It will always be so: this moment,
the sunlight, the long afternoon, the blackbirds,
Joachim with his maps, Thora in her garden.

Notes

1. All references to Walter Benjamin in this essay are to his 'Theses on the Philosophy of History', in Hannah Arendt. (ed.), *Illuminations* (London: Collins/Fontana Books, 1973), pp. 255–66. Citations of Ken Smith's poetry are identified by volume throughout the text.

6

Dance of Being:
The Poetry of Peter Redgrove

Neil Roberts

A few years ago Peter Redgrove published an article called 'Why the Bomb is Real but not True',[1] in which he argued that nuclear weapons and the ethics of modern warfare are made possible by a model of scientific thought which holds as an axiom that the thinker's subjectivity must be rigorously excluded. He calls this a 'monstrous cosmic detachment...which is held to describe the ground of our universe, and modern behaviour,'[2] and points out that an alternative model has been proposed, based on the so-called 'holographic paradigm', of a world the whole of which (including our own subjectivities) is 'enfolded' like the parts of a holographic image into each region. The word 'enfolded' comes from the physicist David Bohm's book *Wholeness and the Implicate Order*; Redgrove cites Bohm's hypothesis of an 'implicate order [in which] one may say that everything is folded into everything' in contrast to 'the *explicate order* now dominant in physics in which things are *unfolded* in the sense that each thing lies only in its own particular region of space (and time) and outside the regions belonging to other things.'[3]

This will be recognised as the well-known meeting of modern physics and oriental religion (Redgrove also cites, with less enthusiasm, Capra's *Tao of Physics*). Far from satisfying the objective criteria long demanded of scientific thought, it is motivated by pressing psychological need in the face of the 'monstrous cosmic detachment'. Redgrove is exploring the territory opened up two hundred years ago by Blake, who is also quoted in the essay. Unlike myself, he knows enough science to hold an educated opinion of the controversy, and his commitment to the 'implicate order' is fundamental to his recent poetry.

The history of bad poetry is littered with the corpses of poems by writers who attempted to versify current philosophical and scien-

tific ideas. We have to ask whether Redgrove creates, as it were, a
poetic equivalent for these concepts, whether they have entered
into the fabric of his language.

In one of the chapters of *Wholeness and the Implicate Order* David
Bohm projects an experiment with language designed to subvert
the subject–verb–object structure, which enshrines a 'manifest'
structure of functions, and to bestow primacy on the verb, to
convey the notion that the action issues from an order of reality
beyond the manifest agency of the subject. Bohm's specific propo-
sals are impossibly schematic and awkward, but his intentions
illuminate the characteristic movement and syntax of much of Redgrove's best poetry. One might say in ordinary English, for example, 'a mother is breast-feeding her baby during a thunderstorm,
while a moth flutters at the radio' without realising how much
editing has gone into this unexceptionable sentence. In the final
section of Redgrove's poem, 'The White, Night-Flying Moths
Called "Souls"', a moth dances to a humming radio and:

> Our baby, like a moth, flutters at its mother,
>
> Who mutters at her baby, uttering milk
> That dresses itself in white baby, who smiles
>
> With milky creases up at the breast creating
> Milky creases, and milk-hued water
>
> Hangs in the sky, waiting for its clothes,
> Like a great white ear floats over us, listening
>
> To the mothy mother-mutter, or like a sky-beard smiles
> And slips into its thunderous vestry and descends
>
> In streaming sleeves of electrical arms
> To run in gutters where it sucks and sings.[4]

In this sentence there are twelve verbs and five participles, and in
the part of the sentence that focuses directly on the feeding of the
baby the agency passes from the baby to the mother, to the baby
again, to the milk, to the baby again and (possibly) to the breast. At
the same time the pattern of internal rhymes and puns suggests
more than coincidental links between the fluttering of the baby, the

muttering of the mother, the uttering of the milk and even the gutters where the thunderwater babylike 'sucks' and (mother-like?) 'sings', while the mother is punningly linked with the moth and the cross-language pun on 'mutter' emphasises the merging of agent and action. What we experience when reading the passage, then, is not (as in my 'ordinary' sentence) a series of coincidentally or even causally related actions but a nexus in which the human subject is neither the triumphant lord of the verb nor its deterministic victim but a partner in a syntactically notated dance of being.

The passage I have just discussed is an outstanding example of Redgrove's technique in the way that human action is absorbed into the elemental pattern but the human meaning and value are not lost, on the contrary are enhanced. Redgrove makes unusually overt use of sound patterning here, but comparable examples of sentence structure can be found everywhere in his more recent work. Moreover, this principle which we have seen served by long, flexible sentences with many verbs, can also produce strikingly condensed effects:

> Tissues of the earth, in their proper place,
> Quartz tinged with the rose, the deep quick,
> Scrap of the tissue of the slow heart of the earth,
> *Throbbing the light I look at it with,*
> Pumps slowly, most slowly, the deep organ of the earth.

> (my italics)[5]

Here the deviant syntax, focusing on the rare transitive use of the word 'throb', has the effect of distributing the action between the stone, the light and the speaker, again avoiding a fixed structure of subject and object.

These are examples of the 'poetry of grammar' which 30 years ago Roman Jakobson said was 'seldom known to critics', but is perhaps more familiar now.[6] The old Jakobsonian grid-pattern of intersecting axes of combination and substitution, corresponding to the functions of metonymy and metaphor,[7] has its limitations, but it is a powerful model for illustrating the way much poetry works. Take, for example, Craig Raine's notorious 'Arsehole':

> It is shy as a gathered eyelet
> neatly worked in shrinking violet.[8]

This is the New Critical ideal of poetry. Deftly and simultaneously Raine insinuates the double metaphor of arsehole as eye, arsehole as flower; the sides of the metaphor are held together by the mind in tension and paradox to allow a new, more tender and appreciative feeling towards the despised bodily part, but the poem does not question – and would not want to – the actual separateness of those things it brings together for a rhetorical purpose. One recalls that the function of *ostranenie*, 'making strange', was to 'make the stone *stony*'.[9] Our perception of the stone or of the arsehole is changed, but we remain in, or are returned to, an empirically safe world in which stones are stony and arseholes are arseholey.

For Redgrove, we should perhaps replace the grid with his own figure of a spider's web:

> At every intersection and along each boulevard
> Crowded with lenses gazing upwards, pointing light[10]

inspired by the Hindu figure of a necklace of pearls each one of which bears the reflection of every other. The application of this to Redgrove's 'metaphors' would best be illustrated by a poem such as 'Transactions', with its bewildering inter-reflection of mushrooms, electricity, angels, moon and clothing, but the poem is too long and elaborate to be discussed here. A shorter example is the conclusion of 'The Quiet Woman of Chancery Lane':

>   I take
> The blind girl by her night hand.
> With her fingers raised, she traces in the air
> The slow rising of that mountain that hangs, the full moon,
>
> It is like the presence of a fountain, she says,
> Like the fresh aura of falling water, or like
> That full head of the thistle I stroked in the park,
> And its sound is like a fountain too, or like snow thistling.[11]

Metaphor depends for its effect on the things being brought together remaining at the same time separate. Redgrove, like all poets, uses metaphor in this way, but it is not (as it is with Raine) his most characteristic rhetoric. In the passage quoted he uses a series of similes, and simile usually functions like metaphor rather than, say, like metonymy. Nevertheless I would argue that these similes are, in a curious way distinctive to Redgrove, metonymic. They depend on the reader accepting (if only for the duration of the poem) a breakdown of the empirical boundaries between moon, fountain, thistle and snow. The blind girl's uncanny location of the moon in the sky invites us to accept her perceptions as *real*. Whereas in the Raine poem a recognition of likeness-in-unlikeness between arsehole and flower or eye precipitates a change of feeling towards the arsehole, here most readers will not *recognise* any likeness between the moon and a fountain. It can be no more than a charming (or patronising) fancy unless the reader entertains the notion that her heightened and synaesthetic non-visual senses enable her to perceive actual connections of the kind vividly epitomised by the phrase 'snow thistling'.

Redgrove's thinking is profoundly monistic; as he goes on to say in the essay, 'We have no reason, except Irrelativity, which is sometimes called schizoid thinking, for standing outside this complex implicated relationship of everything we know.'[12]

We all know, however, that it's not as easy as that. Redgrove's 'except' covers some of our most deeply ingrained self-conceptions and securities. The consoling vision of the poem and the essay is not an intellectual proposition one can simply take over – it lies, as it were, on the other side of a process of *psychological* transformation which is, in an inevitably untidy way, charted through the course of Redgrove's poetic career.

One of his most successful early pieces is the comic prose fantasy 'Mr Waterman', in the form of a dialogue with a notably reticent psychiatrist, which begins:

> We never really liked that pond in the garden. At times it was choked with a sort of weed, which, if you pulled one thread, gleefully unravelled until you had an empty basin before you and the whole of the pond in a soaking heap at your side.[13]

Here we have figured the exasperation of our ordinary consciousness in the face of the intractably 'implicated' relation of our nature to the rest of the world. The water invades the patient's house, and has the power to take on any shape, most disturbingly that of 'Mr Waterman' himself, a creature of such energy and charm that the patient dreads 'the time (for it will come) when I shall arrive home unexpectedly early, and hear a sudden scuffle-away in the waste-pipes, and find my wife ("just out of the shower, dear") with that moist look in her eyes, drying her hair.'

Eroticism and humour, as we shall see, make a powerful combination in Redgrove's work. But first we must take one or two sightings of the progress of this 'patient' through his poetry. The biggest reason why we can't simply assent intellectually to the vision of the later poetry is that it is rooted in the acceptance of death – death is inevitably the most compelling instance of transformation for all of us. Death is horror to the ego, however sweet-natured and 'unegotistical' the ego may be. No ego could be more sweet-natured than that of the protagonist in Redgrove's earliest poems, who bends his will to the protection of his family against the vision of death in an old house where many have died.

> 'This is no place to bring children to'
>
> I cried in a nightmare of more
> Creatures shelled in bone-white,
> Or dead eyes fronting soft ermine faces,
> Or mantled in carnation, dying kings of creation,
> Or crimson mouth-skirts flashing as they pass.[14]

These early poems are confessional: their strength is the exposure of trauma, but they are trapped within the trauma. The attempt in this poem at a superior point of view can only back away from the vision by calling it a 'silly agony'.

The way forward for Redgrove, artistically, was to dramatise the trauma, to move from confession to fable. The fruit of this development and the corresponding development of vision can be seen in 'The Case' from his fourth book *The Force*, one of the most powerful of all his poems. Here the protagonist's senses have been opened, by the example of his mother, to the overwhelming reality of the natural world:

And I swam in the thunderstorm in the river of blood, oil and
    cider,
And I saw the blue of my recovery open around me in the water,
Blood, cider, rainbow, and the apples still warm after sunset
Dashed in the cold downpour, and so this mother-world
Opened around me and I lay in the perfumes after rain out of the
    river

Tugging the wet grass, eyes squeezed, straining to the glory,
The burst of white glory like the whitest clouds rising to the sun
And it was like a door opening in the sky, it was like a door
    opening in the water,
It was like the high mansion of the sky, and water poured from the
    tall french windows.
It was like a sudden smell of fur among the flowers, it was like a
    face at dusk
It was like a rough trouser on a smooth leg.[15]

This rhapsody is punctuated, however, by two threatening repeated phrases, 'Oh shame', and 'It was something about God'.
The first is an abbreviation of the mother's own exclamation, when
the flowers were 'pumping their natures into her': 'What a shame
we have to die.' The more we love life the more we dread
the thought of death, and so the speaker's love of nature comes
to be dominated by an upward, world-spurning movement, like
the spirit of Marvell's 'On a Drop of Dew' disguised as celebration
of the world:

One with the birds that are blue-egged because they love the sky!
With the flocks of giraffes craning towards the heavens!

The mother who is immersed in nature but afraid of death has to be
complemented by the father who is outside nature, who is notable
for his 'silent invisibility' and 'virile restraint'. The result is not a
balance but a split in the protagonist's nature, and at the end of the
poem he blinds himself in order to 'live unseeing, not watching,
without judging, called "Father".'
    'The Case' is an extremely complex poem that blends psychiatry
and myth to create a figure who is both an archetype and a
psychiatric 'case'. He is impelled by the mother to search for the
absent father – we are not in the archaic world where the male sky
unendingly embraces the female earth to create life, but the familiar
Christian one where God is at least partly sickened by the 'mother-
world wet with perfume' and has turned away from it. The hero is
condemned, accordingly, to be celibate, that is to be cut off from the
prime saving experience in Redgrove's universe.
    The protagonist of the earlier poetry is understandably male.
He is also archetypally 'masculine' in that he feels threatened by
the teeming changefulness of nature and strives to order it in

accordance with his ideal conception of himself. In 'The Case' he says he is a gardener, and there are echoes of Marvell's 'Mower Against Gardens' as well as 'On a Drop of Dew'. Redgrove's poetry, from this point on (and perhaps, implicitly, even earlier), is pervasively concerned with and structured by his beliefs about the psychology of gender. Psychological differences between men and women are biologically determined – 'Every month, all through the month, the woman goes through a series of bodily changes of ineffable sensitivity that are the total response of her being, arguably more deeply actual and rooted in this physical world than any man can attain'[16] – but exaggerated and perverted by culture and religion. Redgrove sees his 'mission as attempting to arouse the feminine energies in men, and the feminine modes of perception.'[17] *The Black Goddess* begins with the statement, 'I've always known we are surrounded by invisibles', and he recalls the perplexity he felt about a religion whose 'invisibles' were always called 'He' when for himself 'the most compelling invisibilities somehow came through women', most importantly his mother who, he says, swam in the sea when she was carrying him and said to the unborn child, 'You must be brave if you can, and learn to ride the waves.'[18]

The relation of the woman to the male protagonist in his poetry moves from that of antagonist and/or victim to teacher and eventually partner. In this process she is frequently associated with a group of related motifs – blindness, blackness, defilement – that symbolise her affinity with the 'invisibles' and her rootedness in the world. This conception of femininity, and its use as a psychological category available to men, is bound to arouse suspicion, but I will defer discussion of its ideological aspects until I have given some examples.

In Redgrove's first volume, *The Collector*, where the typical protagonist is fixed in 'masculine' psychology, there is a poem about a woman that intriguingly anticipates the development I have described. It is an unassuming poem, almost like a creative writing exercise, about what it is like to 'do without eyes'. The result is a synaesthetic enhancement of the other senses.

[She] Heaves the heavy bulging of the water-jug,...
With clinking nails scrabbles for the body of the sprawling soap,
Rubs up the fine jumping lather that grips like a mask, floods it
    off...

Bloods and plumps her cheeks in the springy towel, a rolling
variable darkness
Dimpling the feminine fat-pockets under the deep coombs of bone
And the firm sheathed jellies above that make silent lightning in
their bulbs.[19]

This poem stands alone in *The Collector*, uniquely and modestly
exemplifying the 'feminine' experience that becomes explicit in the
poetry ten years later.

Redgrove's first four volumes were published over a period of
seven years, culminating in *The Force* (1966) which contains, in 'The
Case' and 'The Widower', his most subtle portrayals of the 'masculine' consciousness. He did not publish another major collection
until 1972, when *Dr Faust's Sea-Spiral Spirit* appeared, to be followed in 1973 by *The Hermaphrodite Album* and his first and most
innovative 'novel', *In the Country of the Skin*. By now his personal
and creative association with Penelope Shuttle had begun, whose
first explicit product was *The Hermaphrodite Album*, but which un-
doubtedly influenced this whole new phase of his work.

One can extract from *Dr Faust* a close-knit group of poems that
continue the 'story' of the male protagonist in earlier poems. The
key development is that he is now intimate with a woman who, by
word and example, guides him out of the tormenting psychological
and metaphysical fix that finally drove 'The Case' mad. In some of
them the woman seems to have died, but her lesson outlives her. In
two of them the women are referred to as 'witches', and one of the
most startling claims of *The Wise Wound* is that 'witchcraft is the
subjective experience of the menstrual cycle'.[20]

In one of the most successful of these poems, 'The Youthful
Scientist Remembers', the woman makes one brief remark, which
has an ostensibly disproportionate effect on her lover:

> You pointed out that the lily
> Was somebody's red tail inside their white nightie
> So much so
> That I am still sober and amazed at the starlight
> glittering in the mud,
> I am amazed at the stars, and the greatest wonder of them all
> Is that their black is as full as their white, the black
> Impends with the white, packing between the white....[21]

The woman's lesson is like the one that Lawrence's Birkin tries more ponderously to instil in the famous classroom scene in *Women in Love*, here the more effective for its colloquial humour and brevity. The lover's whole response to the world is changed and intensified by the sharply lateral vision ('their black is as full as their white') that her words inspire in him. At the beginning of the poem he has said, 'You have mud on your jersey,/This pleases me, I cannot say why.' This mudstain is a less flamboyant version of the woman's demonstration in 'The Idea of Entropy'; it is, for Redgrove, a menstrual symbol – therefore (but also independently of such symbolism) a badge of the 'more deeply actual and rooted' existence.

'The Idea of Entropy at Maenporth Beach' is Redgrove's most popular and anthologised poem. It is also one of his best poems. Although it is quite a simple poem, to reach it we have to pass through a thicket of allusions: via the title to Wallace Stevens's 'Idea of Order at Key West', via the epigraph, 'C'est Elle! noire et pourtant lumineuse', to Baudelaire's 'Un Fantôme', and via the dedication to John Layard, the Jungian teacher with whom Redgrove underwent analysis. The poem can be read as a retort to Stevens, though not a disrespectful one. Instead of the remote, statuesque and abstract feminine personification of 'The Idea of Order' who 'sang beyond the genius of the sea' we have a blonde woman in a white dress, not indeed quite real but certainly physical, who immerses herself in mud; and instead of the solemn sonorous diction of Stevens we are humorously bombarded with onomatopoeic Anglo-Saxon and colloquial monosyllables:

> If it were a white dress, she said, with some little black,
> Dressed with a little flaw, a smut, some swart
> Twinge of ancestry, or if it were all black
> Since I am white, but – it's my mistake.
> So slowly she slunk, all pleated, into the muck.[22]

Baudelaire's black but shining 'fantôme' is found among the shadows of 'les caveaux d'insondable tristesse'.[23] She is clearly, on Redgrove's reading, the Black Goddess, and this discovery of the most precious thing in the depths of sadness recalls Layard's aphorism, often quoted by Redgrove, 'depression is withheld knowledge.'

The poem immediately establishes that its female figure is not, like Stevens's, 'beyond' the material world: 'Slowly she slipped into the muck.' While she certainly functions as an exemplification of the idea of entropy, and is never quite 'real' as a person, the action and diction of the poem maintain a certain quizzicality towards the word 'idea' itself. The woman immerses herself in mud, obliterating her blonde hair, white dress and the diamond at her throat, emerges as a 'black Venus' and runs along a sandy beach sprinkling the mud and ending up 'streaky white'. The effect is a humorous version of a pagan baptismal ritual rather than the post-Cartesian metaphysics of Stevens's poem. The diction – 'muck', 'stank', 'smut', 'slunk', 'swart', 'snotty' – draws attention to itself while it insists on the brute physicality of the action. Yet, by the end, Redgrove rises to a rhetoric much less remote from Stevens's:

> The black rooks coo like doves, new suns beam
> From every droplet of the shattering waves,
> From every crystal of the shattered rock.
> Drenched in the mud, pure white rejoiced,
> From this collision were new colours born,
> And in their slithering passage to the sea
> The shrugged-up riches of deep darkness sang.

That Redgrove's final word is the keyword of Stevens's poem cannot be an accident. It is perhaps a not entirely ironic homage, for both poems are concerned with transformation and creativity, but we might suspect that he is implicitly rebuking the elder poet by making the femininity of his figure so much more vital and central to the poem's meaning.

The drift of male–female relations in Redgrove is entertainingly summarised in the *Hermaphrodite Album* sequence 'Six Odes', which also provides the occasion for considering the Redgrovian feminine in a more ideological light. The sequence moves from overt male domination of the feminine to participatory celebration; what is celebrated in the concluding poems is the woman/nature topos, inviting comparison with such poems as Ted Hughes's 'Crow's Undersong' and Lucio Piccolo's 'Veneris Venefica Agrestis' (translated by Charles Tomlinson in *Written on Water*). This topos is well-known to be characteristically circular and self-sustaining: the woman is 'natural' in comparison with the man, and nature is thought of as 'feminine'. Redgrove's interest in the feminine, of course, does not rest on a tired poetical convention, and his poems draw strength from the investigations that were to result in *The Wise Wound*. Nevertheless the topos should not go unquestioned.

Supported by the influence of Jung and Graves (the latter of whom, it will be remembered, thought the role of Muse barred women from writing poetry), it is extensively present not only in Redgrove's poetry but also in that of the two most popular living UK poets, Hughes and Heaney. Its basic structure, which explains its circularity, is that woman and nature are both locations of what 'man' (with all the ambiguity of that word) lacks and needs. Its psychological content is paralleled by its cultural content: that the main motor of our civilisation has been the privileging of 'masculine' intellect over 'feminine' body, feelings, intuition, accounting for many of the deformations of civilisation, and most especially the destructive exploitation of the natural world. Many aspects of this critique are powerfully argued in *The Wise Wound* and *The Black Goddess*, especially in the chapter of the former that deals with the suppression of witchcraft. Redgrove and Shuttle's version of this argument can certainly claim to be a feminism and *The Wise Wound* is, in its way, a not unpolitical work. Nevertheless, the problem of the whole topos is encapsulated in the Jungian Erich Neumann's assertion, in his classic study *The Great Mother, an Analysis of the Archetype*, that 'in both sexes the active ego consciousness is characterised by a male symbolism, the unconscious as a whole by a female symbolism.'[24] (The unconscious and nature are regularly spoken of in tandem in Jungian discourse.) In the words of Simone de Beauvoir, 'He is the Subject, he is the Absolute – she is the Other.'[25]

But in Redgrove this is not entirely so. The woman in 'Without Eyes' is emphatically experiencing herself: there is no need to refer to any male consciousness. There is more of a sense of an observer, possibly male, in 'The Idea of Entropy', but still the experience belongs primarily to the woman. In 'Six Odes' there is certainly a male perspective, but Redgrove's distinction can be illustrated by comparing the final poem in the sequence, 'Coming-Lady', with Ted Hughes's more famous 'Crow's Undersong'.

She cannot come all the way...

She comes singing she cannot manage an instrument
She comes too cold afraid of clothes
And too slow with eyes wincing frightened
When she looks into wheels

('Crow's Undersong')[26]

She comes like a seashell without a skin,
She comes like warm mud that moves in sections.
She comes with long legs like a tree-frog clambering
Towards some great fruit, niddip, niddip.
A small acrobat lives inside her flower;
The canopy blooms.
She has an underground belfry tolling the bushes
Which shakes the ground,
It is full of shivering bats that fly out and return.

('Coming-Lady')[27]

The Hughes poem is justly celebrated. The play of the chant urged by the repetition against the various rhythmic restraints is superbly handled, and the poem as a whole is tender and moving. In the present context, however, it is notable that the female figure is not human, and that although feelings are attributed to her she is presented from another, and obviously masculine perspective: a perspective that she cannot 'come all the way' to share. The difference in the use of the word 'come' in the two poems is revealing. Much has been made of the sexual connotations of the word in 'Crow's Undersong', but even though a later line states that she has come 'amorous', these connotations seem to me secondary to the spatial, especially when we take full account of the privative spatial metaphors with which the poem opens. For all the sensuous allure of much of the poem's language, the controlling metaphor is one of distance, and the implied 'here' to which she 'cannot come all the way' can only be understood as the 'active ego consciousness' and its world of clothes, wheels, houses and cities, which is 'characterised by a male symbolism'.

In Redgrove's poem the sexual meaning of 'come' is of course dominant almost to the exclusion of other meanings. Consequently the human identity of the female and the humanity of the situation are dominant: it is a poem about two people making love. Redgrove strengthens the humanity of the poem by leavening the natural imagery with ribald humour: 'Her knickers come off like opening party invitations'. For all the natural similes, she is a woman 'coming'; this coming is experienced both by her and by her lover: the language can be read both ways, enacting the sense of participation. Unlike Hughes's woman/Goddess she can 'come all the way', or rather she and her lover can come all the way to each other. There is nothing ambivalent about her humanity, and so Redgrove's man can say 'I have lost dread there longer than a man reasonably may'.

The female in 'Crow's Undersong' is frightened of wheels and 'cannot count'. However much the poet values her, and however much he may discredit the ability to count (as in 'Crow's Account of St George' and 'Revenge Fable') we know that the power will always be with those who can count and can control wheels. Nature may triumph in the end, at our expense, but that is no consolation to women, who are part of 'us', not of hypostasised Nature. Hughes knows this but I think that Redgrove's poetry has been more successful in exploring the territory of 'the feminine', in absorbing the Jungian influence without implicitly diminishing the humanity of women, or forgetting that the invention of the wheel and the ability to count are aspects of our humanity, of our femininity as much as of our masculinity.

Notes

1. P. Redgrove, 'Why the Bomb is Real but not True', in David Martin and Peter Mullen (eds), *Unholy Warfare* (Oxford: Blackwell, 1983), pp. 141–6. See also N. Roberts, 'Peter Redgrove: The Science of the Subjective', *Poetry Review*, Vol. 77, No. 2, 1987, pp. 4–10 (an extract from an interview with Redgrove conducted in October 1986).

2. P. Redgrove, 'Why the Bomb is Real but not True', in *Unholy Warfare*, op. cit., p. 141.

3. D. Bohm, *Wholeness and the Implicate Order* (London: Routledge, 1980), p. 177, quoted in *Unholy Warfare*, p. 144.

4. P. Redgrove, *The Apple-Broadcast and Other New Poems* (London: Routledge, 1981), pp. 69–70; also in *Poems 1954–1987* (Harmondsworth: Penguin, 1989).

5. P. Redgrove, 'Minerals of Cornwall, Stones of Cornwall', in *Dr Faust's Sea-Spiral Spirit and Other Poems* (London: Routledge, 1972), p. 3; also in *Poems 1954–1987*, op. cit. Compare Bohm: 'The subject–verb–object structure of language, along with its world-view, tends to impose itself very strongly in our speech, even in those cases, in which some attention would reveal its evident inappropriateness ... Thus, instead of saying, "An observer looks at an object", we can more appropriately say, "Observation is going on, in an undivided movement involving those abstractions customarily called 'the human being' and 'the object he is looking at'." (Bohm, op. cit., p. 29.) 'Minerals of Cornwall' was written several years before even the original publication of this passage in 1976. Red-

grove, I should say, never lapses into the Pseuds' cornerish prosiness of Bohm's discursive style here.

6. R. Jakobson, 'Linguistics and poetics', in D. Lodge (ed.), *Modern Criticism and Theory* (London: Longman, 1988), p. 53.
7. See R. Jakobson, 'The metaphoric and metonymic poles', in D. Lodge, op. cit., pp. 57–61.
8. C. Raine, 'Arsehole', in *Rich* (London: Faber, 1984), p. 26.
9. V. Shklovsky, 'Art as Technique', in L.T. Lemon and M.J. Reis (eds), *Russian Formalist Criticism: Four Essays* (Lincoln, Nebraska: Bison Books, 1965).
10. P. Redgrove, 'My Father's Spider', in *The Apple-Broadcast*, op. cit., pp. 5–6; also in *Poems 1954–1987*, op. cit.
11. P. Redgrove, 'The Quiet Woman of Chancery Lane', in *The Man Named East and Other New Poems* (London: Routledge, 1985), p. 11; also in *Poems 1954–1987*.
12. Martin and Mullen, op. cit., p. 143. Cf. 'Einstein was not able to obtain a unified field theory which *related* human beings to the universe or each other...So it appears that Einstein's basic work should be called "Irrelativity", and like other mechanistic theories it is a recipe for alienation.' (Ibid., p. 142–3).
13. P. Redgrove, 'Mr Waterman', in *The Nature of Cold Weather and Other Poems* (London: Routledge, 1961), p. 54; also in *Poems 1954–1987*, op. cit.
14. P. Redgrove, 'Old House', in *The Collector and Other Poems* (London: Routledge, 1959), p. 11; also in *Poems 1954–1987*, op. cit.
15. P. Redgrove, 'The Case', in *The Force and Other Poems* (London: Routledge, 1966), p. 80; also in *Poems 1954–1987*, op. cit.
16. P. Shuttle and P. Redgrove, *The Wise Wound: Eve's Curse and Everywoman* (New York: Marek, 1978), p. 26.
17. P. Redgrove, unpublished letter to Neil Roberts, 19 December 1977.
18. P. Redgrove, *The Black Goddess and the Sixth Sense* (London: Bloomsbury, 1987), p. xi.
19. P. Redgrove, 'Without Eyes', in *The Collector and Other Poems* (London: Routledge, 1959), p. 52; also in *Poems 1954–1987*, op. cit.
20. Shuttle and Redgrove, op. cit., p. 209.
21. P. Redgrove, 'The Youthful Scientist Remembers', in *Dr Faust's Sea-Spiral Spirit*, op. cit., p. 18; also in *Poems 1954–1987*, op. cit.
22. P. Redgrove, 'The Idea of Entropy at Maenporth Beach', in *Dr Faust's Sea-Spiral Spirit*, op. cit., p. 20; also in *Poems 1954–1987*, op. cit.
23. C. Baudelaire, 'Un Fantôme', in E. Starkie (ed.), *Les Fleurs du Mal* (Oxford: Blackwell, 1962), p. 37.
24. E. Neumann, *The Great Mother, an Analysis of the Archetype*, translated by R. Mannheim (London: Routledge, 1953), p. 28.
25. Simone de Beauvoir, 'Introduction' to *The Second Sex* (1949, reprinted in E. Marks and I. de Courtivron (eds), *New French Feminisms, an Anthology*, Amherst: University of Massachussetts, 1980), p. 44.
26. T. Hughes, 'Crow's Undersong', in *Crow, from the Life and Songs of the Crow*, 2nd edn (London: Faber, 1972), p. 56. In T. Gifford and N. Roberts, *Ted Hughes: A Critical Study* (London: Faber, 1981) I praised

this poem unreservedly. I do not withdraw that praise, but the reading prompted by the Redgrove comparison seems to me completer and less naive.

27.   'Coming-Lady' (Part 6 of 'Six Odes') in P. Redgrove and P. Shuttle, *The Hermaphrodite Album* (London: Fuller d'Arch Smith, 1973), p. 49; also in *Poems 1954–1987*, op. cit.

7

Seamus Heaney:
From Revivalism to Postmodernism

Alistair Davies

In one of the most important and wide-ranging of recent essays on
Seamus Heaney, the Irish philosopher, cultural historian and literary critic Richard Kearney, who writes with the added authority
of a working association with Heaney, describes what he takes to
be the dominant reading of him.[1] 'Heaney's primary inspiration,
we are told, is one of place his quintessentially Irish vocation, the
sacramental naming of a homeland. Hence the preoccupation with
images of mythology, archaeology and genealogy, of returning to
forgotten origins.'[2] It is a reading which Kearney sets out to challenge and he does so, in a vocabulary derived from the hermeneutic philosophy of Martin Heidegger, because he believes that it not
only misrepresents Heaney's work but also obscures the significance of his achievement for contemporary Irish culture. We can
grasp the intended scope of Kearney's revisionary account if we
give due weight to the following distinction, for he asks us to
reconsider Heaney's work in a radically new perspective and, at
the same time, to shift even more radically the grounds upon
which we choose to assent to that work. Following from its Heideggerean presuppositions, this involves less a rereading than the
owning up to new possibilities of individual and collective existence.

It is, of course, not difficult to understand how the reading to
which Kearney objects has come about. The poems of Heaney's
first and widely noticed volume, *Death of a Naturalist* (1966), conveyed with all the intensity and exaggeration of childhood imagination and remembrance the particularity and mysteriousness of
place, of the rural world of hedge, barn and farmyard in which he
had grown up. When Heaney himself praised Ted Hughes (with
whom he was immediately associated) for bringing 'back into
English poetry an unsentimental intimacy with the hidden coun-

try',[3] it seemed as if he was describing his own work as well. Like Hughes, he went beyond mere recollection to touch upon a deeper, undisclosed power underlying the world he described. His account of various skills – his grandfather's turf-cutting, his mother's milk-churning, his father's ploughing – pictured the age-old, closely-knit rural Ireland by which he was formed and continued to be sustained; but he placed the adult practitioners of these skills – of cultivation and of making – within a timeless pattern of struggle with a hallowed, if capricious, land:

> Centuries
> Of fear and homage to the famine god
> Toughen the muscles behind their humbled knees,
> Make a seasonal altar of the sod.

> 'At a Potato Digging'

Even with a reference to 'forty-five' and the great Irish famine, we are here present, as the poet states unequivocally, at a centuries-old ritual, first of gathering and then, as the concluding lines of the poem make clear, of grateful libation as the harvest is safely gathered in. This is the poetry of intimate preposition, for Heaney makes available to the reader both the precise details of the scene and the unconscious and enduring feelings and apprehensions of those who inhabit it. Heaney's perspectives, it is clear, owe more to anthropology rather than to history.

In succeeding volumes, *Door into the Dark* (1969), *Wintering Out* (1972) and *North* (1975), he explored further the ancient forms which animate everyday life. 'So I began to get an idea of bog as the memory of the landscape, or as a landscape that remembered everything that happened in and to it,'[4] he explained. By digging, the poet would uncover the remains laid down in the alluvia of the bog, remains which had been left by the various invasions of Ireland, of which the most important had been that of the English; but even this, it seemed from the stark and unconfortable poetry of *North*, would be assimilated and endlessly resisted within the bottomless bog and by the adherents of its tribal goddess.

> I stand at the edge of centuries
> facing a goddess.

> This centre holds

and spreads,
sump and seedbed,
a bag of waters
and a melting grave.

'Kinship'

The consequence of this was to translate history into saga, event
into endless but meaningful repetition. There is here none of the
modernist anguish voiced by Yeats, laureate (if not the inventor) of
the aristocratic Anglo-Irish tradition, in his most famous poem:
'Things fall apart; the centre cannot hold' ('The Second Coming').

Heaney made clear why this should be the case. The act of digging
uncovered the origins of Ireland, but the movement, as he indicated
in 'Bogland', the first of the Bogland series (published in *Door into
the Dark*), was 'inwards' as well as 'downwards', resolving his own
as well as his nation's quest for identity.[5] By exploring the bog in
North, he revealed the 'word-hoard', the buried treasure of linguistic
and cultural resources, with their different allegiances and entail-
ments, available to him as an Irish poet:

I push back
through dictions,
Elizabethan canopies.
Norman devices,
the erotic mayflowers
of Provence
and the livied latins
of churchmen

to the scop's
twang, the iron
flash of consonants
cleaving the line.

'Bone Dreams'

He could identify at one moment with the victims, at another, with
the victors of Irish history, entering into the lives of all. Nevertheless, his poems, he stated, came up 'like bodies out of the bog of
my own imagination.'[6] While this allowed him to place himself

imaginatively and linguistically outside one particular tribal anonymity, it also pointed to a profound passivity before the most deeply rooted material of the past. Even his account of the etymological diversity of the language echoes he could exploit suggested the stratification of the word-hoard upon one underlying and irreducible structure.

Kearney challenges this dominant reading by turning to the hermeneutic philosophy of Martin Heidegger. Heidegger might at first sight seem an unusual figure to choose for such a revisionary task. Had he not recommended a return to origins occluded in the course of history? Had he not, from his earliest work, traced the anxiety which troubled individuals in the modern world, even if they tried to evade it, to the feeling of *Unheimlichkeit*, of 'not-being-at-home' in this world? *Unheimlichkeit* 'is the basic kind of Being-in-the-world,' he explained in *Being and Time*, 'even though in an everyday way it has been covered up.'[7] Could we not explain the appeal of Heaney (as of Hughes) by pointing to the ways in which they stilled that anxiety through the poetic restoration to us of the feeling of being-at-home? Does their work (like the philosophy of Heidegger himself) not satisfy a powerful and persistent nostalgia (literally 'homesickness') for a primordial home which has for most of us in contemporary society been lost but which is felt to persist on the margins, in rural, pre-industrial worlds?

Heidegger, however, had also made clear from his earliest work that the feeling of 'not-being-at-home' in the world was an unavoidable condition of being-in-the-world, and not the specific consequence of historical conditions. Even if the individual in modern society felt acutely the 'homelessness' which had resulted from the metaphysical choices made at the beginning of the modern era and in the eras which preceded it, there is no suggestion that we can go back to pristine origins. Human beings, as self-conscious individuals existing in time and limited to and by the concepts and the languages they inherited, were fated to the feeling of 'not-being-at-home' in the world. Nevertheless, if we cannot hope for the recovery of an origin (which we are driven to seek because it is absent), we can at least put an end to mere wandering or to our captivation by false concepts of home by reinterpreting the past in the hope of shaping and sustaining an authentic future. For the very experience of 'homelessness' brings a countervailing moral response. 'The call of conscience,' Heidegger also explained in *Being and Time*, 'existentially understood, makes known for the

first time what we have hitherto merely contended: that *Unheimlichkeit* pursues Dasein and is a threat to the lostness in which it has
forgotten itself.'[8]

This is the Heidegger to whom Kearney appeals. He interprets
Heaney's use in *North* of the mythic struggle between Hercules,
'sky born and royal ... his future hung with trophies', and Antaeus,
'the mould-hugger', as an act of creative becoming between pro-
spective and retrospective visions.[9] Hercules, the figure of reason,
provides the 'estranged detachment' by which an address to origins enables the 'liberating advent of homecoming' rather than the
inauthentic satisfactions of 'tribal nostalgia'.[10] No origin is given,
nor is any destination fixed. All those alerted to 'homelessness' are
at the same time motivated by the call of conscience to 'homecoming', to the quest for a less alienated and alienating future.
This may be an endless task, beset by the risk that individuals
may resolve to overcome inauthenticity by turning to what is
'familiar' and 'near-at-hand' – 'pap for the dispossessed' in Heaney's concluding phrase to 'Hercules and Antaeus'.

There follow, of course, a number of important consequences
from viewing Heaney in this way. It allows Kearney to contradict
the view that Heaney is an anti-intellectual, merely intuitive poet. It
allows him to contradict the view that he is (by comparison with
Derek Mahon, John Montague, Michael Longley and Thomas Kin-
sella) technically limited, a writer who avoids the interrogation of
language and its relation to reality which is central to other contemporary Irish poets. 'Far from subscribing to the traditional view
that language is a transparent means of representing some identity
which precedes language – call it *self, nation, home* or whatever –
Heaney's poetry espouses the view that it is language which perpetually constructs and deconstructs our given notions of identity.'[11] But it allows him above all to reverse the concepts of
history and of the poet's relationship to it implied in the dominant
reading. History is not a pattern preordained by prehistorical tribal
myths and the endless legacies of enmity and strife which they
authorise, nor is the poet's consciousness the passive receptacle of
the dreams and symbols associated with these. 'The wet centre',
Heaney reminds us in 'Bogland', 'is bottomless'.

What distinguishes Kearney's essay, however, is the cultural and
political framework within which he places his philosophical reading. For the dominant reading against which he argues is, in the
context of Irish politics and culture, the revivalist one, which he

associates with the 'backward look' of nationalist myths and ideology, a nationalism which has for him been rendered out of date by
the social and economic modernisation of the Irish Republic in the
1970s and 1980s. 'The Irish Republic is becoming, in spite of resistance to constitutional change, a secular state of the European
community.'[12] Ireland is in a state of transition, faced, on the one
hand, by the challenge to its traditions, on the other hand, by the
possibilities of change and pluralistic redefinition brought about by
the rational procedures of modernity. This experience is for Kearney the very condition of postmodernity and he gives to the series
of essays in which his essay on Heaney appears the title *Transitions*.
In such a condition, the postmodernist artist – and he numbers
Heaney among contemporaries in drama (Friel), fiction (Banville)
and film-making (Jordan, Murphy) who are engaged in a common
enterprise – has the particular task of 'rewriting the old as a project
of the new'. Postmodern myth, to be distinguished from the
revivalist apotheosis of myth as 'unitary tradition' and the modernist critique of myth as 'mystifying dogma', construes myth as 'a
two-way traffic between tradition and modernity'.[13] It encourages
us 'to reread tradition, not as a sacred and inviolable scripture, but
as a palimpsest of creative possibilities which can only be rean-
imated and realized in a radically pluralist culture.'[14]

The reasons for rereading Heaney in this way are clear. The poet,
aware of the inevitability of 'homelesseness', not only puts under
question the revivalist myths upon which all nationalist traditions
are based but also makes available from that questioning the possibility of a more authentic, and more plural community:

> Balor will die
> and Byrthnoth and Sitting Bull.

> 'Hercules and Antaeus'

Yet this rereading may entail less of a reversal than Kearney believes, for it shares with the revivalist tradition the same assumption about the poet's function. In each case, the poet puts into
words and thereby gives substance to the idea of a community.
'The word alone gives being to the thing,' Heidegger stated in 'The
Nature of Language',[15] and this notion underlay the answer he
gave to the question: 'What are poets for?' Their function in the
derelict present, he suggested, was to construct through language

no less than 'a house of Being'. The attractiveness of Heidegger's view of the function of the poet lies precisely in the fact that it grants poetry a cultural centrality which, even in contemporary 'high culture', it no longer possesses. By considering Heaney as a figure founding a world, the critic not only obscures the marginal social and cultural conditions within which he produces, but also the marginal social and cultural conditions out of which he writes.

We might think that Heaney's ironic self-representation in 'Singing School, 6, Exposure', 'weighing and weighing' amidst the turmoil of Northern Ireland 'my responsible *tristia*', involves the very acknowledgement of the marginality of the poet. The poet can make nothing happen. He may well complain that the language and the forms in which he writes are not his own, but then the native 'guttural muse' was, he had conceded in 'Traditions' in *Wintering Out*, 'bulled long ago' by the invaders' alliterative tradition. Is he not the poet of the play of their differences, possessing and possessed by both? His technical innovations within the lyric form might be seen as a subtle form of resistance to the English lyric tradition, but they could not undermine its massive authority nor its admirable commitment to the spirit of ambiguity and of necessary delay. Was he not destined, like the manumitted slave he describes in 'Freedman', to a career made up of biting the hand that fed him?

Yet this irony reflects less the ineffectuality of all poets within a particular historical situation than his failure, on account of the immobility engendered by divided affiliations, to give adequate voice to something which remains central to him and to his fellow kin – the spirit of place violated by the invasion of the English and the imposition of their cultural forms:

> Iambic drums
> Of English beat the woods where her poets
> Sink like Onan.

> 'Ocean's Love to Ireland'

His irony is the product of self-enfeeblement, and even though he can seek compensation for this by identifying with the Viking warriors of the North or envisage the overthrow of England's political and cultural forms through an apocalyptic combination of natural and linguistic forces, this last dream, as we can see in

Wintering Out, is significantly set in train by a Wordsworthian encounter not with a Highland lass but with a Gaelic-speaking girl from Derrygarve:

> But now our river tongues must rise
> From licking deep in native haunts
> To flood, with vowelling embrace,
> Demesnes staked out in consonants.

'A New Song'

Heaney's irony appears the Rousseauite-Wordsworthian confession of an artificial man who has lost his naturalness and his natural strength by the very act of writing, by creating images of the self to circulate within urban and urbane society. He is haunted by the loss of his power over that primal song which in turn binds utterance and place, place and the community which inhabits it.

By enclosing his career within one continuous process of perpetual detour, a Heideggerean reading of Heaney not only draws our attention away from such politico-sexual self-figurations but also obscures the degree to which he begins to dismantle them in his recent work. The publication of *Station Island* (1984) marks, I believe, a profound transformation. This judgement might seem too assertive for a volume which Helen Vendler found on its appearance a 'verbally firm and assured but psychologically beset and uncertain mid-life recapitulation'.[16] There is certainly a mid-life recapitulation in the central Dantesque sequence, 'Station Island', from which the volume takes its title. Here the poet-speaker imagines a series of encounters with the dead – with Irish writers, William Carleton and James Joyce, and with friends and relatives, some killed in the sectarian violence in Northern Ireland – during a pilgrimage on Station Island, or St Patrick's Purgatory, a small island in Lough Derg, Co. Donegal, which has been a place of pilgrimage for Irish Catholics since mediaeval times. He had, in his youth, undertaken the pilgrimage three times; now, in imagination and in middle age, he seems, in the phrase of his clerical interlocutor in canto IV, to be there 'taking the last look'.[17]

He is, it is true, saying farewell, but not with the uncertainty Vendler describes. He is saying farewell because, like the disillusioned priest, he is a man who realises that the choice of his vocation was not 'freely chosen but convention'. The poem is

Heaney's belated renunciation: I will not serve. He can no longer function as the kind of poet his background demands, providing what he mocks the priest for providing:

> 'You gave too much relief, you raised a siege
> the world had laid against their kitchen grottoes
> hung with holy pictures and crucifixes.'

'Station Island, IV'

This leave-taking is more, however, than a rejection of old habits on the way to a more fulfilling new life. This would be to concede too much to the spiritual significance of the pilgrimage itself and to the embodiment of the idea of pilgrimage, in different but distinctive forms, in the poetry of the middle way of Yeats, Kavanagh and Eliot, the intertextual ghosts of Heaney's own rite of passage. His leave-taking involves the much more fundamental rejection of the social, cultural and religious conventions by which the poet has been bound because he recognises that they are not freely chosen but the constricting codes and discourses of a social majority. The fact that they have taken their precise form under siege and in response to the oppression of the colonialism of the plantation does not make them any less codes articulated by power. The very feelings of dispossession make the need for their enforcement all the more acute. 'The more capitalism follows its tendency to "de-code" and "de-territorialize",' Felix Guattari usefully reminds us, 'the more it seeks to awaken or re-awaken artificial territorialities and residual encodings, thus moving to counteract its own tendency.'[18]

We might find an explanation for this radical change in the fact that Heaney had been displaced by education, by travel, by the very success of his career as a poet and academic. The journey from being a pupil at Anahorish School to the Boylston Professorship of Rhetoric and Oratory at Harvard is certainly as far and as dislocating as those traversed by other poets of his generation – I think of Tony Harrison and Douglas Dunn – who have reflected upon the ambiguous nature of the opportunities offered to them as working-class children by the Butler Education Act of 1944:

> Everywhere being nowhere,
> who can prove
> one place more than another?

'The Birthplace'

We might find an explanation for this in *Field Work* (1979), in the failure to find an affinity with the newly-acquisitive South in which he had made his home:

> My people think money
> And talk weather. Oil-rigs lull their future
> On single acquisitive stems.

'Triptych, II, Sibyl'

No longer preoccupied with the dispossession of his native realm, he is, like Joseph Brodsky or Czeslaw Milosz, liberated in the space of exile, between worlds, in 'my free state of image and allusion' ('Sandstone Keepsake'). Empowered by the shade of James Joyce, the most exuberant exile of them all, he writes 'for the joy of it' ('Station Island, XII').

Such an explanation, I think, simplifies the nature and the consequences of the transformation described in *Station Island*. The poet who had in his earlier work employed the perspectives of the anthropologist, captivated by the strength of myth and ritual, now writes as a semiologist analysing the hidden means by which and the oppressive ends to which myth and ritual function in the family, in Catholicism, in the educational system, in nationalist culture, and in the larger social system of divisions and hierarchy:

> 'I hate how quick I was to know my place.
> I hate where I was born, hate everything
> That made me biddable and unforthcoming,'

('Station Island, IX')

With such knowledge of their determining effect, he explores the ways in which codes and discourses, including literature itself, operate in order to make the subject biddable and he includes in his interrogation of the social and cultural production of subjectivity both the lyric and the autobiographical poem.

There is, however, no possibility of finding some pure and originary point of consciousness which pre-exists the imposition of such codes and discourses. 'Master, what must I do to be saved?' The rich young man's question to Christ is not only at the heart of the pilgrimage: it is echoed in the last of the 25 lyrics in the first section of the volume and in the last of the 20 Sweeney poems in the third and final section of the volume. For Heaney, the answer lies not in divestment but in dissonance, in juxtaposition, in unsettling codes and discourses by disclosing their artificiality. He cannot reclaim reality: it is always prefigured. He can, however, delight in the variety of modes by which he can recover it, embellishing that reality in the very act of constituting it. In the first poem of the volume, 'The Underground', he recalls a moment on his honeymoon, racing through the underground to arrive on time for a concert at the Albert Hall, but he complicates that moment by redescribing it through the perspectives of a Pan, a Hansel or an Orpheus. Each perspective carries its own enriching implication, but together, they function to unsettle the notion of poetic authority. The poem does not offer us the satisfying shelter of Heidegger's 'house of Being' but it does give us a pleasurable awareness of the artifice of all poetic constructions.

With *Station Island*, Heaney becomes a postmodern poet, not in the sense defined by Heideggerean hermeneutics, but in the sense defined by Roland Barthes in his own postmodernist exercise in autobiography, *Roland Barthes by Roland Barthes*, by means of the concept of 'diffraction':

> This is why, when we speak today of a divided subject, it is never to acknowledge his simple contradictions, his double postulations, etc.; it is a *diffraction* which is intended, a dispersion of energy in which there remains neither a central core nor a structure of meaning: I am not contradictory, I am dispersed.[19]

Within the volume as a whole, we confront a multitude of selves, each one, as we can see from the opening poem, enunciated within specific scenes of language or explicitly defined by the processes of displacement and resistance. In an earlier poem in *Field Work*, 'In Memoriam Francis Ledwidge', on the nationalist poet killed fighting in France in 1917 in the British army, Heaney had found in the circumstances of his death all the strains of Irish culture crisscrossed in 'useless equilibrium'. In this volume, there is no such sense of immobilising contradiction. He places himself beyond the preordination of social, cultural and religious binaries which ensures that each Irish identity is shaped and reduced by a repudiated Other and he finds an appropriate persona in the sceptical and myriad Sweeney.

When we read 'Making Strange' (a poem whose title evokes the Russian formalist Shklovsky's concept of 'defamiliarisation'), we can see that such a practice of the self is strikingly at odds with that of the hermeneutic philosophy of Heidegger.[20] The poet-speaker, revisiting the rural world in which he has grown up, stands between an outsider, 'the one with his travelled intelligence/and tawny containment', and another, a local:

> unshorn and bewildered
> in the tubs of his wellingtons,
> smiling at me for help,
> faced with this stranger I'd brought him.

> 'Making Strange'

The encounter seems to invite an Heideggerean gloss. Should we not sympathise with the silent figure, who is ill at ease with the discourse of the outside world? Is he not right to refuse the idle talk of the rootless modern outsider? 'Ontologically this means that when Dasein maintains itself in idle talk, it is – as Being-in-the-world – cut off from its primary and primordially genuine relationships-of-Being towards the world,' Heidegger had argued in *Being and Time*.[21] The smiling look is at once a sign of disguise and a signal of hidden affiliation with the poet who had made his name by mediating the unworded experience of this fixed and rooted world. By means of a new poetic language, he had made strange the habitual perception of things; and by making familiar things unfamiliar, he had brought the reader closer to a realisation of the authenticity which had been lost, had set the reader in the uncomfortable awareness of 'homelessness' upon the task of 'homecoming'.

Yet this mediation does not take place. As a 'cunning middle voice' suggests, these are two different worlds, both structured by exclusive and limiting sets of codes. There is no sense, as there was in Heaney's earliest poetry, that this rural world was the first world, in some way more real and valuable. Art may well be a way of changing and enlarging perception through making the familiar strange, but it achieved this, as Shklovsky made clear, by drawing our attention to its own specific processes. Heaney extends the implication of this idea to the act of writing itself. For, in using what he recognises to be pre-existing codes, the poet becomes strange to himself, self-estranged and metamorphosed into another identity. These are ' "departures you cannot go back on' ".

Here, the figuring and refiguring of the poetic subject is framed through and by a meditation on academic and philosophic concepts. This does not mean that the poem is, in the pejorative sense, an academic or philosophical poem. The procedure, fully alert to and taking pleasure in the constituting power of discourse, resembles that of Roland Barthes, who wrote of himself that 'he rarely starts from the idea in order to invent an image for it subsequently; he starts from a sensuous object, and then hopes to meet in his work with the possibility of finding an *abstraction* for it, levied on the intellectual culture of the moment.'[22]

After *Station Island*, Heaney's writing occupies a new kind of cultural context and relies upon a new kind of reading. For the poet, analysing and enacting the construction of the subject through various cultural codes, is concerned to establish by this the concept of an infinitely dispersed subject existing in a verbal space in which no one code or discourse is dominant. In his succeeding volume, *The Haw Lantern* (1987), this leads Heaney, with a considerable levy on recent deconstructionist and reader-response theory, to play (perhaps most notably in 'Parable Island' and 'From the Canton of Expectation') not only with language but also with the expectations of the reader.

Yet, as with Barthes, Heaney's aim is to write from the margin in order to share with his readers a more multiple and less constrained subjectivity. He contests the codes which trap him within social, tribal, professional or familial expectations; but, at the same time, he does not envisage a position where these will be abolished. As the shade of James Joyce advises in the final canto of 'Station Island':

> 'You lose more of yourself than you redeem
> doing the decent thing. Keep at a tangent.'

> ('Station Island, XII')

Heaney is, in Barthes' phrase, 'like an *intermittent* outsider' who can 'enter into or emerge from the burdensome sociality, depending on my mood – of insertion or of distance.'[23] He writes not for a community in which he would be subject to Barthes' oppressive 'spirit of likelihood' but for that dispersed audience which shares and understands his own intermittent position.

Notes

I would like to thank Norman Vance for his advice in the preparation of this essay.

1. Richard Kearney, 'Heaney and Homecoming', in *Transitions: Narratives in Modern Irish Culture* (Manchester: Manchester UP, 1988), pp. 101–12. The essay is followed by an appendix: 'Heaney, Heidegger and Freud – The Paradox of the Homely', pp. 113–22.
2. Ibid., p. 106.
3. Seamus Heaney, 'Deep as England', *Hibernia*, 1 December 1972, quoted in Robert Buttel, *Seamus Heaney* (Lewisburg, W. Va.: Bucknell UP, 1975), p. 30.
4. Seamus Heaney, 'Feeling into Words' in *Preoccupations: Selected Prose 1968–1978* (London: Faber, 1980), p. 54.
5. For a discussion of this, see Terence Brown, 'A Northern Voice', in Harold Bloom (ed.), *Seamus Heaney: Modern Critical Views* (New Haven, Conn.: Chelsea, 1986), pp. 25–37. For an analysis of the politics of language in Heaney, see Blake Morrison, *Seamus Heaney* (London: Methuen, 1982). For a more recent interpretation of Heaney and of his relationship to Irish traditions, see Norman Vance, *Irish Literature. A Social History: Tradition, Identity, Difference* (Oxford: Blackwell, 1990), pp 241–60.
6. Quoted by Terence Brown, op. cit., p. 33.
7. Martin Heidegger, *Being and Time*, trans. John Macquarrie and Edward Robinson (Oxford: Blackwell, 1967), p. 322. I have left *Unheimlichkeit* in its original form.
8. Ibid., p. 322.
9. Richard Kearney, op. cit., p. 107.
10. Ibid., p. 108.
11. Ibid., p. 102.
12. Ibid., pp. 9–10.
13. Ibid., p. 278.
14. Ibid., p. 280. For a more detailed exposition of his views on postmodernism, see Richard Kearney, *The Wake of Imagination* (London: Hutchinson, 1987).
15. Martin Heidegger, 'The Nature of Language', in *On the Way to Language*, trans. Peter D. Hertz (New York: Harper & Row, 1971), p. 62.
16. Helen Vendler, ' "Echo Soundings, Searches, Probes" ', in Harold Bloom, op. cit., p. 178. This essay originally appeared in *The New Yorker*, 23 September 1985.
17. See Neil Corcoran, *Seamus Heaney* (London: Faber, 1986), p. 159. This study provides invaluable biographical information on Heaney.

18. Felix Guattari, *Molecular Revolution: Psychiatry and Politics*, trans. Rosemary Sheed (Harmondsworth, Middlesex: Penguin, 1984), p. 36.
19. Roland Barthes, *Roland Barthes by Roland Barthes*, trans. Richard Howard (London: Macmillan, 1977), p. 143.
20. See Gerald L. Bruns, *Modern Poetry and the Idea of Language* (New Haven, Conn.: Yale UP, 1975), pp. 74–7. This study gives an excellent account of the conflict between Orphic (Heideggerean) and Hermetic (Mallarmean) views of poetic language in the High Modernist period.
21. Martin Heidegger, *Being and Time*, op. cit., p. 214.
22. Roland Barthes, op. cit., p. 99.
23. Ibid., p. 131.

8

'Some Sweet Disorder' – the Poetry of Subversion: Paul Muldoon, Tom Paulin and Medbh McGuckian

Elmer Andrews

Making a significant contribution to the 'extension of the imaginative franchise'[1] which Blake Morrison and Andrew Motion have identified as a salient feature of contemporary British poetry are those poets outside the dominant social wisdom – not necessarily in overtly political terms, but in the sense of having at their disposal historical or symbolic resources, allegiances and affiliations denied to those who write straight out of the depthless, dehistoricised English mainstream. This may be a matter of class (Dunn, Harrison) or race (Braithwaite, Markham) or gender (Selima Hill, Carol Rumens, Medbh McGuckian) or region (Muldoon, Paulin). This essay examines three of the younger Ulster poets in whose writing the marginal becomes central, to both memorable and subversive effect. For the work of these poets may be seen to have a countercultural ambition, a transgressive function, in giving voice to what lies outside the law, outside the dominant (social and linguistic) value system. In their different ways, these poets open up, for a brief moment, onto disorder and illegality, tracing the unsaid and the unseen of culture, that which is silent, invisible, made 'absent' because it lies outside the dominant categories. Given the traditional rigidity of the Ulster social formation out of which these poets wrote, and seeing the disastrous consequences of such obduracy, there were perhaps added incentives for an Ulster poet to try and extend the 'imaginative franchise'.

Looking into a fishmonger's window, the speaker in Paul Muldoon's 'Paul Klee: They're Biting' sees a waist-thick conger which seems to mouth the word 'No'.[2] The negative is charged with political meaning in Northern Ireland: 'Ulster Says NO', 'No Surrender', 'Not an Inch'. In '7 Middagh Street' the ghost of Louis MacNeice is 'assailed' with 'a charm of goldfinches', and recognises in 'their "Not an inch"/and their "No", and yet again, "No"' (*MB*, p. 58) the voice of Sir Edward Carson. The last word in the poem (and the book) is with another sternly negative voice, that of a sectarian Belfast shipyard worker: ' "MacNeice? That's a Fenian name"./As if to say, "None of your sort, none of you/will as much as go for a rubber hammer/never mind chalk a rivet, never mind caulk a seam/on the quinquereme of Nineveh"' (*MB*, p. 60). This is the voice of oppressive authority, of exclusion and suppression. Poetry's sumptuous quinquereme has to be protected from the subversive influence of MacNeice's 'sort'.

Early on, Muldoon demonstrates a resistance to narrow categorisation and definition. 'The Mixed Marriage' is a poem which continually shuttles back and forth between dark, primitive instinct, a native *pietas* personified by the speaker's father, and civilised, cosmopolitan value represented by his mother. The poem's hair-balances, its subtle shifts of tone and nuance, dramatise the complexity of the speaker's allegiances. These formal satisfactions, we are to understand, are the product of the speaker's 'in-between' (moral, political, cultural) position. He eludes and overflows any simple categorisation, refuses any particular obsession, remains continually open to alterity.

The 'mixed marriage' theme is extended beyond the merely personal in more recent poems such as 'Chinook' and 'Meeting the British', which tell of the uneasy confluence of different languages and cultures. Meeting the British is a violent affair, the natives receiving six fishhooks and two smallpox-infested blankets. Early poems, however, tend to emphasise the advantages of heterogeneity. In 'Mules', which reiterates the fascination of 'what was neither one thing nor the other', the speaker asks: 'Should they not have the best of both worlds'.[3] 'The Right Arm' is an intriguingly subtle sonnet which asserts the sufficiency of 'wedged' or 'sleeved' – 'in-between' – existence. The octave recalls a time when as a child in the family shop at Eglish, the speaker reached into a sweet-jar for a bit of clove-rock. 'Clove-rock' is ambiguous, suggesting safety and security ('Rock of Ages', 'a cleft in the rock'), but also something that has been split in two. At the time, the speaker was 'three-ish', an 'in-between' age; 'three-ish' rhymes with 'Eglish', which is close to, but not quite, 'English', the place, like the speaker, also 'in-between': 'I would give my right arm to have known then/how Eglish was itself wedged between/*ecclesia* and *eglise'*. Awareness of the 'in-between' state, as that first odd line suggests, is a mark of maturity. The linguistic and cultural problematic that is focused in the name 'Eglish' undermines the simplicity and complacency of the evocation of the childhood world. But the 'in-between' state has its own paradoxical wholeness: the Eglish sky was 'its own stained glass vault'; and the glass sleeving the speaker's arm, though it may be easily shattered, and though it creates a space offering only a very limited room for manoeuvre, nevertheless provides a structure within which specific goals may be attained. This limited, fragile glass space which the poet has found for himself gives transparently onto the wider world and, like the Eglish sky above, has its own beauty and completeness. Imaginative power lies between, rather than in, things.

Muldoon challenges single or unitary ways of seeing, introducing alternatives and confusion. 'Lunch with Pancho Villa' makes explicit the problems of establishing 'reality' and 'meaning'. The speaker foregrounds his own signifying practice, thus betraying his version of the 'real' as a relative one, which can only deform and transform experience. Thus, the 'real' is exposed as a category, as something articulated by and constructed through the poem. The poem conveys Muldoon's scepticism about 'truth', and enacts his retreat from any kind of fixity, including taking up any fixed position on the Troubles in Ireland. Part 1 stages a confrontation between 'I' and 'My celebrated pamphleteer' (*SP*, p. 19) who berates the speaker for his lack of political commitment. Part 2 undoes this staging, denying the solidity of what we have been persuaded to take for real: 'No one's taken in, I'm sure,/By such a mild invention'. But as soon as the poem's self-cancelling movement begins to gather momentum, it, too, is blocked and revised. The 'reality' the speaker had conjured up in Part 1 is perhaps not so 'preposterous' after all. No definitive meaning or vision is allowed, everything remains equivocal. Even the 'I' in the poem is uncertain, and differs in the poem's two parts. In Part 2 the 'I' is 'author' ('All made up as I went along') rather than actor, but the last stanza anticipates a reinsertion of the 'I' into the fiction, when the speaker imagines himself, in a mirror-image of the original encounter described in Part 1, in the role of host wondering how to deal with his visitor, a young poet who will doubtless be rambling on about 'pigs and trees, stars and horses'. The shifting 'I's keep us at a distance. They have as cause and effect an uncertainty of vision, a reluctance or inability to fix things as explicable or known. The poem is constructed on the recognition of emptiness. Its unsettling power comes from the sense we are given of the mixture of too much and of nothing, from the interplay of unreality and the solid, four-square confidence of the octosyllabic ten-line stanza, with its vigorous rhymes and rhythms, and its colloquial familiarity.

In 'The Big House' the interrogation of the real is given a cultural and historical inflection. The poem asserts a secret knowledge that undermines and relativises an official, public sense of reality. This secret knowledge is in the possession of an 'I' (also an 'eye') which is submerged or excluded ('I was only the girl under the stairs', 'I slept at the very top of that rambling house,/A tiny room with only a sky-light window' (SP, p. 22)). Marginalised, confined, in service to a ruling class, the 'I' passively observes, its perspective one that is at a significant angle either above or below the plane of the main action. It is an 'I' which is again uncertain, mixing Irishisms ('haggard') and Americanisms ('He swayed some'), and expressing itself in a discordantly and disconcertingly elliptical, associative, digressive manner. Pronouns are left unidentified; exact knowledge always remains a rumour. Nothing is stable, forms merge together. Rational sequencing is subordinated to verbal and rhetorical play. 'People will always put two and two together', the speaker says, and this is indeed what the reader is left to do. The Muldoon poem, we come to see, characteristically lies inside closed systems, opening spaces where unity had been assumed. Breaking single, reductive 'truths', tracing a space within society's cognitive frame, it proposes latent 'other' meanings or realities behind the known or the possible.

'Cass and Me' (a poem which bears comparison with Heaney's 'Follower') tells of escaping from conventionalised ways of seeing and of the achievement of an alternative (childlike) mode of vision which leads to a renewed appreciation of the strangeness of the ordinary. The poem begins disconcertingly, refusing to yield much sense till 'father' in the third line provides a referent for 'his' in the second. Again, we are immediately drawn into the process of constructing meaning, and alerted to the unreliability of the speaking voice. We are told of an impersonation, a transvestism, a desire to experiment with identity, which is typical of children's play. The poem is, in fact, a celebration of this childlike openness to new experience. When he climbs onto the adult's back, the child is hoisted onto a new plane of perception. His perspective, now interestingly changed, assumes an epic, legendary quality. The adult Cass is touched by the boy's sense of wonder. Escaping from the tyranny of normal perception, man and boy share a momentary expansion of consciousness which Muldoon describes with resonant economy.

The childlike world-view is the subject of 'Duffy's Circus'. To the child, the circus is a place of magical metamorphosis while to the father it is an affront to God and nature. But it is the world 'beyond the corral' (*SP*, p. 33), the world as circus, rich and strange and full of shifting possibilities, which interests Muldoon. His poetry has much in common with Bakhtin's concept of carnival. For Bakhtin, carnival was a temporary condition, a ritualised suspension of everyday law and order. It dissolved differences, allowed for the intermingling of different ranks, broke sexual taboos and merged together 'all the things that were closed off, isolated and separated in carnivalistic contacts and combinations'.[4] Similarily, Muldoon defies reason and inverts the rules, introduces the unexpected, presents the 'abnormal' and hallucinatory, poses a potentially re-volutionary challenge to the dominant way of seeing and ordering. The big difference is that Muldoon's carnival has no communal base.

'Our Lady of Ardboe' describes the people's longing for new vision, for something other than the limited known world: 'Our simple wish for there being more to life' (*SP*, p. 28). But absence, silence, lack, unsatisfied desire are at the semantic centre of the poem. The last two lines shift the focus onto the speaker himself standing in a field waist-deep among purples and golds with one arm as long as the other – suggesting perhaps that out of the riches of the world he inhabits he must provide for himself, at the level of imagination, what he has lost at the level of faith. Retreating from a transcendental role, Muldoon's poetry is an interrogation of limits rather than a search for totality. It continues to articulate desire, but the ends of that desire are unknown. The poetry refuses to be definitive or knowing, it lacks finality, it interrogates authoritative truths and replaces them with something less certain. It aspires to endless carnival, a deconstructive Utopia.

Traditional wisdom is dismantled. In 'Aisling', the inspiring woman of the traditional Irish vision-poem, once she is put under pressure from intimate, personal experience, loses identity. Cathleen ni Houlihan metamorphoses into Aurora, Flora, Artemidora, Venus, eventually becoming Anorexia – a destructive neurosis, and presiding deity of the contemporary hunger-strikers. As the disenchanted central line has it: 'It's all much of a muchness'. There is the same refusal to be bound by traditional *pietas* in 'Armageddon, Armageddon' II, where the speaker identifies with a demystified Ossian. Where 'Cass and Me' revealed the enchantment of the ordinary, 'Armageddon, Armageddon' II works in the opposite way, unmasking the ordinariness of the legendary. Muldoon moves back and forth between these two poles, both movements having this in common that they are a form of 'defamiliarisation' or 'estrangement'.

Similarly, Muldoon plays with and subverts literary tradition to which he is nonetheless indebted. In doing so, he seeks to escape what Harold Bloom calls 'the anxiety of influence', and clear a space for his own imagining. Thus, 'Identities' parodies a Chandleresque narrative of intrigue. The Chandleresque style reappears as the basic idiom of 'Immram', applied to a version of the Old Irish legend *The Voyage of Mailduin*. 'The More a Man Has the More a Man Wants' is based, we are told, on the Trickster cycle of the Winnebago Indians, and reworks a wide range of prior texts, among them Mahon's 'Knut Hamsun in Old Age', Montague's 'A Meeting' and Heaney's 'Broagh'. The poem, a violent, free-wheeling fantasy in which images of the Troubles merge with those of American drug-culture, is organised in the perversely constrained and authoritarian shape of 49 sonnets. Moreover, it represents one of Muldoon's most ambitious experiments in handling unstable, shifting identity. The central character is called Gallogly who is related to a previous Muldoon character called Golightly (the name emphasising the need for movement, but also advising caution) and to Gaelic gallowglass warriors and to the Sioux braves of the Oglala tribe. The title is an assertion of endless desire, a proverbial denial of closure and completion.

For Muldoon, circularity is a dominant structural principle. 'Immram' (literally 'rowing around') is a picaresque, digressive search-poem. The conversational, anecdotal tone is constantly being subverted by changes of mood and tense, and the narrative is fragmented and elliptical. The object of desire remains elusive, and the poem ends where it began. So does '7 Middagh Street', which begins and ends with the 'quinquereme of Nineveh'. The poem comes freighted with a rich variety of idiom, a protean vitality of language, a diffuse cargo of gossip, reminiscence, fantasy and ironic meditation on the relation between art and politics. It comprises seven monologues (the scarcely differentiated voices of a famous group of itinerants and émigrés – Auden, Gypsy Rose Lee, Benjamin Britten, Chester Kallman, Dali, Carson McCullers and MacNeice – all of whom were associated with 7 Middagh Street in New York in the 1940s) and refuses to place authority with any one of them. (The same technique, the same refusal of direct, personal statement, when Muldoon extends it into his editorial and critical writing – in, for example, his Introduction to the Faber anthology of Irish poetry, which consists merely of a juxtaposition of two opposite opinions, one expressed by F.R. Higgins, the other by Louis MacNeice – has not been met with much enthusiasm.) The interplay of points of view prevents us from ever thinking we can easily chart the course of poetry's quinquereme. Where Yeats's central poetic symbol was the rooted tower, Muldoon invokes the circumnavigating quinquereme, and specialises in a poetry which is a free-wheeling exposition of cross-cultural freedom.

The Muldoon persona and poem are both characteristically in transit. In the early 'The Mixed Marriage' he speaks of himself 'flitting' between a hole in the hedge and a room in the Latin Quarter. 'The Soap-Pig', a very fine elegy to a respected friend and colleague, Michael Heffernan, refers to many different kinds of departure: the speaker's own 'successive flits' (*MB*, p. 27), the time 'Mary was leaving', Heffernan's arrival and subsequent 'escape' from Belfast to London. The soap-pig, a gift from the dead friend, gradually melts from 'pig-shaped bar' to 'soap-sliver' to 'lather'. The speaker remembers his friend deliberating

> on whether two six-foot boards
> sealed with ship's
> varnish and two tea-chests
> (another move) on which all this rests
>
> is a table; or this merely a token
> of some ur-chair,
> or – being broken –
> a chair at all . . .

Identity, meaning, is no more stable than one's corporeal existence. Words flow in on other words close to them ('or' – 'ur' – 'chair');

idiomatic syntax runs on across the line endings; the literal slides into the metaphorical and the symbolical ('(another move) on which all this rests'; 'a table; or...merely a token'), the 'real' into the ideal; different orders of being finally collapse toward nothingness ('or – being broken – /a chair at all...'): in all sorts of subtle ways the poem memorably dramatises the process of our own dissolution.

Muldoon's 'reality' does not have the stability of the early Heaney's densely textured, minutely detailed sensuous world. Where Heaney's images of a rural childhood confirmed and celebrated a sense of roots, Muldoon's filial piety has never been so convincing. His 'stars and horses, pigs and trees' have never, like Heaney's, been simply naturalistic: they dissolve in fantasy ('The Coney') or convert to myth ('Dancers at the Moy'). The sonnet 'Quoof' tells of how the 'family word' (*SP*, p. 77) for a hot-water bottle is 'carried' into 'strange' bedrooms. The octave emphasises roots and continuity, and suggests the way language 'naturalises' what is 'strange'. The sestet, however, discovers the point where language is no longer able to define or domesticate the Unknown. All that lies beyond the reach of the available language is conceptualised only in negative terms, as alien, irrational, monstrous, unnameable –

> the smouldering one-off spoor of the yeti
> or some other shy beast
> that has yet to enter the language.

(*SP*, p. 77)

In contrast to Heaney's memorialising tendencies, Muldoon pushes toward confrontation with the 'other'.

In 'Gathering Mushrooms' the speaker confronts the native and modern polarities of his experience. On one hand, there is the father's mushroom farm; on the other, hallucinogenic experience. Under the influence of the mushrooms the rural scene is psychedelically deranged, but the poem ends, rather uncharacteristically, by affirming *pietas*: the speaker recalls us to harsh reality and the need 'to negotiate with bare cement' (*SP*, p. 73). The fantastic element is even more pronounced in the most recent volume. 'The Coney' is another poem about the speaker's father. Halfway through there is an abrupt swerving of tone and direction which

introduces into the speaker's reminiscence of his father's skill as a
mower the broad, comic fantasy of Bugs Bunny. The talking coney
calls to 'Paddy Muldoon' (the name of the poet's father) to join him
in the swimming-pool. The coney, it would seem, has confused the
speaker with his dying father. The whole poem represents a radically playful refusal of the structures and 'syntax' of rational order,
including even the notion of fixed, single identity.

'Something Else' (the title indicating the perennial object of Muldoon's poetic enterprise) is a defiant statement of the primacy of
the free, wayward, self-delighting imagination untrammelled by
rational consideration, moral obligation or preconceived purpose
of any kind. A lobster being lifted out of a tank makes the speaker
think 'of woad,/of madders, of fugitive indigo inks', then of Nerval
promenading with a lobster 'on a gossamer thread', then of Nerval
hanging himself, 'which made me think/of something else, then
something else again' (*MB*, p. 33). Coherent narrative is replaced by
an endless, opportunistic carnival of free association. The same
bold refusal to be bound by rational considerations is found in
'Sushi'. An apprentice who has scrimshandered a rose's exquisite
petals from the tail-end of a carrot, offers his 'work of art' to the
Master Chef for his inspection:

> Is it not the height of arrogance
> to propose that God's no more arcane
> than the smack of oregano,
> orgone,
> the inner organs
> of beasts and fowls, the mines of Arigna? –
> the poems of Louis Aragon? –

> (*MB*, p. 34)

This is poetry without an object, demonstrating the potential of
language to generate meanings out of itself. The signifier is not
secured by the weight of the signified, but floats free. The relation
of sign to meaning is hollowed out and free rein is given to
semiotic play. As these lines show, meaning can often be the
product of chance linkages that are made on the basis of sound
rather than sense. But the 'work of art' does not escape critical
analysis. It is 'gravely weighed' by the Master, who has 'the look
of a man unlikely to confound/Duns Scotus, say, with Scotus

Eriugena'. Indeed, Muldoon's best work maintains a severe tension between free imagination and reason, order and disorder, mystery and craft.

The fear that life is frozen into unalterable inertness is the entropic nightmare at the heart of Tom Paulin's poetry: the possibility of escaping from the malign, destructive, external forces is what the poetry explores. For one of Paulin's central assumptions is that we live in a historical period which has so total a control of our discourses that it all but precludes any account of change. Literature, he believes, is a kind of free space in which actuality need not be so terribly insisted upon as it usually is in the historical world: it allows for the exploration of other possibilities. He praises Muldoon for positing a Northern vision 'which lies beyond a self-regarding, emotional Irish nationalism and an equally self-regarding British complacency'. Clearly, the kind of poetry Paulin admires is that which flees the high ground of orthodoxy, which acts as a revelation of potential that is denied or constantly threatened by circumstances, a poetry which occupies the interstices of the prevailing codes and discourses, and gives voice to suppressed or marginalised life. The centre is denied its monopoly on 'truth': 'Only nationalists, whether British or Irish, claim monopoly on "truth".'[5]

In 'The Other Voice' he writes of 'the fear of necessity/In an absolute narrative'.[6] Making history into freedom, and not bondage, is an imaginative as well as a political project. 'What is Fixed to Happen' is a poem written against fixity, determinism and passive acquiescence in familiar assumptions and values. What is obvious, clear and familiar need not necessarily be true, for ideology is inscribed in the way we see, talk, write and think: 'The eye is such a cunning despot/We believe its wordless travelogues/And call them *History* or *Let it Happen*' (*SM*, p. 34). Raising the question of whether history is fact or fiction in 'Martello' (in *The Liberty Tree*), he prefers to deal in concrete experience:

> And the answer that snaps back at me
> is a winter's afternoon in Dungannon...[7]

One notices in this poem how easily the Calvinist sense of sin and damnation slips into a secular mode. Fear, guilt, the atmosphere of menace, a latent violence: these – the feelings of that winter afternoon in the Dungannon police barracks where the speaker has come to report an accident – are the unmistakable conditions of Paulin's poetry.

'A Just State', from his first volume *A State of Justice*, is an early example of his tough, caustic manner:

> Its justice is bare wood and limewashed bricks,
> Institutional fixtures, uniforms,
> The shadows of watchtowers on public squares...[8]

This poem establishes the typical imagery, mood and tone of Paulin's early poetry. In *The Strange Museum*, his second collection, a poem entitled 'Surveillances' focuses on the 'blank watchtowers' (*SM*, p. 6) of a prison camp and a circling helicopter probing streets and waste ground with its long beam of light. 'Purity' (in *The Strange Museum*) ends with the troopship's sinister encroachment upon pastoral myth. 'A Partial State' describes the uneasy 'stillness' of a regime which refuses to recognise and accommodate the 'Other', and relies on violent repression to maintain itself in defiance of the will of nature, man and 'the gods' (*SM*, p. 19). Underneath the pretence of order is a frightening, irrepressible energy which breaks through the tight constraints, and which the authorities are ludicrously unable to deal with. Despite all the machinations of 'the chosen', they cannot obliterate the spirit of revolt. 'The chosen' whom Paulin denounces are most obviously Ulster's 'loyalists', but there is no difficulty granting the poem a wider application. Paulin's wastelands are sometimes explicitly Ulster, sometimes anywhere in the world. Belfast is 'a northern capital', 'the guarded capital'; Ulster is the gruesomely ironic 'just state', 'the lost province' and 'a partial state'. Other poems speak of 'a violent district' and even 'the town of Z—'.

Wherever they may be, it is in the eerie stillness of stiff, parched landscapes or cold, wet streets, in the shadow of the watchtowers and in the glare of the searchlights, under the gaze of the uniformed and helmeted enforcers, that the poet must go about his business. The chaos which erupts in scenes of sexual madness and violence conveys Paulin's sense of the outcome to which all suppression is finally leading. 'Under the Eyes' (in *A State of Justice*) describes a highly mechanistic ('clockwork') concept of human relations. Everything is measured, known. Inevitably, however, suppressed energy breaks free of constraint in horrific outbursts of violence. The church is part of the machinery of oppression. 'Inishkeel Parish Church' enacts the sense of release and dilation on moving from the 'packed church' (*SJ*, p. 15) out into the bracing natural world.

The greatest fear of all is that we have lost the capacity for fresh idiom, that heroic potential has passed from us forever. 'Gael and Protestant' (in *A State of Justice*) ends with a cry for rebirth, for some new initiative to redeem the wasteland. And 'Atlantic Changelings' concludes on a similar note: 'I cry out/For a great change in nature' (*SM*, p. 28). If we are to transform our situation we must first reinscribe ourselves in history. The refusal of history is presented in terms of a passionless sexuality, as in 'Civil Lovers' (in *The Strange Museum*), which describes a retreat from passion and a return to dull politeness and the wish to sleep. The 'stillness, without history' of which Paulin speaks in 'A Partial State' is also the subject of 'Before History' (both in *The Strange Museum*). The protracted, insistent rhythms of that poem's last stanza carry us to the very brink of cataclysm, when history can no longer be ignored.

One of Paulin's most accomplished poems in *The Strange Museum* is 'The Harbour in the Evening', which is an elegiac evocation of an old woman's lost past. History, like personal memory, has buried energies which Paulin wants to summon and release into the present. In particular, he wants to revive the suppressed revolutionary potential of eighteenth-century Protestantism. Conscious of the anguished vacuum at the heart of Protestant identity – 'There is so little history/we must remember who we are' ('After the Summit', *LT*, p. 29) – he follows Yeats in creating his own pantheon of dead heroes. Paulin's heroes are the Presbyterian freethinkers who embody the rebellious republican spirit of the 1790s. 'Presbyterian Study' (in *The Liberty Tree*) celebrates a forgotten breed of Presbyterian radicals. In 'Desertmartin', modern-day 'loyalist' Protestantism represents a debasement of an original energy:

> I see a plain
> Presbyterian grace sour, then harden...
> A harsh, ignoble ethic has left its mark on the landscape:
> Here the Word has withered to a few
> Parched certainties...
> These are the places where the spirit dies.
>
> ('Desertmartin', *LT*, p. 16)

The enemy is not hard to identify: 'Paisley's plain tongue, his cult/ of Bunyan and blood/in blind dumps like Doagh and Boardmills –/that's the enemy' ('And Where Do You Stand on the National Question?', *LT*, p. 67).

'Dead', 'bitter', 'baked', 'withered', 'parched', 'charred', 'tightens', 'black', 'blind' this is the vocabulary of 'Desertmartin': a contrasting imagery of fragrance and sweetness – 'cinnamon things' and 'sweet yams' ('Father of History', *LT*, p. 32) – emphasises the exoticism of radical Presbyterianism in a contemporary context. In 'The Book of Juniper', Paulin's ideal, taking the form of a Jacobin Tree of Liberty, is imaged by a fragrant 'Phoenician juniper' (*LT*, p. 25). In this poem Paulin passes from critique to celebration, thereby demonstrating that a radical poetry need not be limited to counter-discursive guer-rilla manoeuvres of a subversive nature, but can accommodate (however warily) the 'singing line':

> now dream
> of that sweet
> equal republic...

One might well ask how the exorbitance of this vision can be reconciled with Paulin's careful emphasis elsewhere on concrete experience as the proper ground of poetry. He is so absorbed in a Utopian model of redeemed Presbyterianism that he blinds himself to complication. His myth of the United Irishmen has little in common with orthodox Republican politics, and his attempt to associate Republican Socialism with Protestantism has no relation whatever to contemporary reality. Might not the submerged (Pro-testant) life be more realistically conceived? Is Paulin not prevented from unearthing this real secret life because his anger and indig-nation do not let him get close enough to what he seems simply to revile? How far is he trying to change a debased Protestant culture, and how far is he simply holding it up to ridicule?

In 'Under Creon' the speaker identifies with those who took the Jacobin oath on the black mountain. Making his way to the secret rendezvous, he 'searched out gaps/in that imperial shrub' (*LT*, p. 13). Here, the searcher/poet is looking at history/language from the outside, from the point of view of a potentially different his-tory/language. He operates in the danger zones of margins and boundaries, at the intersection of different codes, where it may be he can release new energies from the dead hand of history and state power (one of his poems is called 'Cadaver Politic'). Traditionally, the English poet experiences himself in his own language in an utterly different way from the Irish poet. The Irish poet fights for the renovation of submerged elements that have remained outside the centralising and unifying influence of the artistic and ideological norm established by the dominant literary language. Paulin emphasises that these processes of linguistic shift are inseparable from social and political struggle.

Dialect poetry centres the peripheral. Paulin's use of words like 'keeks', 'boul', 'sheugh', 'glooby', 'choggy', 'scroggy', 'clabbery', 'jeuked', 'slegging', 'jap', 'dwam' might be expected to assure us of roots and traditional value. But as Paulin uses these terms they acquire a literary and self-conscious quality. His version of Ulster dialect is combined with an abstract and theoretical language of 'the subterfugue text', 'the chthon-chthon that spells must', 'that spiky *différance'*. He is inside and outside his subject at the same time, able to celebrate local character in all its rugged vitality and still distance himself from orthodoxy. What we have is an insolent, logophiliac, extremely nervous poetry that is very aware of itself, a transitional poetry, war poetry, shock poetry, its violence and disjointedness enacting the confusions of a mutilated province.

Paulin's next collection, *Fivemiletown*, bolder and brasher, more risk-taking than ever, marks a considerable development in his exploration of the potential of poetic language to revolutionise our ways of seeing the world. Using a great variety of first-person personae, he switches roles, histories, idioms with bewildering speed. Versions of Tsvetayeva, Goethe, Sophocles, Mayakovsky, Strindberg and Heine are pressed into the service of his central themes. 'Voronezh', a version of a poem by Anna Akhmatova, dramatises a condition of 'permafrost' where growth and movement have been arrested. Paulin's vernacular is calculated to relocate Russian conditions in a more immediate context: 'this scroggy town/where every line has three stresses/and only the one word, *dark'.*[9] In an environment where the possibilities of expression have been so drastically curtailed, the need is for a new language which will allow for greater variety, for change, for the emergence of new meaning.

In order to resist the determinism of 'an absolute narrative', Paulin seeks to evolve a poetic style which destabilises meaning and single identity, and disrupts the normal connections between poetry, history, community and self. We are constantly being thrown off balance. The metaphor is wholly relevant for, as Paulin says in 'The Defenestration of Hillsborough', written in the wake of the signing of the Anglo-Irish Agreement, there is a choice:' Either to jump or get pushed' (*F*, p. 54). To jump is to liberate the self from the rigid structures by which consciousness is determined, to escape from a constricting environment. Paulin enacts this 'jump' in the structures of his poetry by disrupting the usual ways of constructing meaning. The many shifts, breaks, jumps to different places, people and times, the verbal playfulness, promote a poetry of subversive anti-rationalism and relentless complication. Meanings, life itself, like the Metro rails in '11/11/84', 'Zip away/into a black hole' (*F*, pp. 35–6). Following this poem's roller-coaster progress, we are struck by the vividness of its flashing, epiphanic images as we are carried in a sweep to the end. When we get there we realise there has been no climax, that there is no conclusion. We search desperately for the link between the poem and its cryptic epigraph: 'The public knows very well the distinction between wrestling and boxing; it knows that boxing is a Jansenist sport based on a demonstration of excellence'. The poem is a highly complex tissue of different idioms. It is as though Paulin has constantly to destroy the prevailing languages, and as constantly to reconstitute the fragments in the process of making his poem. His indeterminate structures allow new connections and therefore an enlargement of imaginative vision. We are invited to enjoy the spontaneity and independence of constructing our own system. Paulin exploits the improper, and in this impropriety poetry becomes less a call to action than a meditation on complexity itself.

'Sure I'm a Cheat Aren't We All?' mocks the possibility of enlightenment and order. Neither 'England' nor the 'Church' (*F*, p. 40) nor the scholar's efforts to systematise our knowledge can keep chaos at bay. There is an unruly, sexual energy, a deadly libidinal compound of jealousy and pretence, which undermines any stable meaning. The speaker spends a morning filing titles in the Bodleian, but the forces of disorder soon reassert themselves. Conventional speech is in a bad way in this poem. Distinctions of time and of place are collapsed. As the opportunities for 'speech' are 'suspended prorogued done away with', grammatical structures crumble under the increasing pressure, punctuation disappears, and memories and thoughts tumble in on one another in wild profusion. Paulin is trying to give us a world beneath or beyond syntax and all that that implies. The whole poem's elaborate word-play proclaims the radical potential of words dissolving and forming new, unexpected combinations.

Much of Paulin's poetry embodies his dissenter's ambivalent attitude to form. One part of him longs for form: he wants to 'refine/Whatever gabbles without discipline' ('A Nation, Yet Again', *LT*, p. 45). As he says in 'And Where Do You Stand on the National Question?', 'I want a form that's classic and secular/the risen *République*/a new song for a new constitution' (*LT*, p. 58). 'To the Linen Hall' celebrates 'a style and discipline' (*LT*, p. 77) which he longs to recover, but which have long since disappeared from everyday life. The dream of grace and reason having degenerated beyond recognition the classical procedures which would re-enact it are inappropriate now. A new form is called for: 'We live in a time when the spirit/hungers for form' ('Before History', *SM*, p. 1). What Paulin fears is being trapped in particular forms. Forms, he insists, must constantly be renewed if we are to avoid 'the sense of being lost/In a soured countryside that clings/To idols someone else imagined' ('Going in the Rain', *SM*, p. 22). His images of parched landscapes or permafrost emphasise this fear of arrest and congealment, of becoming fixed in the given patterns of response. His compulsive deployment of different styles calls into question the value of any one style – indeed of style itself. It is perhaps indicative of a suspicious unwillingness to get too involved in any particular idiom or version of reality. Apparently at home in many styles, he seems to trust none.

Throughout his poetry we come across details of linear arrangements, geometrical shapes and designs, references to compasses, rules, theorems, grids and matrices. It is one of the most enduring of all human dreams to feel that we live amid geometry. Geometry testifies to our capacity to overcome and order shapeless space. But in Paulin's calculus, there are dangers here too. 'Yes, the Maternity Unit' presents an image of man-made order imposed upon the natural world: 'A geometry of poplars sifts in the wind,/their tight theorem almost surprised/as it fences ten flat playing-fields' (*LT*, p. 36). The trees lift their heads into a transcendent realm of 'plumed stillness' beyond geometry, but in the 'secular republic of observations' they are assimilated to a quite different reality of civil and military imperatives: the thin trunks become corporation railings or a sentry's fixed bayonet. The sound of a boy's stick trilled along the railings is a burst of machine-gun fire, the release of pent-up feelings by one 'Bored by enclosures'. Once again, violence is activated

by sheer desperation to break into new freedoms. The poem becomes a cry for help, a call for a new aesthetic.

Paulin's poems are heavily populated by designers, builders and
organisation men. The mason is a recurrent figure, making his first
appearance in 'Monumental Mason', a poem that is reminiscent of
Wallace Stevens's 'Like Decorations in a Nigger Cemetery'. The
mason is a decorator, a figure of the artist who, against the pressure
of reality, affords a glimpse of 'tenderness/on bald stone, some
dead letters' (*SJ*, p. 46). As the pun suggests, there is no radiant
faith in art's transforming power here. The artist's communications
are partial at best, and continually subject to the greater power of
reality: while the mason works, the sound of the undertaker making a coffin can be heard from next door. Paulin doesn't allow us to
forget that under the mason's decorative gilt there is the cold truth
of the void.

In *Fivemiletown*, the mason reappears in 'Symbolum', and in
'Now for the Orange Card': 'a mason/wanting to express *freedom*'
(*F*, p. 10). The mason merges with the freemason, whose secret
organisation has been a conspicuous failure as any kind of genuinely subversive force in society. Hence, the Jacobin ideal outlined
in the poem's first three lines remains unfulfilled. The second
section of the poem considers the sad possibility that no 'underground' activity may be able to affect the daylight world – not even
the efforts of the illustrious Achilles who chose glory, was fated to
die young and is now on 'his night journey' to the Underworld.

Paulin aims to free imagination from traditional forms and constraints – almost but not quite into meaninglessness. Poetry is a
subversive act, a defiance of a linguistic and literary order designed
for the ideological suppression of potentially rebellious impulses. It
is a paradigmatic gesture of spontaneity in an increasingly manipulated world. The poet is an underground resistance fighter (underground movements, secret societies, secret signs, coded messages –
these recur throughout Paulin's work) in a bleak, cold country
occupied by foreign powers. As such, he has sabotaged many of
the main lines of communication which the occupying armies
would otherwise use. But he has not blown up all the lines of
communication. He avoids the even greater terror of total formlessness. There is enough coherence left for us to experience the
poems as communication, and enough linguistic sport for Paulin to
demonstrate his own freedom from control. Championing a mor-
ality of flexibility, the creative faculty itself, he uses his poetry to

inculcate something between the rigidity of dogma and the fluidity of endless, indifferent play.

All three of the poets considered here have been met with a good deal of wariness and suspicion, but it is Medbh McGuckian's work which has proved to be the most controversial. To Patrick Williams, the poetry is 'risible', 'inane'; he believes 'these fey, twee, drifting diaphanous pages convey far more of the author's apparently terminal egoism than anything else.'[10] He further refers to 'the counterfeit authority and wry knowingness of her images', the 'large claim implicit in the tone', 'the vast amorphous implications and sheer pretentiousness'. Comparing her work to Paulin's, Williams concludes: 'Paulin writes with energy and intelligence and an actual thought-process is discernible in his work. McGuckian's concoctions of endless poeticisms are non-visionary, and the funny, sealed little worlds where harmless cranks parley with themselves in gobbledegook won't impinge on the real world of loot and dragons.' Catherine Byron, on the other hand, asks us to take our time and refuse to despair at difficulty so that we can reorient our sensibilities to respond to McGuckian as an exponent of 'the woman's sentence': 'There is no-one else writing poetry quite like McGuckian's in Britain or Ireland. Trust her. Be patient.'[11]

Formal constraint is an opportunity for Muldoon's playful ironies; Paulin is prepared to push syntax to its limits, to the point of rupture, his desire for 'something else' tending towards annihilating conventional poetic structures. The countercultural implications of these disruptions are far-reaching, for they represent a dislocation of culture's signifying practices, the very means whereby it establishes meaning. By contrast, McGuckian is an ostensibly much more conservative writer, quieter, less brash, respectful of syntactic structures. But what we find in her poetry is that the logicality signalled by the apparently strict syntactic patterning is essentially gestural or parodic, undermined by the illogicality of the content. The conventional structures of reason are made to hold what they are not normally required to hold, and the resulting pull between logic and illogicality gives the poetry its peculiar tension.

One of her poems is called 'The Princess of Parallelograms'. Two things immediately strike us about the title – its invocation of geometrical shape and ordering, and the surreal incompatibility

of its two terms. It does, however, set up a (ambiguous) relation
between 'princess', with its feminine and fairy-tale connotations,
and notions of mathematical order in 'parallelograms':

> Light circled each side of the river,
> Like mouths into which grapes were pressed:
> A necklace sensationally broken
> I associate with her nearness,
> Who, denied her own dreams
> So she could enter
> The stainless dreams of others,
> Was chiefly charmed by those
> Of her metaphysical child.
> More than him she feared
> To sleep in a motionless bed,
> So she measured down beside me
> Like a boatswain.[12]

Having read the poem, we are also struck by the lack of organic
relationship between title and poem, though 'circles', 'side' and
'measured' provide some marginal relation with 'parallelogram'.
The poem, consisting of two carefully constructed sentences, is
framed by two similes and gestures towards a logic of cause-and-
effect in the two 'so's. Neither of the similes, however, helps us to
visualise the original proposition any more clearly. 'Like', in fact, is
a parodic logical counter, acting subversively to diffuse and confuse our thinking instead of helping to stabilise and clarify it. The
poem remains resistant to visual interpretation. Indeed, one of the
central features of McGuckian's poetry is its refusal of empirical
reality. As soon as a concrete reference is established it is quickly
undermined by incongruity and illogicality. 'I associate' in the
poem's fourth line alerts us to a major compositional principle,
but the association that is made defies interpretation because the
story (made all the more urgent by 'sensational') which lies behind
the broken necklace is withheld. Pronoun identities are likewise left
vague. And who is 'her metaphysical child'? The male symbolic
order represented in the poem by the 'parallelograms'? Is the poem
suggesting that the greatest of all dreams (the word occurs twice in
the poem) is the dream of order? What we can say with more
confidence is that this is a poetry which resists any complacent
reliance on the available order or methods of ordering, while refus-

ing to give up on them entirely. It is this instability in the poetry
which gives it its vertiginous, dream-like quality, and which constitutes the (female) threat it poses to the dominant (male) social
and symbolic order.

The poetry offers an account, and many succinct and startling
images, of its own idiosyncratic methods. The female speaker in
'Vanessa's Bower' is Swift's Vanessa, who lays claim to a stringent
independence from (Swift's) patriarchal authority: 'Don't put me
into your pocket: I am not/A willow in your folly-studded garden/
Which you hope will weep the right way' (*VR*, p. 10). 'Star' expresses a similar need to preserve an independent mind: 'I make a
show of going out/Under my own manless law, to save me/Going
over to your camp' (*VR*, p. 45). 'This oblique trance is my natural/
Way of speaking' (*VR*, p. 29) the speaker in 'Prie-Dieu' declares,
while in 'Sabbath Park' the poet outlines both a geometry and an
architecture for her work: 'I put faith/In a less official entrance, the
accidental/Oblongs of the windows that I find/Have neither catch
nor pulley' (*VR*, p. 54). McGuckian aspires to the kind of poetry she
describes in 'On Ballycastle Beach': 'As meaningless and full of
meaning/As the homeless flow of life/From room to homesick
room'[13] – lines which illustrate two key elements of the McGuckian
aesthetic: its emphasis on fluidity, and its basis in the woman's
world of houses and rooms which, nevertheless, contain the whole
world – planets, histories, ghosts of the dead: 'The room is a kind
of travel also' ('Apple Flesh', *OBB*, p. 13). 'The Dream-Language of
Fergus' also provides an image of the 'dream-language' of
McGuckian, a language flowing within the main current but offering a resistance to it – with exciting results: 'So Latin sleeps, they
say, in Russian speech,/So one river inserted into another/Be-
comes a leaping, glistening, splashed/And scattered alphabet/Jut-
ting out from the voice' (*OBB*, p. 57). She sees her poetry as
an irruption of the inadmissible within the changeless everyday
flow:

> Your lips were always a single line of time
> Flowing through a single place – day after day,
> Like kisses bestowed on both cheeks, they
> Fastened the years together, when I would like
> To have prised them, ever so gently apart.

('Something like the Wind', *VR*, p. 53)

Undoing those unifying structures and significations upon which (male) social order depends, McGuckian's poetry gives voice to what has been suppressed, and thus functions to subvert cultural stability. In 'Venus and the Rain' the speaker, arguing for her own personal, idiosyncratic vision, refers to her 'gibbous' voice 'retelling the story/Of its own provocative fractures' (*VR*, p. 31). Coming across the word 'gibbous', the reader may think of 'gibberish', or a gibbet and the idea of hanging or execution; or perhaps the word will suggest a wildly-leaping gibbon. Actually the word 'gibbous' means 'unequally convex on two sides, as the moon between half and full', the word thus relating to a characteristic assymetry in McGuckian's poetic, perhaps even hinting at one of her favourite tropes – pregnancy as a metaphor for creative fecundity. This equation of art and motherhood informs one of her best poems, 'Next Day Hill'. Here, the speaker, whose 'poems thicken in the desk' like a foetus, longs 'to get back/To the proper size':

> I wanted so much
> To get down again to a place full of old
> Summers, Mexican hats, soft fruitwood
> Furniture, and less moon, the porch-light
> And the leaves catching one another's glance,
> Firm clouds not pulled out of shape by wind.[14]

'The Sitting' declares an aesthetic. The painter's model, her half-sister, questions the principles of representation assumed by the painter. The 'half-sister' (*VR*, p. 15) resists the fixed, the posed. This resistance is brought to a climax in the strenuous rhythms of the last few lines which recapitulate and adroitly rework earlier images:

> She calls it
> Wishfulness, the failure of the tampering rain
> To go right into the mountain, she prefers
> My sea-studies, and will not sit for me
> Again, something half-opened, rarer
> Than railroads, a soiled red-letter day.

Succeeding poems often derive from this refusal of fixity. The best, however, maintain a severe tension between freedom and fixity. McGuckian dismantles and recombines the real, but she does not escape it. The most successful poems exist as a spectral presence, suspended between the real and the unreal. One is reminded of Coleridge's remarks on the dissolving activity of 'Fancy', its re-creating of the real: 'Fancy has no other counters to play with but fixities and definites... It is a mode of memory emancipated from the order of time and place, blended with and modified by that empirical phenomenon of the will, which we express by the word *choice*.'[15]

It is important to see that McGuckian's feminine mode is a process *within* the (male) symbolic order, each questioning the limits of the other. The poetry, that is, refuses to stereotype relations and, instead, keeps fluid the oppositions between male and female, logic and emotion, constraint and freedom, waking and dream. 'The Hollywood Bed', a marriage poem, and one of the best poems in the first collection *The Flower Master*, opens with a characteristic progression toward dream:

> We narrow into the house, the room, the bed,
> Where sleep begins its shunting. You adopt
> Your mask, your intellectual cradling of the head,
> Neat as notepaper in your creaseless
> Envelope of clothes, while I lie crosswise,
> Imperial as a favoured only child,
> Calmed by sagas of how we lay like spoons
> In a drawer, till you blew open
> My tightened bud, my fully-buttoned housecoat,
> Like some Columbus mastering
> The saw-toothed waves, the rows of letter 'm's'

> (*FM*, p. 17)

The 'narrowing' doesn't lead to a complete mergence of identities. The speaker develops a contrast, hinging on 'while' in line 5: there is a male order which privileges intellect, self-possession and control – 'while I lie crosswise'. She is the personification of natural process which refuses to be bound by (male) constraint; he is the epitome of masculine will and 'mastery', which extends even to the realm of symbolisation. But if we look again at those lines we see that the female 'cradling' is used to describe the male posture, while the female is described in emphatically male terms as 'imperial'. The female, we further note, is 'calmed by sagas' (such as might feature Columbus?), sagas being a distinctly 'male' literature. However, 'calmed' links the speaker with the traditional female symbol of the sea, which Columbus may 'master' but never 'calm'. The second stanza, beginning with the pivotal 'Now', revises the earlier version of maleness. The male, who has now slipped the conscious controls and habitual forms, is 'skewed' (as the female was earlier) by 'your piquancy of dreams', but still capable of imposing an 'outline' that the female would gratefully accept.

It is in a spirit of affection and witty amusement that the speaker gives voice to her uniquely personal apprehension of sexual relations. This takes the form of a complex web of ironies and interfusions that depends on a language of great subtlety and flexibility. The poetry evinces a defiant fluidity, a lack of discretion. The very fine 'Harem Trousers' makes explicit the poet's desire to eliminate the 'I' altogether, to escape from a rational, unified self in order to become ex-centric, heterogeneous, capable of spreading into every contradiction and (im)possibility. The poem testifies to a desire to undo the linguistic order which creates and constitutes a whole self, a total body, an identity, a desire to reverse or rupture the process of ego formation, and to attempt to re-enter what Lacan calls the 'imaginary' phase, before differentiation: 'Asleep on the coast I dream of the city./A poem dreams of being written/Without the pronoun "I"' (*OBB*, p. 43). What follows is an interplay of forces – inner and outer, dream and reality, self and other, male and female – with no secure concrete referent. Submerged psychic dream-forces find objective embodiment in nominally exterior things like the 'river' (which picks up the geographical theme introduced by the opposition between 'coast' and 'city' in the first line) and 'staircase'. To some extent, these are metaphorical projections, but McGuckian's metaphors do not behave expectedly. 'The river bends lovingly/Towards this one, or that one, or a third', its movement a soft, easy meandering, without specific destination, the repeated 'or' signalling openness and flexibility. With the 'staircase', not even a tenuous connection with empirical reality is maintained: 'It straightens, stands, it walks/Timid and incongruous/Through roadblocks and breadlines'. Sound and rhythm, the succession of compound or near compound words ('staircase', 'nevermentioned', 'ladder shape', 'anything', 'overflows', 'roadblocks', 'breadlines') dramatise a surreal will to power. The penultimate stanza presents the speaker now 'Unkempt, hysterical' and alienated, and we are made to see the negative aspect of the meandering river and feel what a lack or loss of control and direction can also mean. Then, in the final stanza, a fragile order is re-established, much to the speaker's relief:

> Your room speaks of morning,
> A stem, a verb, a rhyme,
> From whose involuntary window one
> May be expelled at any time,
> As trying to control a dream
> Puts the just-completed light to rest.

The final awareness is that 'trying to control a dream' can put out the light which dream lets into experience.

Muldoon's, Paulin's and McGuckian's different scandals and eccentricities have this in common that they destroy conventionalised ways of looking at the world; they form a breach in the stable, normal course of human affairs and events, and free human behaviour from predetermining norms and motivations. Their poetic fantasies tell of a longing for that which does not exist, or which has not been allowed to exist, the unheard of, the unseen, the imaginary, as opposed to what already exists and is permitted as 'really' visible. What Bakhtin terms carnivalistic and official selves can be made equivalent to Lacan's psychoanalytic distinction between two stages of development, the imaginary (the stage of undifferentiation, before signification) and the symbolic (the stage of insertion into the social order and its signifying practices). These poets set up possibilities for radical transformation by dissolving the boundaries between these two realms. In doing so, they replace familiarity, comfort and rationality with estrangement, the irrational. They demonstrate the potential for revolution by daring to speak the socially unspeakable; but they also register epistemological confusion, an apprehension of the partiality and relativity – the fictionality – of meaning. Their poetry, which does everything in its power to deflect the mere intellect, exists to repair the simplicity of the analytic thought of the programme-builders, the politicians, the system-makers and the theorists. More is demanded of us to understand this poetry than to understand any purely logical proposition: these poets require the use of all our faculties, intellectual, emotional and imaginative, in conjunction.

Notes

1.   'Introduction', *The Penguin Book of Contemporary British Poetry*, eds Blake Morrison and Andrew Motion (Harmondsworth: Penguin, 1982), p. 20.
2.   Paul Muldoon, *Meeting the British* (London: Faber, 1987), p. 32. Hereafter, the abbreviation *MB* will be used, and page references incorporated into the text.
3.   Paul Muldoon, *Selected Poems 1968–1983* (London: Faber, 1986), p. 34. Hereafter, the abbreviation *SP* will be used, and page references incorporated into the text.
4.   Mikhail Bakhtin, *Problems of Dostoevsky's Poetics*, translated by R.W. Rotsel (Ann Arbor: Ardis, 1973), p. 101.
5.   Tom Paulin, 'Introduction', *Faber Book of Political Verse*, ed. Tom Paulin (London: Faber, 1986), p. 43.
6.   Tom Paulin, *The Strange Museum* (London: Faber, 1980), p. 44. Hereafter, the abbreviation *SM* will be used, and page references incorporated into the text.
7.   Tom Paulin, 'Martello', *Liberty Tree* (London: Faber, 1983), p. 55. Hereafter, the abbreviation *LT* will be used, and page references incorporated into the text.
8.   Tom Paulin, *A State of Justice* (London: Faber, 1977), p. 24. Hereafter, the abbreviation *SJ* will be used, and page references incorporated into the text.
9.   Tom Paulin, *Fivemiletown* (London: Faber, 1987), p. 25. Hereafter, the abbreviation *F* will be used, and page references incorporated into the text.
10. Patrick Williams, 'Spare That Tree!', *The Honest Ulsterman*, No. 86, Spring/Summer 1989, pp. 49–52.
11. Catherine Byron, 'The Carpentry of the Sea', *Poetry Review*, Vol. 78, No. 3, Autumn 1988, pp. 63–4.
12. Medbh McGuckian, *Venus and the Rain* (Oxford University Press, 1984), p. 32. Hereafter, the abbreviation *VR* will be used, and page references incorporated into the text.
13. Medbh McGuckian, *On Ballycastle Beach* (Oxford University Press, 1988), p. 59. Hereafter, the abbreviation *OBB* will be used, and page references incorporated into the text.
14. Medbh McGuckian, *The Flower Master* (Oxford University Press, 1982), p. 42. Hereafter, the abbreviation *FM* will be used, and page references incorporated into the text.
15. S.T. Coleridge, *Biographia Literaria*, first published 1817 (London, J.M. Dent: 1965), p. 167.

9

The Gaelic Renaissance:
Sorley Maclean and Derick Thomson

Christopher Whyte

Interaction between Gaelic-speaking culture and the other cultures of the British Isles has been powerfully influenced by the distorted images the latter have of the former. First among these is the concept of Gaelic as an 'old' language with an 'ancient' literature, due to a large extent to the continuing effects of the Ossianic controversy which raged in the late eighteenth and early nineteenth centuries. Working from a slim handful of traditional ballads he did not always fully understand, James Macpherson produced a radically different literary artefact which was then projected back onto a culture to which it was in many ways alien.[1] Far from being 'old', Scottish Gaelic counts among the younger literary languages of Western Europe. It was only upon the definitive breakdown during the seventeenth century of a professional bardic system strongly linked to Ireland, with a shared literary koine, that verse in the vernacular of Gaelic Scotland reached the status of an independent tradition.[2] Since then there have been two periods of particular richness. The first roughly covers the years between 1740 and 1810, with the work of Alasdair MacMhaighstir Alasdair (Alexander MacDonald, c. 1695–c. 1770), Rob Donn (1714–78), Donnchadh Bàn Mac-an-t-Saoir (Duncan Bàn Macintyre, 1724–1812) and Uilleam Ros (William Ross, 1762–?91).

The second begins in 1943, with the appearance of *Dàin do Eimhir agus Dàin Eile* ('Poems to Eimhir and Other Poems'), the first collection by Somhairle MacGill-Eain (Sorley MacLean, 1911–). He is one of a group of five poets who introduced modernist, and eventually postmodernist, perspectives, as well as an internationalist outlook to Gaelic poetry. The others are Deòrsa Caimbeul Hay (George Campbell Hay, 1915–85), Ruairidh MacThòmais (Derick Thomson, 1921–), Iain Mac a' Ghobhainn (Iain Crichton Smith, 1928–) and Dòmhnall MacAmhlaigh (Donald MacAulay, 1930–).

The flowering they initiated continues in the work of the younger poets, eight of whom feature in the anthology *An Aghaidh na Sìorraidheachd/In the Face of Eternity*, published early in 1991.[3] This essay will concentrate on the work of MacLean and Thomson, both major poets whose work has had an important influence on those coming after, and deserves to be better known and more closely read beyond the confines of Scotland and of these islands.

MacLean was born on the island of Raasay, which lies between Skye and the Applecross peninsula, north of Kyle of Lochalsh.[4] He was a monoglot Gaelic speaker when he began school at the age of six, and came from a family that was particularly rich in singers, pipers and tradition-bearers. The family store of songs played a crucial part in the formation of MacLean's sensibility. He is not a singer himself, but has commented that, if he had been, he might well have created melodies rather than poems. He claims that he was able to remember after a single hearing the words of any Gaelic song he particularly liked. Another important influence was the Free Presbyterian church. MacLean was exposed both to the richness of its pulpit oratory and to its grim hostility to the arts, and the doctrine that only an infinitesimal portion of humanity would at the last be saved inspired in him a hatred of all elitism as well as a profound sense of pessimism and compassion for the lot of mankind. The political radicalism dating from his early teens relates to the charismatic figure of John Maclean, the great Marxist teacher and Clydeside radical who was nominated consul in Scotland by Lenin and imprisoned for his beliefs. It is not surprising that, among the English Romantic poets, MacLean was particularly drawn to Shelley and Blake as well as Wordsworth.

In 1929 a bursary took him to Edinburgh University, where he studied English rather than Celtic for strictly economic reasons. Grierson was professor at this time, and the influence of the Metaphysical poets, and specifically of Donne, can be traced in the often contorted and tortuous intellectual striving of MacLean's Gaelic love lyrics. He read Eliot and Pound, who strongly influenced the English verse he wrote alongside work in Gaelic during these years. He came to feel, however, that the former was both derivative and over-sophisticated, and made a conscious commitment to write in Gaelic henceforth. In Edinburgh he met James Caird and the philosopher George Davie, author of *The Democratic Intellect* and *The Crisis of the Democratic Intellect*, fundamental texts for understanding the intellectual culture of Scotland in the last two centuries. They introduced MacLean to Hugh MacDiarmid (penname of Christopher Murray Grieve (1892–1978)), leader of the Scottish Renaissance Movement, a nationalist and a Marxist and the dominant figure in Scottish literature between the wars. The two poets became firm friends, and MacDiarmid's *A Drunk Man Looks at the Thistle* convinced MacLean of the primacy of the lyric, as well as inspiring in him the desire 'to write a long medley with as many lyric peaks as might grow out of it.'[5]

The biographical situation underlying the *Dàin do Eimhir* began to delineate itself in the years after MacLean graduated from Edinburgh and took up teaching posts, first at Portree in Skye, and then at Tobermory on the island of Mull. Living on the latter island was a particularly heart-breaking experience, given that he was surrounded by evidence of the wholesale manner in which the native people, many of them bearing his own name, had been cleared from their ancestral territory. The cycle of poems to Eimhir is underpinned by a tension between commitment to the struggle against fascism on a European level, expressed in the specific possibility of going to fight in defence of the Spanish Republic, and burningly intense love for a woman who does not reciprocate. A third theme, articulated almost *sotto voce* but nevertheless important, is MacLean's growing certainty of his poetic vocation and his stature as a poet. But the biographical elements are transmuted and heightened in the cycle. As many as three women are subsumed in the single figure of Eimhir, while MacLean has made it clear that 'certain circumstances, family circumstances, prevented me from going to fight in the International Brigade. It wasn't a woman fundamentally that kept me from going though there was one.'[6] The economic and family concerns that weighed so heavily are not mentioned in the cycle:

My mother's long illness in 1936, its recurrence in 1938, the outbreak of the Spanish Civil War in 1936, the progressive decline of my father's business in the Thirties, my meeting with an Irish girl in 1937, my rash leaving of Skye for Mull late in 1937, and Munich in 1938, and always the steady unbearable decline of Gaelic, made those years for me years of difficult choice, and the tensions of those years confirmed self-expression in poetry not in action.[7]

In January 1939 MacLean took up a post at Boroughmuir High School in Edinburgh, and was enlisted in the Signals Corps in September 1940. He was seriously wounded at El Alamein in November 1942, and spent the following nine months in hospital. As a result the preparation of *Dàin do Eimhir agus Dàin Eile* was entrusted to others, principally to Douglas Young, lecturer in Greek at Aberdeen University until 1941, a nationalist who suffered imprisonment for his refusal to be conscripted by a British government. MacLean's letters to Young are deposited in the National Library of Scotland,[8] and throw valuable light on the emergence of the cycle, as well as on the textual problems connected with it. In the 1943 collection, the first poem is numbered 1, the last 60, with a short 'Envoi' following, but 12 poems are missing from the sequence. While MacLean was unsure about the quality of some of these, others, first published in 1970,[9] were probably excluded because of their highly intimate content. Both *Reothairt is Contraigh: Taghadh de Dhàin/Spring tide and Neap tide: Selected Poems* (Edinburgh 1977) and *O Choille gu Bearradh/From Wood to Ridge: Collected Poems in Gaelic and English* (Manchester 1989) reprint only a selection of items from the 'Dàin do Eimhir', which are given titles and divided into sections in such a way as to obscure their function within the original cycle. This evidently expresses MacLean's current attitude to the text, although Derick Thomson has written that 'it is a matter for regret that the love sequence has been reshuffled and only partly reproduced in the 1977 volume.'[10] I myself have argued at some length that, in their original form, the 'Dàin do Eimhir' are MacLean's masterpiece, and that individual lyrics can only be fully understood when restored to their context in the cycle as a coherent, interlocking whole.[11] The 1943 collection is by now a very rare book, and as it carries only a few English translations, it is inaccessible to MacLean's English-language admirers. It is significant that Iain Crichton Smith based his splendidly creative translations *Poems to Eimhir* (Newcastle 1971) on the 1943 text, including several poems MacLean himself did not choose to reprint.[12]

What makes *Dàin do Eimhir agus Dàin Eile* such an important book? Crichton Smith has written of the excitement he felt when, in 1945, he received it as a Gaelic prize from

> an unusually enlightened Gaelic teacher ... I was overwhelmed by the combination of music and imagery that I found in the book, and indeed it is the volume of poems to which I have

returned most often, long after I sensed in Auden and Spender flaws which I did not find in MacLean... the volume seemed to compose a single poem, the record of a mind and heart engaged in work that was essential to them, and written too in varying forms which seemed suitable to the twentieth century... Gaelic poetry in my experience simply was not like that.[13]

In order to fully appreciate the impact of *Dàin do Eimhir agus Dàin Eile*, one must remember the state of Gaelic poetry as it emerged from the nineteenth century. The failure of the Jacobite Rebellion of 1745 had marked the definitive military defeat of Gaelic Scotland, which was followed by rapid Anglicisation of the Gaelic aristocracy and the introduction of an alien concept of land tenure which made possible the destruction of communities throughout the heartland of the language. The break in continuity, cultural trauma and loss of confidence which ensued meant that the most characteristic poetry of the Victorian period is small-scale, carefully crafted but unambitious verse frequently produced by urbanised Gaels who look back on their homeland with undisguised nostalgia and an uneasy mixture of British patriotism and all too vociferous language loyalty. The three outstanding poets of this era are atypical. Màiri Mhòr nan Oran (Mary MacPherson, 1821–98), a nurse, began composing poetry, much of it strongly political, after the age of 50, and dictated her work to an amanuensis, as she herself was not sufficiently literate in her mother tongue to write it down. Iain Mac a' Ghobhainn (John Smith, 1848–81) was the only one of the three to benefit from a university education, which he interrupted when tuberculosis forced him to return home to Lewis in 1874. Uilleam MacDhunlèibhe (William Livingston, 1808–70), experimented with a kind of free verse and attempted large-scale narrative forms with only partial success. His innovations did not find followers.

So MacLean's poetry emerged against a background of narrowing perspectives, overwhelmingly local concerns and technical unadventurousness. It is only with him that Gaelic poetry is weaned definitively from song, and begins to be written and read rather than composed and recited, although the traditional modes continue to be used within island communities to this very day. We can get an idea of the desacratory quality of MacLean's work from a quatrain printed as 17 of the 'Dàin Eile' (1943: 82). In it he asks how he can aspire to the sensual enjoyment of a woman's body while the Red Army is struggling against Hitler, and faltering, on the banks of the Dnieper. It is typical of him to yoke together a moment of tenderness and vulnerability with large-scale historical tragedy in this way, and typical, too, that he should see the two as irreconcilable. This brief lyric breaks the decorum of the Gaelic tradition and also speaks a subject-matter it had considered beyond its reach for over a century. Who would have thought that events on the Russian front would resound within Gaelic Scotland, or that a Gaelic poet could have things of import to say about them? There were two strands of poetry within the Gaelic tradition: a public, bardic utterance which addressed political leaders and the community as a whole, and a body of anonymous song, often concerned with love, where the expression of deeply intimate contents was allowed and made possible precisely because the authors were anonymous. MacLean brings these together in a way that must be perceived as deeply disruptive, as no less a transgression than his own eventual, hard-won admission that love will always take precedence over the demands of ideology and politics.

The power of the cycle lies, however, not so much in the conclusion it reaches as in the violence with which it states its dilemmas. The opening lyric dates from August or September 1930, while in May 1941 the last four and the 'Envoi' had still to be written. Lyric 2 is dated May 1932 and is entitled 'A' Chiall 's a' Ghràidh/Reason and Love' (1989: 4/5). It sets out from the ambivalence of the word 'ciall', which in Gaelic both means 'reason, meaning' and serves as a term of endearment, like 'darling':

> Nuair dhearc mo shùil air t' aodann
> cha do nochd e ciall a' ghràidh,
> cha do dh' fheòraich mi mu 'n trian ud.

> When my eye lighted on your face
> it did not show the reason in love,
> I did not ask about that third part.

Although the poem is about an attempt to integrate reason and emotion, and ends with a perhaps too easily achieved conciliation of the two, what resonates with the reader is the imagery of bisection and division, the sense of a polarisation within the personality leading to alienation and painful struggle. Lyric 18, 'Urnuigh/Prayer' (1989: 16–17) develops this splitting in the context of the fascist victory in Spain. Rupert·John Cornford, who fought in the defence of Madrid and was killed near Cordoba in 1936, is taken as a type of the hero who distances himself from love so as to be fully committed to political struggle. But MacLean's plea to be cleansed from love and attain heroic stature chokes in his throat:

> An iarr mi mo chridhe bhith glainte
> bho anfhannachd mo ghaoil ghlain ghil,
> an iarr mi spiorad 's e air fhaileadh
> eadhon gum faighear anns a' bhoile mi
> cho treun ri Dimitrov no ri O Conghaile?

> Will I ask that my heart be purified
> from the weakness of my pure white love,
> will I ask for a flayed spirit
> even in order that I be found in the madness
> as brave as Dimitrov or as Connolly?

(MacLean deliberately links the Edinburgh-born hero of the 1916 Easter Rising in Dublin with the man accused of setting fire to the Reichstag in 1933, as part of his project to relocate Gaelic culture in a European and contemporary context.) Because he has not flayed his heart, and has preferred a woman to the challenge of history, his prayer is both blasphemous and futile, and he turns to the language of Calvinist theology to make the point explicit:

> Cha ruigear a leas ceistear no sgrùdair
> a dh'fhaicinn nach eil 'nam ùrnuigh
> a' Ghairm Eifeachdach no 'n Dùrachd,
> 's ged tha mi soilleir anns an fhìrinn
> nach eil mo spiorad aon-fhillte.

> No catechist or examiner is needed
> to see that there is not in my prayer
> Effectual Calling or sincerity,
> and though I am clear-sighted in scripture
> that my spirit is not one-fold.

Words from this poem echo throughout the cycle. Indeed, a study needs to be done of the semantic patterns MacLean creates and which give the 'Dàin do Eimhir' so much of their cogency. The close of 18 opposes 'slàn' ('whole') and 'sgàinte' ('split'), and the idea of flaying ('faileadh') inspires the Puritanism of 32 'Sgatham/ Let me lop...' (1989: 136–7), where he resolves to strip all ornament from his verse until it is as bare and chill as the death of Liebknecht. This lyric speaks specifically of burning tree branches. When the same image returns at the close of 43, 'Am Mùr Gorm/ The Blue Rampart' (1989: 142–3), we understand that the flaying has remained a mere aspiration:

> Agus air creachainn chéin fhàsmhoir
> chinn blàthmhor Craobh nan Teud,
> 'na meangach duillich t' aodann,
> mo chiall is aogas réil.

> And on a distant luxurious summit
> there blossomed the Tree of Strings,
> among its leafy branches your face,
> my reason and the likeness of a star.

'Ciall' harks back to 2, while the star is an anticipation of the galactic imagery which will dominate the poems from 50 onwards. The split is between reason and emotion, between passion and intellect, but links in to a deeper conviction that love and ideology cannot be reconciled. Love will always be destabilising, disruptive, an energy that undermines structures of belief and the action consequent on them. As early as 3 'Am Buaireadh/The Turmoil' (1989: 6–7) he had complained that her beauty cast 'sgleò/air bochdainn 's air creuchd sheirbh/agus air saoghal tuigse Leninn' ('a cloud/ over poverty and a bitter wound/and over the world of Lenin's intellect'). Lyric 4, 'Gaoir na h-Eòrpa/The Cry of Europe' (1989: 8–9), is couched in a series of agonised questions, rising from a troubled *mezzo forte* to an almost deafening *fortissimo* at the close. Can her beauty and the beauty of the music she sings blot out the sliding towards fascism of Scotland and of Europe as a whole, 'a' bhrùid 's am meàirleach air ceann na h-Eòrpa' ('the brute and the brigand at the head of Europe')? At the beginning of the poem, these horrors seem to be somewhere behind her, hidden from us by her physical presence, but the balance gradually tips until MacLean characteristically atomises 'gach cuach de d' chaul òr-bhuidh' ('every lock of your gold-yellow head'), which can in no way counterbalance the mass tragedies of Gaeldom and of Europe. In

8 'An Clogad Stàilinn/The Steel Helmet' (1989: 10–11) he accuses his love, beneath an epigraph from Yeats, of perhaps unconscious fascist sympathies. One of the few celebratory poems in the cycle is 30, 'Am Boilseabhach/The Bolshevik' (1989: 134–5) (and the word, like 'bùirdeasachd' for 'bourgeoisie' later in the poem, is a Mac-Lean coinage). It envisions a free socialist republic in Scotland, yet insists that the poet would proclaim his loved one queen, striking an ideologically dissonant note even in the context of triumph.

Atomisation returns in 42 'Tràighean/Shores' (1989: 140–1), with the poet measuring the sand, grain by grain, on Homhsta Shore in Uist, waiting for the sea to ebb drop by drop, then combining drop and grain in 'cochur gaoil dhut' ('a synthesis of love for you'). But the apotheosis of fragmentation comes with 45, 'An Sgian/The Knife' (1989: 144–5):

> Rinn sgian m' eanchainn gearradh
> air cloich mo ghaoil, a luaidh,
> is sgrùd a faobhar gach aon bhearradh
> is ghabh mo shùil a thuar.

> The knife of my brain made incision,
> my dear, on the stone of my love,
> and its blade examined every segment
> and my eye took its colour.

Love is a jewel, a precious stone pick-axed from the speaker's body, and the blade, the flame and the glass that test it, as well as the scrutinising eye, are elements of his own personality in its state of fragmentation. If the testing comes over almost as an attempt to destroy the jewel (intellectual scrutiny can find the flaws and weaknesses in love), the ultimate effect is to emphasise its wholeness. A series of paradoxes seem to be catching each other's tails, and the reader's difficulty in understanding mirrors the intellectual strain embodied in the poem:

> Agus 's e a' chlach tha briste
> an leug shoilleir shlàn
> nuair phrannar i le eanchainn
> gu barrachd cruais a gràidh.

> And the stone that is broken
> is the clear whole jewel

> when it is pounded by a brain
> to a greater hardness of its love.

At the opposite end of MacLean's expressive range is the hypnotic, almost automatic writing of the closing section of 'An Cuilithionn/ The Cuillin', the marvellously incantatory whispering lines that begin with a repeated 'Có seo' ('Who is this', 1989: 128–31), and of 'Coin is Madaidhean-Allaidh/Dogs and Wolves' (1989: 134–5), numbered 29 in the Eimhir sequence. MacLean wrote to Young in March 1942 that he had written 28 and 29 in the form we now have them upon waking around 2 or 3 in the morning, under the impression that he had composed them in sleep. A similar claim is made for the 'Có seo' lines in the prefatory note to 'An Cuilithionn'.

The dogs and wolves are a symbol of the poems he has not written, pursuing the white deer of Eimhir's beauty across a desolate landscape of mountains and wilderness. The traditional vocabulary of hounds and hunting is being pressed into use to express a psychological reality which reiterates the potential destructiveness of the speaker's desire. If his hounds were to reach the deer, they would presumably tear it to pieces. Nothing happens in the poem. The pursuit has an endless, circular quality which reminds one of Nastagio degli Onesti in Day Five of the *Decameron*, without having that tale's bloody close. The words 'tòir' and 'tòrachd', meaning 'hunt, pursuit', have echoed through the earlier part of the cycle. Lyric 52, 'Tri Leòis/Three Rays' (1989: 154–5), makes a substitution which is vital to the sense of the whole:

> Cha b'ann fada bha an tòir
> a thug còrr 's deich bliadhna
> an uair a bha an fhaodail còrr
> 's na dh'fhóghnadh dòchas Sìorruidh.

> The pursuit was not long
> that took more than ten years
> when the treasure-trove was more
> than would suffice for an eternal hope.

'Faodail' is explained by Dwelly as 'goods found by chance', 'thing found', 'stray treasure'.[14] If the 'Dàin do Eimhir' began as an impassioned quest for Eimhir's love and for physical possession of her, the scenario has subtly changed, as the speaker becomes conscious of the poetry that has come into being over a span of ten years. He knows by this stage that she can never be his. The perspective has widened, however, and one wonders if the real drama of the cycle has not consisted in the making of a poet more than in the failure of a love. Lyric 56 speaks of a 'dàn air faodail' (1943: 43), a poem come upon by chance, and 59 (1989: 164–5), celebrating 'gach faodail a fhuair thu' ('every treasure you chanced on') in the collection of Gaelic lore made between 1855 and 1899 by the exciseman Alexander Carmichael (subsequently published as *Carmina Gadelica*), compares MacLean's 'ealaidheachd òir gun luasgan' ('peaceful golden lyric') to the Hymn of the Graces Carmichael had transcribed from recitation, almost as if the two were equally 'found' objects.

The referential world of 'Dàin do Eimhir', in geographical and political terms, was a profound innovation for Gaelic poetry. In literary terms, too, MacLean was able to turn his bicultural background (Gaelic in the home community, Scottish and English through obligatory formal education) to a source of enrichment rather than of alienation. Lyric 20 (1943: 21) speaks of a trio of unhappy lover poets who can function as models: William Ross, Aleksandr Blok and Yeats. Blok is perhaps mediated through MacDiarmid's use of his work in *A Drunk Man Looks at the Thistle* and through MacLean's general sympathy for the Russian Revolution and the Bolsheviks. Yeats' love for Maud Gonne, with its resonances of frustration and of political waywardness, must have been frequently present to MacLean when writing the 'Dàin do Eimhir'. Indeed, he told Young in a letter written in November 1941 that Yeats's 'Where had her sweetness gone?' (from 'Quarrel in Old Age') was the germ of the poem which is the cycle's climax, 57 'An Tathaich/The Haunting' (1989: 158–9). But the cycle sends roots back deeper into the European tradition of love poetry, towards Guido Cavalcanti, Petrarch and Ronsard. His knowledge of Pound would have brought MacLean into contact with the troubadours. Though 13 'A' Bhuaile Ghréine/The Sunny Fold' (1989: 12–13) only makes the briefest mention of 'an Audiart a bhuair De Born' ('the Audiart who plagued De Born'), it is in fact a subtle meditation on the warrior poet's 'dompna soisseubuda', a composite lady put together from the best qualities of a range of noblewomen he admired. MacLean aspires to put every effect

a thug Lochlann is Eire
is Alba àrsaidh do mo dhaoine
a chur cuideachd an caoine
agus an ìobairt do 'n ìoghnadh
tha geal dealbhte an clàr t' aodainn.

that Norway and Ireland
and old Scotland gave to my people
together in mellowness
and to offer them to the wonder
that is fair and shapely in your face.

Lyric 19 (1943: 20) is a more classical poem, with its proud boast to
have both received immortality from Eimhir and conferred it on
her, and its echo of Horace's monument more lasting than bronze
from Book III of the *Odes*. The last quatrain is breathtaking, refor-
mulating the *carpe diem* of baroque poetry with its macabre graveyard imagery through Baudelaire's 'La Charogne' in what sounds
like both a celebration and a kind of revenge:

is ged bhios tusa aig fear-pòsda
is tu gun eòl air mo strì-sa,
's e do ghlòir-sa mo bhàrdachd
an déidh cnàmhachd do lithe.

and, though you will be married to another
and ignorant of my struggle,
your glory is my poetry
after the slow rotting of your body.

In 57, the longest and perhaps the greatest poem in the cycle,[15]
the roles in the hunt have been reversed. If at the beginning of the
'Dàin' Eimhir was indifferent to his pursuit, now it is her face that
haunts him night and day, posing him the anguished problem of
forgetfulness. She is convinced that this interval of time is not
subject to change or corruption, but he does not see how it can
outlast the limits of an individual human consciousness:

Is dé a' chàil thar chàiltean
a mhothaicheas an àilleachd,

'n uair nach nochd sùil no cluas i
blas, suathadh no fàileadh...

Mur faighear, air chor's gum mothaich,
aon chàil eile no seòl-tomhais,
am bi cruth no bith aig t' àilleachd
an àrainn tìme 's domhainn?

And what sense beyond senses
will perceive their beauty
when neither eye nor ear will show it,
nor taste nor touch nor smell...

If there is not found, for perception,
one other sense or dimension,
will your beauty have form or being
in the bounds of time and the eternal deep?

(1989: 162–5)

The mounting tide of questions receives no answer, but the last two quatrains communicate a kind of arrival which is also a defeat or a surrender: not the Red Army in its struggle by the Dnieper, but this face obsessively haunting him is closest to MacLean's heart.

My discussion of MacLean's work has concentrated on the 'Dàin do Eimhir' because I believe them to be his masterpiece, a love cycle on a par with the work of Catullus or Petrarch or Ronsard, and a great long poem which he produced almost unawares while struggling consciously to produce a kind of epic in 'An Cuilithionn'. The latter was begun in spring or early summer of 1939 and broken off abruptly in December of that year. The events of the Polish insurrection in 1944 put paid for ever to the idealism about the Red Army as potential liberators of Europe that had inspired the piece. MacLean published 'what I think tolerable of it' in *Chapman* magazine between 1987 and 1989. We have no way of understanding how the seven sections were to relate to the plan of the whole as originally conceived by MacLean. The pervading image is of the bare rock outcrop of the Cuillin Mountains in Skye, a symbol of human hope and heroism contrasted with the bogs and quagmires which have overflowed the surrounding land.

MacLean is by his own declaration not a professional poet, but one who writes in spite of himself. The bulk of his work comes from the decade leading up to the publication of *Dàin do Eimhir agus Dàin Eile*, and includes a sizeable body of lyrics related thematically to the main cycle, as well as the section 'Blàr/Battlefield' in *O Choille gu Bearradh* (1989: 205–15), bringing together his poems from North Africa. It can be argued that the finest British poetry to have emerged from the Second World War was written in Gaelic. George Campbell Hay's poems, also from North Africa, and inspired by a deeply humanitarian, if not specifically pacifist perspective, are unsurpassed in this respect.

High points of MacLean's production since 1943 are 'Hallaig' (1989: 226–7), using the traditional tree imagery of Gaelic poetry to repopulate a cleared village in Rassay thanks to a potent magic which, however, seems limited in time to the duration of the poet's own consciousness, and the splendid elegy to his brother Calum, one of Scotland's greatest collectors of folklore and a convert to Catholicism, the 'Cumha Chaluim Iain Mhic Gill-Eain' (1989: 264–5). MacLean is at present working on a further extended poem on a motif from Gaelic tradition, 'Uamha 'n Oir' ('The Cave of Gold'), three sections of which are printed in the 1989 volume (282–3).

The impact of MacLean's 1943 collection was strong enough for it to be a distinct influence on the early poetry of Derick Thomson, only ten years his junior. Thomson was born in Bayble village in Point, Lewis (the home of both Iain Crichton Smith and Anne Frater (1967–)). His father James (1888–1971) was headmaster of Bayble School and a poet himself, whose work is collected in *Fasgnadh* (Stirling 1953). Thomson attended the Nicolson Institute in Stornoway from 1934 to 1939 before proceeding to Aberdeen University, where his studies were interrupted by service as a radar mechanic in the RAF from 1942 to 1945. Since 1948 he has held a series of teaching posts in Scottish universities, holding the Chair in Celtic at Glasgow University from 1964 to 1991. He is probably the country's leading Celtic scholar, as well as being a central figure in Gaelic publishing over four decades and co-founder and editor of Scotland's longest-running literary magazine, the Gaelic quarterly *Gairm*.

Thomson has published four collections: *An Dealbh Briste* ('The Broken Picture', Edinburgh 1951), *Eadar Samhradh is Foghar* ('Between Summer and Autumn', Glasgow 1967), *An Rathad Cian* ('The

Far Road', Glasgow 1970) and *Saorsa agus an Iolaire* ('Freedom and the Eagle', Glasgow 1977), and a fifth is said to be in preparation.[16] While the greater part of MacLean's production dates from the 1930s and the first years of the war, Thomson's belongs mainly to the postwar world and spans nearly thirty years, so that a distinct development can be perceived in his method and his themes. It was he primarily who introduced symbolism (in its strictly European sense) to Gaelic poetry, and in what follows the relationship between the vehicle (the thing named or depicted) and the tenor (that which it refers to or means) will be considered in some detail. Allegory and symbolism can be seen as opposite ends of a spectrum, rather than distinct methods of organising poetry. In allegory at its most structured and mechanical, the relationship between vehicle and tenor is explicit and must be clearly grasped if the poem is to be competently read. Symbolism, on the other hand, particularly in the form initiated by Baudelaire and practised by Blok and others, treats the sensual world as an allegory to which we have lost the key. We cannot escape the feeling that sense impressions are a way of saying something else, signs in a language we do not quite have access to. This is why impressions from the different senses can be superimposed and made equivalent through synaesthesia, most famously in Rimbaud's sonnet 'Voyelles'.

For a reader not familiar with the tradition, it is striking that the great Gaelic nature poetry of the eighteenth century, which reached its height in the work of MacDonald and Macintyre, eschews any kind of symbolism. Phenomena are itemised as themselves, building up to a composite picture of a stream or a geographical location. They are never transcended or dissolved in the interests of a higher meaning of which they act as vehicle. It is this quality in the poetry that makes those who know it so impatient of the Celtic Twilight projections of English language poetry. The light of Gaelic nature poetry is clear, limpid and almost pitiless, never weakened by the sentimentalisation that the pathetic fallacy or the figure of the lone wanderer are wont to introduce.

In 'Coin is Madaidhean-Allaidh' ('Dogs and Wolves') MacLean turned the inherited imagery into a vocabulary for psychological processes, but this is not typical of his poetry as a whole. The close of the Cuillin, with its heaping up of abstract concepts in a manner alien to the English ear and alien to any truly organic interaction of vehicle and tenor, is more so:

Thar lochan fala clann nan daoine,
thar breòiteachd blàir is strì an aonaich,
thar bochdainn caithimh fiabhrais àmhghair,
thar anacothrom eucoir ainneart ànraidh,
thar truaighe eu-dòchas gamhlas cuilbheart,
thar ciont is truaillidheachd, gu furachair,
gu treunmhor chithear an Cuilithionn
's e 'g éirigh air taobh eile duilghe.

Beyond the lochs of the blood of the children of men,
beyond the frailty of plain and the labour of the mountain,
beyond poverty, consumption, fever, agony,
beyond hardship, wrong, tyranny, distress,
beyond misery, despair, hatred, treachery,
beyond guilt and defilement, watchful,
heroic, the Cuillin is seen
rising on the other side of sorrow.

(1989: 130–1)

Human misery and moral conflicts are treated as a landscape in a thoroughly original manner combining MacLean's unashamed high seriousness with the topographical preoccupations of the tradition he inherited. George Campbell Hay's work, with its didactic and nationalistic urge, makes unashamed use of allegorical captioning in an almost mediaeval fashion (he revives the imagery of the Ship of Fools). It remained to Thomson to set vehicle and tenor oscillating, shimmering in a tension which, as his poetry matures, refuses to let either side preponderate, creating in the process a richness and uncertainty of meaning which are profoundly modern in tone.

The 1951 volume sees him, in pieces like 'Leig dhìot an iomagain/Let be anxiety' and 'A' Snìomh Cainnte/Weaving words and weaving dreams', mastering the vocabulary of traditional song, with a plangency and self-deprecation that will echo throughout his work:

A luaidh nan làmh geal, cha dèan mi àicheadh
gur tusa dh'fhàg mi fo phràmh leam fhèin,
a' snìomh bhruadar 's a' snìomh bàrdachd,
's a' call am màireach air sgàth an dè.

I shall not deny, white-handed love, that it was you made me sad
and lonely, weaving dreams and weaving verses, and losing
tomorrow for yesterday.

(1982: 28–9)

'Dà Là/Changed Days' talks explicitly of the problem of finding a
symbol ('samhla') for an emotion. Wordsworth chose a withered
bush for grief, the rising moon for joy. Thomson's vocabulary is
different:

> Ceud gu leith blianna 'na dhèidh sin
> fhuair mise samhla air lèireadh,
> 's ged dh'fhaodadh nach tuig thu mo chàs-sa,
> 'se th'ann *kiosk* air ceann sràide.

> A hundred and fifty years later
> I found a symbol for grieving,
> and though you may not understand my trouble
> it is a kiosk at a street end.

(1982: 28–9)

Joy is the neon lights on the cinemas down one side of Princes
Street in Edinburgh. Thomson is not just wilfully violating the
canon of imagery of Gaelic poetry. One has the sense that the
symbols are not freely chosen, but elements in a love story that
has had this setting. The vehicles are no freer than their tenors.
Rather than being chosen in terms of a preordained meaning, they
belong to a pattern of places and impressions which contains, and
can yield only in part, its own logic of signification, and has its
own, as it were pre-existing, coherence and 'givenness'.

'Achadh-Bhuana/Harvest Field' leaves its real import unspoken,
compelling the reader to complete the pattern of correspondences
him or herself. Its imagery marvellously evokes the transition stage
between adolescence and maturity, just preceding sexual initiation,
as a harvest field that is ripe in some places, in others green, and of
which the speaker cuts only a part. The scythe and blade of the first
quatrain clearly suggest the phallus and the possibility of deflow-
ering. This possibility is deferred, and the second quatrain inhabits
a world of perfect, seemingly timeless equilibrium, rudely disrupted in the third:

Dh' fhàg mi beagan ri bhuain a-màireach
is choisich sinn còmhla eadar na ràthan,
thuit thu air an speal bha fear eile air fhàgail,
is ghearradh do chneas, is dhiùlt e slànadh.

I left a little to cut on the morrow, and we walked together
between the swathes: you fell on a scythe that another had left,
and your skin was cut, and refused healing.

(1982: 52–3)

The world of imagery in the poem is self-contained and fully
congruent, yet points beyond itself to another meaning. Characteristic of Thomson is the delicacy and tenderness, the utter absence of
prurience with which a subject of this kind is treated.

MacLean succeeded in turning to his own advantage a biculturalism that resulted largely from inimical historical forces beyond
his control. The use of English in Thomson's family meant that he
experienced from a much earlier age the split that so often emerges
in those who are truly bilingual for part, if not all of their lives (and
of which Iain Crichton Smith has much to say in his poetry). ''Nam
dhachaigh eadar dhà dhùthaich/In my house between two coun-
tries' (1982: 40–1) opens its first three stanzas with the same formula. The Gaelic heartland is contrasted with industrial central
Scotland as experienced by Highland immigrants, a second world
which they cannot blot out of consciousness even though they may
return from it. The splitting is mortal, irrevocable: 'cha smiùr thu 'n
taigh seo o ghalar bàis dhomh' ('you cannot fumigate this house for
me from its mortal disease'). The second concerns 'my writing,
between two tongues' (''Nam sgrìobhadh eadar dhà chànain'),
characterising Thomson's verse in an image of breathtaking beauty
as 'mar chaile-bianan/ga fhrasadh bho liagh mo ràimh-sa,/'s ga
bhàthadh an cuan na cuimhne' ('phosphorescence being showered
from the blade of my oar, and being drowned in the sea of my
memory'). He frequently speaks of his creative activity as something extremely tenuous and fragile, something passing through
his hands but escaping his grasp, 'weaving words and weaving
dreams', or here in 'Fir-Chlis/Merry Dancers':

ged bhios mise 's mo leithid a' cosg ar n-iarrtais
air binnean corrach gailbheach na tìm seo,

's a' cosg ar làmhan air sìoman dìomhain
a chàradh air stràbhan diomain na tìr seo.

and I and my like expend our desires
on the unsteady stormy pinnacle of this time,
and waste our hands putting useless ropes
over the short-lived straw of this country. (1982: 44–5)

The remainder of the poem concerns love, 'my heart, between two invitations' ('"nam chridhe eadar dhà chuireadh'). It is interesting to contrast the last stanza with the lines from *Dàin do Eimhir* 19 concerning roughly similar circumstances. There is none of Mac-Lean's proud boastfulness and possessiveness, none of his intellectual and emotional violence. Thomson projects himself in his verse as resolutely unheroic ('Bidh eagal orm roimh do mhànran/ 's gum fàg a mhìlseachd mi leòinte', 'I shall be afraid of your wooing, lest its sweetness leave me wounded'), and the pain issues in a strongly elegiac tone and in self-reproach.

Thomson is not a great love poet. Themes of individual love are practically abandoned after his first collection, but the tone and vocabulary he had evolved for them is increasingly employed in poems about his language and culture, and the fate of the Lewis world he grew up in. 'Nam dhachaigh eadar dhà dhùthaich' had set the man caught between two women and the poet caught between two languages in parallel: the latter comes to predominate more and more.

'An Tobar/The Well' (1982: 48–9) is similar in method to 'Achadh-Bhuana', in that it never states explicitly what its real subject is. An old woman asks the poet to fetch her even just a thimbleful of water from the village well, now overgrown with bracken, and he complies with her request. But it all seems like a dream now, for only the bracken is left, and the old woman is dead. Clearly Thomson is talking of those from whom he received the language and its associated culture, and who themselves need renewal from a source that has dried up or been lost. There is an undertow of guilt in the poem, perhaps because the water is taken, not to a new generation, but to satisfy the vanity of a dying woman and bring colour to her cheeks. It is neglect more than violence or historical tragedy that has led to the loss of the well. It is fascinating how the imagery establishes its own organic patterns, as when the wrinkles on the woman's face are described as 'n raineach a' fàs mu thobar a sùilean' ('the bracken growing round the well of her eyes').

In 'Cainnt nan Oghaichean' ('Grandchildren's Talk'), from the second collection (1982: 92–3), the English monoglot grandchildren of our grandchildren have become 'coigrich bheaga' ('little strangers'), and the switching on of electric light which God and Macmillan have made possible is contrasted with the switching off of another light, the loss of 'cainnt am màthar, is beus an daoine' ('their mother tongue, and their people's virtues'). 'Uiseag/The Lark' (104–5) is an elegy on a wounded bird, with almost a pursing of the lips as reason says 'tha do latha dheth seachad,/is dè math bhith gad iargain?' ('it's all over with you,/and what's the good of mourning?'). It may be only a reader's hunch that insists that something more than a bird is intended when the heart shouts in reply: '"O! na faiceadh tu i air iteig/cha sguireadh tu ga h-ionndrain gu sìorraidh"' ('"O! could you but have seen her on the wing/you would go on longing for her for ever."') 'Dùn nan Gall/Donegal' (1982: 102–3) speaks of Gaelic as the language of poverty, of the periphery:

> Cha bheathaich feur a' chànain seo,
> chan fhàs i sultmhor an guirt no 'n iodhlainn;
> fòghnaidh dhi beagan coirce 's eòrna,
> cuirear grad fhuadachadh oirr' leis a' chruithneachd;
> chan iarr i ach, cleas nan gobhar, a bhith sporghail
> os cionn muir gorm, air na bideanan biorach.

> Grass does not nourish this language,
> it does not grow fat in fields or cornyards;
> a little oats and barley suffices it,
> wheat quickly frightens it away;
> all it asks is to clamber, like the goats,
> on sharp rocky pinnacles, above the blue sea.

Taken by the 'ragged children' to England or to Glasgow, the language is doomed to expire 'na h-ìobairt-rèite air altair beairteis' ('a sacrifice of atonement on the altar of riches'). Politically, one has reservations about poems of this kind, which could be seen as an internalisation of characteristics imposed on Gaelic from outside, of a pattern which must inevitably lead to the language's death. Adaptation and transformation are denied to it, yet these are processes even the politically strongest languages must subject themselves to if they are to survive. But on a human and a literary level, Thomson's truth to his own experience and his own very special subject-matter commands enormous respect, nowhere more than in the culminating poem of this series, 'Cisteachan-laighe' ('Coffins') (1982: 122–3).

Its topic, culture death, is fascinating enough. Equally impressive, however, is the way it thematises its own method, the way the processes by which the poem is organised are also what it is about. I have written elsewhere that:

> Thomson has the boon, for a writer, of an accessible childhood, an inexhaustible, supportive and yet disturbing storehouse of sensations, like an unfathomable sea on which the buoy of his adult consciousness floats.[17]

This poem has an almost Proustian beginning, as the scent of sawdust in a city joiner's shop sends Thomson back to his grandfather making coffins in Lewis. There are five distinct scenes, linked by the coffin as reality or as metaphor (as itself or as a vehicle): the initial trigger, his grandfather at work, his grandfather's funeral (when the coffinmaker was himself coffined), the school where he failed to realise that those around him were coffins in whom their culture and language was dying, and the final realisation of himself as a coffin nails are being driven into, not yet dead but on the verge of death. This is to simplify or even mechanise the poem, as its imagery is highly organic, establishing connections between the different scenes in a way that escapes any single, unified correlation. School is a place 'san robh saoir na h-inntinn a' locradh' ('where the joiners of the mind were planing'), and the real remedy after the funeral 'còmhradh, is tea, is blàths' ('talk, and tea, and warmth') returns at the close to highlight ironically the uselessness of such remedies in a metaphorical predicament. Thomson thematises his own failure to see the connections, his failure to understand what was happening before it was too late, before the process was too advanced:

> cha do leugh mi na facail air a' phràis,
> cha do thuig mi gu robh mo chinneadh a' dol bàs.

> I did not read the words on the brass,
> I did not understand that my race was dying.

In the last four lines, he is able to bring together elements which have a tactile reality through their use earlier in the poem, now describing a situation which, were it to be presented in merely intellectual terms, would not affect us with the same sense of urgent tragedy. Taken on its own, a phrase such as 'a locradh a' chridhe' ('to plane the heart') could seem mere rhetoric. Revivified by passing through the child's sensibility, for which there are only vehicles and no tenors, it has an overwhelming power.

'Eadar Samhradh is Foghar' contains some of Thomson's most accessible, attractive and popular poems. 'An Rathad Cian', a sequence of 56 short lyrics which appeared only three years later, has claims to be regarded as his major achievement to date. It marks a distinct leap forward in technique, where the relationship between vehicle and tenor, which until now had to be resolved within the span of a single poem, is left to reverberate throughout the book, clarification of the balance between them being almost indefinitely postponed. Lewis is what the cycle is about, yet also the vehicle for a range of meanings often concerning the poet's emotional and intellectual attitudes to the island.

'An Rathad Cian' is very much a cycle about middle age, at once a celebration and a leavetaking, written at a time when Thomson was beginning to realise he would never return home as a resident. There is a slightly obsessional quality to the writing, evident in the religious imagery of the opening poem:

> O uilebheist mo dhomain,
> tha mi tighinn thugad le m' adhradh,
> le mo shùilean prabach, leis a' chainnt
> a dh' ionnsaich mi aig d' altair,
> leis na briathran
> a choisrig mi 'na do sheirbheis
>
> O monster of my world,
> I come to you in worship,
> with red-rimmed eyes, a language
> learnt at your altar,
> the words
> I consecrated to your service

The imagery is more pagan than Christian. Thomson's representation of Lewis jolts us because it goes beyond the conventional to exploit the differing strata of the island's history. The Bayble priests are still saying mass in Latin (2), an old woman at Brenish is a nun with a plaid in place of her veil (27). He sets 'cràbhadairean Eilean Beag Donn na Gaoithe' (22) ('the pious prattlers of the Little Brown Isle of the Wind' – and 'wind' has at least two senses) in a context of ideologies which moves beyond the Hebrides to Russia, Tibet and China, interestingly linking religious obsession and the internalisation of guilt to being on the receiving end of colonial exploitation (11). Thomson's attitude to Presbyterian extremism is detached and, if not tolerant, at least ironical. Lyric 11, entitled 'A' Cluich air Football le Fàidh' ('Playing Football with a Prophet') focuses on one of the lighter moments of a gathering for communion and preaches a broad ecumenism. Lyric 18, 'Am Bodach-Ròcais' ('Scarecrow') splendidly evokes the coming of nineteenth-century evangelical Christianity as the arrival of a scarecrow in the cèilidh-house, who blighted the telling of tales and singing of songs although

> thug e òran nuadh dhuinn,
> is sgeulachdan na h-àird an Ear,
> is sprùilleach de dh'fheallsanachd Geneva,
> is sguab e 'n teine à meadhon an làir
> 's chuir e 'n tùrlach loisgeach nar broilleachan.

> he gave us a new song,
> and tales from the Middle East,
> and fragments of the philosophy of Geneva,
> and he swept the fire from the centre of the floor
> and set a searing bonfire in our hearts.

Lyric 12 speaks of the Callanish stones and the children's sacrifices they may have witnessed, lyric 40 of the arrival of the Norsemen in islands where their homesickness at last abandoned them. This contextualisation offers a very different perspective on themes, one could almost say obsessions of contemporary Gaelic culture, which Thomson manages to treat in a new way: the guilt of the exile and *déraciné*, the terrible prospect that one's native culture may disappear permanently, longing for a childhood world with which all hope of continuity has been lost.

Different approaches help to construct an overall picture of what Lewis means, or may mean, for Thomson. Winning free by emigrating is a freedom almost equivalent to disorientation ('tha mi saor anns an speur,/'s mi tuiteam', 'I am free in the sky,/falling' (3)), and poems from the city (6, 35) have a wry humour, also directed at the returned exile who addresses his dog in Spanish (17). There are powerful tributes to Murdag Mhòr or 'Mucka' (41), the school cleaner, and to Cotriona Mhòr (38), women of a genera-tion to whom Thomson evidently feels a tremendous debt. The imagery has a dissonance, an incongruity, that one comes to recog-nise as typical of the cycle:

> leis a' ghliocas sin
> nach robh an eisimeil leabhraichean,
> leis an àbhachdas, leis a ghearradh-cainnt
> a bha a' leum à cridhe a' chinnidh
> mus deach a chèiseadh,
> mus deach a valve ùr ann
> a chumadh ag obair e anns an t-saoghal ùr.

> with that wisdom
> that flourished without books,
> with the fun, the cleverness-with-words
> that leapt from the heart of the race
> before it was encased,
> before it had the new valve in it
> to keep it going in the new world.

There are portraits of men, too (20, 23), as well as a crucial poem on the funeral of the poet's mother (34), which could also be read as a protest of loyalty to the place he comes from. Losing her and losing Lewis are linked phenomena, viewed with the same ambivalence, for she remains 'Glaiste ann an ùir mo bheatha' ('Locked in the earth of my life'), despite the swiftness of her death. In 49, disori-entation returns in terms that clearly have a multiple resonance:

> Chaidh mi mach á tarraing do phlanaid,
> chan eil mo cheum trom, ged is trom am meadhon-latha,
> air na ròidean eòlach sin,
> tha mi seòladh ann a fànas leam fhìn.

> I escaped the pull of your planet,
> my step is weightless, heavy though middle age may be,

on these well-known roads,
I float alone in space.

From the lines quoted, it will be clear how active Thomson's
imagery is: the rather simpler example and caption technique of
his earliest work is transformed, and the imagery now vehicles a
whole series of tenors, competing with one another in importance
and interrelatedness.

The rich, calm physicality which energises his memory emerges
clearly in 'Dh'fhairich mi thu le mo chasan' ('I got the feel of you
with my feet' (7)), where the contact of the child's bare soles with
the grass of Lewis is likened to his rubbing himself against his
mother in search of peace, and where the middle-aged adult refuses to wash the mud away from between the toes of the boy, to
shed the detritus, the sediment, of his early years in that place. An
elegiac resignation prevails as the cycle moves to its close. Thomson accepts the role of Lot's wife (53), commenting that 'mura
bitheadh an galar sin/bhiodh galar eil' ann' ('were it not that
disease/it would be another one' (49)). (His mother's disease?
The disease of his own obsession with Lewis, at once alienation
and inability entirely to let go?) The cycle becomes a handful of
peats thrown on the fire so as to keep the light going a little
longer (51), and, in an unforgettable image, Thomson rows away,
'Mo chùl ri mo cheann-uidhe/m'aghaidh ris na th'air mo chùl'
('My back turned to my destination,/facing what lies behind
me'), before the oars turn to bier-poles 'tulgadh 's a tulgadh
air bàrr cuimhne' ('rocking and plunging on the surface of memory' (55)).

An Rathad Cian does not richly orchestrate and exploit European
tradition in the fashion of *Dàin do Eimhir*, and its dynamic range is
more limited (from *pianissimo* to a *mezzo forte*, with a tendency to
fade into silence at the close of each lyric). Its dissonances and uncertainties, however, make it very much a work of the postmodern
age, with an originality for which Thomson has still to receive full
credit. His fourth collection, enigmatic and even more subdued,
though moved at times by a stern and savage political anger,
impresses one as a moment of regrouping and assimilation of the
advances made. It does not announce a new manner the way *An
Rathad Cian* so memorably did. Perhaps the poetry Thomson has
written since *Creachadh na Clàrsaich* will develop the seeds contained in it.

The relation of these poets' work to that produced in the rest of Scotland, not to say the rest of Britain, is problematic and still to be defined. Are they part of Scottish literature? And does that literature therefore embrace work in different languages? Does it make sense to talk of an entity such as British poetry, and if so, what place would they find in it? These are not merely cultural questions but political ones and questions of cultural politics, which the development of relations between Scotland and the rest of Britain may serve to unravel. Maybe the greatest tribute to the achievement of the two is the very lively state of Gaelic poetry today, exemplified in the work of poets in their twenties, thirties and forties, who have benefited no less from the intensity and European ambition of Sorley MacLean than from the delicate subjectivity and sustained experimentalism of Derick Thomson.

Notes

1. See D.S. Thomson, *The Gaelic Sources of Macpherson's Ossian* (Edinburgh and London 1952) and F. Stafford, *The Sublime Savage* (Edinburgh 1988).
2. See D.S. Thomson, *An Introduction to Gaelic Poetry*, 2nd edn, (Edinburgh 1990) and D.S. Thomson (ed.), *The Companion to Gaelic Scotland* (Oxford 1983).
3. There is an overview of the work of this generation, with an introductory critical essay, in D. MacAmhlaigh (ed.), *Nua-Bhàrdachd Ghàidhlig/Modern Scottish Gaelic Poems* (Edinburgh 1976). The younger poets are anthologised in C. Whyte (ed.), *An Aghaidh na Sìorraidheachd: Ochdnar Bhàrd Gàidhlig/In the Face of Eternity: Eight Gaelic Poets* (Edinburgh 1991). Both anthologies have English translations facing the text of the original.
4. For fuller biographical information, see J. Hendry 'Sorley MacLean: The Man and his Work', in R.J. Ross and J. Hendry (eds), *Sorley MacLean: Critical Essays* (Edinburgh 1986), pp. 9–38; A. Nicolson 'An Interview with Sorley Maclean', in *Studies in Scottish Literature* Vol. XIV, 1979, pp. 23–36; and the essay 'My Relationship with the Muse', in W. Gillies (ed.), *Ris a' Bhruthaich: The Criticism and Prose Writings of Sorley MacLean* (Stornoway 1985), pp. 6–14 (originally published in *Chapman* magazine in 1976).
5. *Ris a' Bhruthaich*, op. cit., p. 11.
6. *Studies in Scottish Literature*, op. cit., p. 28.
7. *Ris a' Bhruthaich*, op. cit., p. 12.
8. Acc. 6419, Box 38b.
9. Three poems, numbered 40, 46 and 47, appeared in *Lines Review*, Vol. 34, 1970.

10. *The Companion to Gaelic Scotland*, op. cit., p. 171.
11. C. Whyte 'The Cohesion of "Dàin do Eimhir"', in *Scottish Literary Journal*, Vol. 17, No. 1, May 1990, pp. 46–70.
12. In the discussion which follows, poems are quoted from the 1989 Carcanet volume, which gives the most generous selection from the 'Dàin to Eimhir', adding the original roman numerals at the end of each poem, and carries English translations by MacLean himself. 'Dàin' not in this collection are quoted from the 1943 text. In the interests of brevity, quotations are merely followed by a date (1943 or 1989) and page number.
13. I.C. Smith, 'A Poet's Response to Sorley MacLean', in *Sorley MacLean: Critical Essays*, op. cit., pp. 45–6.
14. E. Dwelly, *The Illustrated Gaelic–English Dictionary*, originally 1901–11 (Glasgow 1973), p. 412.
15. Those with no Gaelic have the choice of three versions in which to read the poem. MacLean's own (1989: 159–65), Crichton Smith's in *Poems to Eimhir* (Newcastle 1971), pp. 60–5, and a Scots version by Douglas Young in *A Braird of Thristles* (Glasgow 1947), pp. 34–7.
16. The four collections are reproduced (only *An Rathad Cian* in its entirety) in the bilingual publication, Ruaraidh MacThòmais/Derick Thomson, *Creachadh na Clàrsaich, Cruinneachadh de Bhàrdachd 1940–1980/Plundering the Harp, Collected Poems 1940–1980* (Edinburgh 1982). The book also includes 'Anns an Ospadal/In the Hospital' and a section of new poems 'Dàin às ùr'. Texts are quoted from this source, with numbers alone given for poems from the *An Rathad Cian* sequence. See also D. Thomson, 'A man reared in Lewis', in M. Lindsay (ed.), *As I Remember: Ten Scottish Authors Recall How Writing Began For Them* (London 1979), pp. 123–40; C. Whyte, 'Derick Thomson: Reluctant Symbolist', in *Chapman*, Vol. 38, Spring 1984, pp. 1–6; I.C. Smith, 'The poetry of Derick Thomson', in *Scottish Review*, Vol. 37, February/May 1985, pp. 24–30; and F. MacFhionnlaigh, 'Borbhan comair: ath-sgrùdadh air bàrdachd Ruaraidh MacThòmais', in *Gairm*, Vol. 124, An samhradh 1985, pp. 259–71.
17. C. Whyte, 'Thomson's *An Rathad Cian*', in *Lines Review*, Vol. 112, March 1990, p. 6.9

10

Edwin Morgan:
Messages and Transformations

Roderick Watson

Edwin Morgan is an extremely various poet. His work takes many different directions in subject-matter, style and perceived 'seriousness'. Having written sonnets about spaceships, and concrete poems about Shakespeare, he might seem to specialise in unlikely juxtapositions, not least in the witty title of one of his best known collections: *From Glasgow to Saturn*. Some readers have been positively disconcerted by the element of play in Morgan's work, and others by its sheer variety. The poet knows this:

> I think people like to have a thematic centre, like to know where they are. They feel more comfortable if they know what is central to any poet they're reading or thinking about. But I would like to defend what I do ... I have always had the sense that I should do different things, both in subject and in form ... The very fact that one person is responsible for all these poems means that there's some sort of unity about them.[1]

Morgan doesn't say what that 'unity' might be, and it's not my purpose to propose a seamless and final coherence either. Nevertheless, the theme of 'messages and transformations' does seem to relate to something central in this writer's imagination, and it runs through what is often taken to be the very different genres to be found in his poetry. The thesis is, then, that we can discern a central creative preoccupation at work in Morgan's 'love' poems, his 'Glasgow' poems, his 'concrete' poems, his 'science fiction' poems, his 'instamatic' poems and even in his sonnets. This preoccupation has to do with 'messages and changes': that is to say, with messages *of* change, and with messages that are themselves changed or changing.

Morgan's variations on the theme of message and change bring us to the roots of art itself, and in particular to that analysis of creativity which was redefined for our century by the Russian Formalists as 'defamiliarisation'. Morgan has declared an interest in Russian Formalism, and I believe that many of his poems offer a popular contemporary development of their desire to disturb our familiar modes of perception by foregrounding or subverting conventional verbal and phonic structures. Of course creative 'estrangement', transformation and even transfiguration have always been with us:

> Full fathom five thy father lies;
> Of his bones are coral made;
> Those are pearls that were his eyes:
> Nothing of him that doth fade,
> But doth suffer a sea-change
> Into something rich and strange.
> Sea-nymphs hourly ring his knell:
> [Ding-dong]
> Hark! now I hear them – ding-dong, bell.

Ariel's song is very much to do with the 'sea-change' of art. Its subject is a metamorphosis as old as Ovid and as disturbing as any described by Kafka. (Compare, for example, Morgan's own treatment of the transformation scene at the end of *The Winter's Tale* in 'Instructions to an Actor', in which he sees the boundaries between gender, causality and even life and death to be triumphantly and joyfully transgressed.) Such transformations lie at the heart of the creative act, and in *The Tempest* Alonso, King of Naples, has indeed been unforgettably changed. His eyes have become pearls and his bones coral, and these organic substances – the product of living creatures – are both 'alive' and 'dead'. More than this, their status as jewels or objects of rarity and worth make them analogues of continuing value, symbols of something rich and strange even beyond death. At one level, of course, Alonso's mortal fate has simply become immortal song – more lasting than bronze. But Ariel's lines are a still more subtle model of the artist's transforming relationship with truth and the material world, not least in their paradoxical dishonesty, for of course Ferdinand is misled, his father isn't dead, and Ariel has told him a fib!

Shakespeare's Renaissance images offer us something rare, decorative and valuable. Many modern poets have tried the sea-change another way – to show value in the unregarded debris of

our urban lives. This is what Yeats recognised towards the end of
his life, when he reassessed his preoccupation with mythic Celtic
heroes in 'The Circus Animals' Desertion':

> Those masterful images because complete,
> Grew in pure mind, but out of what began?
> A mound of refuse or the sweepings of a street,
> Old kettles, old bottles, and a broken can,
> Old iron, old bones, old rags, that raving slut
> Who keeps the till. Now that my ladder's gone,
> I must lie down where all the ladders start,
> In the foul rag-and-bone shop of the heart.

Morgan's engagement with the same insight was early stated in
'To Joan Eardley',[2] from his key 1968 collection *The Second Life*.
In Glasgow in the 1960s, the agents of mortality and sea-change
were indeed the pick and the bulldozer, for the city was under-
going massive urban redevelopment at the time. Indeed, urban
change – demolition and rebuilding – was one of the themes in
the title poem 'The Second Life', and although Morgan has since
qualified his early optimism about those civic projects, he still
values his sense that new things suddenly seemed to be possible
in Glasgow – 'The old coats are discarded./The old ice is loosed./
The old seeds are awake.' *The Second Life* was a key collection in
this regard – it marks Morgan's arrival as a mature writer, and it
makes several references to a new sense of personal change, sexual
identity and even rebirth, as experienced by a man in his forties.[3]
    In 'To Joan Eardley', however, it is art which brings life, with its
paradoxical power to make us experience an energy which
has 'vanished', or to fill an otherwise '*un*echoing close' with the
cries of departed children. Those 'rags and streaks' are both the
fabric of the painting itself – the literal canvas and pigment – and
the ramshackle lives depicted upon it. Thus Eardley, Morgan and
the reader too are 'mastered' by life transfigured into art, or perhaps by life itself, or by both. The ironic and ambiguous connotations of 'mastered' in the context of fine art are clear, especially
when we remind ourselves that Eardley's 'Glasgow children' paintings have their roots in a style of expressionist but compassionate
social realism.[4] Morgan's interest in the transforming power of art
(and in the challenge of its relationship to the workaday world) is
never solely theoretical or aesthetic.

out. Time passes and records are lost, or they become fragile and unclear. The very word 'generation' degenerates before our eyes, and the visual effect is like a long, narrow banner frayed and tattered at the end. 'Space Sonnet and Polyfilla', from *The New Divan*, offers two 14-line poems, the first of which has gaps in its text which the second one ('Polyfilla') supplies. This is done in such a way that if one were to lay the second on top of the first the gaps would be filled. The completed whole speaks of delirium on the surface of Mars, but with each poem standing on its own the effect is once again of a fragmented or static-ridden message.

'Unscrambling the Waves at Goonhilly' uses a 'printout' format to run through a scrambled set of morphemes to do with fish and stars. (The receiving dish at Goonhilly Down picked up the first satellite TV broadcast across the Atlantic in 1962.) Constructions such as 'telfish' 'sarphin' and 'doldine' gradually rearrange themselves until the poem concludes and confirms itself with 'dogfish' and 'telstar'. 'The Computer's First Christmas Card' runs through combined pairs of two syllable morphemes in similar fashion, all of them formed around 'happy', 'merry', 'jolly', 'berry', etc. But the machine falls at the last fence, for just as clarity seems about to be triumphantly achieved – it wishes us a 'M E R R Y C H R Y S A N T H E M U M'. In similar fashion, 'Spacepoem 3: Off Course' offers a series of adjectival phrases to do with free-fall conditions in a space capsule ('the golden flood'; 'the weightless seat'; 'the orbit wisecrack'; 'the hot spacesuit', etc.), and then permutates them into increasingly surreal or 'off-course' combinations. 'The Tower of Pisa' offers a more evolutionary approach to mutation by setting a complete line, and then following it with a structural and phonetic echo of itself for as long as the process can be sustained without losing some sort of semantic sequence: 'this is the cold base cut/this cold base is no cult/this is the cold old rock/this is the culled rock face...'

Mutation and permutation are the operating principles behind these and most of Morgan's 'concrete' or 'sound' poems, from *Gnomes* (1968) and *The Horseman's Word* (1970), to pieces such as 'The Hanging Gardens of Babylon' in *Themes on a Variation* (1988). Morgan particularly likes to use repeating lines (each one slightly changed from the one before) in order to liberate phrases, words, morphemes, and ultimately phonemes from their conventional semantic sequences. 'Opening the Cage' might even be taken to be an ironic comment on the freedoms offered by such (de)composition, for it consists of 14 different permutations of the 14 words in John Cage's line 'I have nothing to say and I am saying it and that is poetry'. The sheer 'literariness' of such a point of view would satisfy the most stringent Formalist.

Morgan's eye for accidental visual-semantic effects led him to write a sequence of nine poems called 'Interferences' in which key words suddenly suffer an unexpected deviation – as if altered by a typesetter's 'literal'. Yet the change is curiously effective, with a power of its own:

> and she took his hand
> placed it on her womb
> 'I am your virgian bride'
> with a smile worlds away

The poet found similar inspiration in two actual misprints in poems by Norman MacCaig. 'A Jar Revisited' is a highly intertextual poem which meditates on what 'fictitious spaec' might be (taken from a literal in MacCaig's poem 'Painting – The Blue Jar' which is itself an echo of Wallace Stevens); while 'Little Blue Blue' is a surreal exploration of 'blueness' prompted by the misprinted title of another MacCaig piece which should have been called 'Little Boy Blue'.

Morgan took this interest in 'found' material a stage further in his 'Newspoems (1965–1971)', subsequently published in *Themes on a Variation*. In these he set out to look for eye-catching phrases or graphic shapes embedded in the daily ephemera of newspapers or advertisements, constructing his lines by extracting irregularly shaped patches from the page. The ensuing cut-outs were photocopied and enlarged to give a set of 50 poems some of which are offered as 'Found Concrete' poems, or 'Unpublished Poems by Creeley'. Morgan recognises that such work springs from the concrete movement of the late 1950s, going back to Italian Futurism and Russian Constructivism in the first two decades of the century. In America Brion Gysin and William Burroughs also worked with 'found' material, but their use of fold-in and cut-up techniques was consciously random, whereas Morgan's method has been much more creatively selective. His aim is to 'dis-cover' alternative 'Newspoems' from within their original texts in much the same way as another kind of message ('i am thoth/i am ra') was found to be embedded in Christian scripture.

It is tempting to connect this fascination with buried, subverted or encoded messages with Morgan's sexuality, for his fine love poetry has contained veiled references to his own homosexuality for years, although he has not spoken about it in public until a recently published interview with Christopher Whyte.[7] In an interview with Robert Crawford from the same year (1988), Morgan responded with enthusiasm to the suggestion that episodes from his own life were indeed 'embedded' in his poetry, most notably in the long and difficult sequence 'The New Divan'.[8] He went on to say that after all 'poetry *is* a man's life' and not just a matter of linguistic metaphysics or readerly experience as certain critics would have it. Nevertheless, I would still point out that there are broader forces at work here, for structural destabilisation in the shape of change, fluidity and simultaneity has been central to modern experience after all, and to the modernist art which most appeals to Morgan. Having said that, it still may be no coincidence that gay writers such as Whitman, Hart Crane, Lorca and Genet have had so much of value to say about the instability of our times by way of celebration, turbulence, transmutation or subversion.

A more active engagement with metamorphosis is used for comic effect in 'The First Men on Mercury'. In this poem a newly landed Earthman addresses a Mercurian with the traditional banalities: 'We come in peace from the third planet./Would you take us to your leader?' The Mercurian replies in its own tongue '— Bawrr stretter! Bawr. Bawr. Stretterhawl?' But things start to mutate and to interpenetrate as the dialogue develops. By the end of the poem it is the Earthman who is speaking gibberish, while the Mercurian can now be read in clear, advising the humans to return, observing that 'nothing is ever the same', and promising that 'You'll remember Mercury'. (As a chemical element Mercury is notably fluid, of course; and as Hermes, messenger to the gods, he is equally quick, playful, ingenious and even unstrustworthy.)[9]

The same gradual linguistic interpenetration – a slow invasion of meaning – characterises a later poem, 'Shaker Shaken' from *The New Divan*. In this case the opening stanza is taken from a Shaker[10] sound poem of 1847. The poem reproduces this stanza no less than five times, but in each repetition Morgan gradually replaces the original nonsense phonemes with structurally matched English phrases and images of his own. The effect is as if the poem were slowly developing, like a clouded photographic print, into clarity and 'sense'. But the final 'message' is itself a surreal poem, full of languorous and haunting images: 'we mixed with the waters, the wily waters/till the tiger swam with us and loved us up' (*Poems*, p. 353).

'Shaker Shaken' demonstrates a unique development from nonsense straight into trans-sense, with a memorably musical effect when read aloud. It is one of Morgan's most successful achievements in the mixture of structural ('concrete') and aural ('sound') genres which he has made his own. In this respect the poet has acknowledged an affinity with Vladimir Mayakovsky and *his* relationship with the Russian Formalists and the poetic experimentalists of the 1920s. Mayakovsky's friend Alexei Kruchonykh advocated *zaum*, for example, as a 'transrational' sound poetry constructed from an imaginary language and hence universally 'intelligible'. Morgan has written about this movement and about these effects in the introduction to his own translation (into Scots) of Mayakovsky's poems.[11]

In both theory and practice, it is the Russian early modernists who have had most to say to Morgan about the nature and the role of metamorphosis in modern life and literature. Morgan acknowledged this in an essay called 'Heraclitus in Gorky Street: The Theme of Metamorphosis in the Poetry of Andrei Voznesensky', which first appeared in 1968, the same year as *The Second Life*. He has valuable insights to offer on Voznesensky, but it is clear that the essay tells us just as much about his own creative wellsprings. Thus it is the artist's 'desire', he observes, 'to "take over" and "make over" nature in metaphor or metamorphosis.'

> Yet we too are being taken over and made over. Values invade us as we them. A poet may have to bury and hide himself like a bulb, for anything to grow. Distraction is continuous, enormous, fascinating and frightening. Roles are adopted and discarded. The self shrinks, shudders, makes covert decisions, asks terrible questions. A poetry which wants meaningfully to interlock with this age must be prepared to be vulnerable, fluid, various, adventurous and searching.[12]

He goes on to discuss Voznesensky's 'Sketch of a Long Poem' from a 1966 collection. The passage he quotes begins with two lines which echo Heraclitus: 'Everything flows. Everything changes./ One thing passes into another'. Morgan comments:

Like the 'unechoing close' in 'To Joan Eardley', Morgan's poems are full of cries and voices, homing-in, haunting or confusing us. And, in true modernist fashion, the artistic transformations that fascinate him are likely to owe as much to found objects, accident or chance as they do to the 'modifying powers of the imagination' as Wordworth saw it.[5] Thus a broken 'Confectionery' shop-sign ('CONFECTIO') can be found to spell out the Latin word for something made – the very 'composition' that the painting of it has itself become. Further subtleties can be found in *conficio*, the root verb, which means to make or to prepare, but can also mean to wear out or to destroy.

Morgan is drawn to 'accidental' metamorphosis of this sort, and he often uses it to comic effect. The poem 'Boxers', in *From Glasgow to Saturn* (1973), seems to be a long-distance telephone call describing the most unlikely happenings. Have we got the message garbled because of background noise, crossed lines or bad reception? Or are these absurd events really happening? The original poem makes no typographical distinction between the two (and finally three) voices involved. The emphasis is mine in the following extract:

> —Who're you with? *Boxers.*—What?
> —*There's something going on here.*—Still can't hear you.
> —*Boxers.*—Look this is impossible, what did you say?
> —*There was that storm last night all night you know.*
> —What's that? What's torn?—*Wires down up-by.*
> *But that's not what you hear here.*—What? Where?
> —*Here. It's the sparring.*—What's that I keep hearing?
> —*I just told you. Boxers.*—There's one word
> you keep using.—*Did you hear that crash?*
> *That was the table, they're spry as cats.*
> *I gave them steaks and the end of the wine.*
> *Sleep? Not them. Up at each other*
> *the four of them like*—what's that you say?
> You said cats. What cats? Where are the cats?
> —*Cats? I'm not speaking about cats. Boxers.*
> —There it is, there's that word...[6]

'Boxers' is a comedy on the difficulties of communication without context. In the first instance the reader has to spot the fact that the poem is a telephone dialogue between Harry and an 'absent' Linda, whose identity is not revealed until the very last word of the poem, but who sets things rolling in the opening line with a question full of sexual suspicion, 'Who're you with?' From now on, like Linda at the other end of the line, we have to struggle to make sense of what a sound like 'boxers' might be taken to signify. And Morgan plays with us by hinting at a succession of possible readings.

First of all, they might be pugilists ('the sparring'); next, perhaps boxer dogs, four of whom have been fed on steak and the end of the wine. (This might explain the noise and the over-turned table.) It's part of the contextual and linguistic fun of the poem that the possibility of the boxers being dogs is conjured up in our minds (in a paradoxical act of Derridean *différance*) by an entirely figurative reference to them being spry as *cats*. But as the poem progresses they start to sing, 'two with belts and two with braces', and a later idiomatic reference to having to make coffee for 'those clowns' restores them to human form – only to bring the possibility of some sort of circus into the picture. By the end of the poem, when 'they're swinging on the pulley', they might be acrobats or monkeys, or even boxer shorts! The game is merci-fully cut short by a crossed line ('Overseas telegrams, can I help you?') and a last desperate cry from the man with the boxers – 'Linda!'

As if all this weren't enough, the poet confounds the contextual confusion of his lines by playing with homophones such as 'storm' and 's'torn', and 'hear/here'. He also foregrounds the oddness of 'up-by', (a common Scots English idiom meaning 'across the way' or 'along the road'), by placing it next to 'down' to make 'Wires down up–by' – a grammatical construction guaranteed to entertain linguists and baffle translators. Morgan returned to the exploration of dislocated contexts and off-centred dialogue with 'The Barrow. A Dialogue' in the same collection.

'Boxers' is typical of a significant number of poems in which the writer delights in the instabilities of language, the unreliability of different mediums of 'communication', and in the twists and turns by which we actively seek to 'read' a text. His concrete poem 'Message Clear' turns all these factors to moving effect. The poem is constructed from 55 lines arranged in a long column, not unlike a narrow computer printout. On closer examination each line can be seen to be merely a repetition of the final line – except that letters and whole sections of the text have been omitted or somehow erased on the page. Only the last line is given complete, when the message is finally delivered 'in clear', as it were. But the lines grow denser as the poem proceeds, gradually building up a sequence of different phrases, longer and more coherent, whose letters are always selected in their proper order from within the simple statement which is the final (and original) line.

The end effect is that the poem seems to assemble itself as it goes along, and the text requires an active effort of decipherment and (re)construction on our part. It is as if we are witnessing some interrupted or static-ridden communication, only gradually patching itself together. Perhaps the sender is having dificulty; perhaps the receiver is faulty; perhaps the atmospheric conditions are unpropitious.

If these fragmented lines are read aloud, it seems proper (and even unavoidable) to enact their difficulty with a halting delivery as we find ourselves groping for coherence and sequence. Such a choice is certainly supported by the meaning of the opening ten lines. Given *en clair* they are simple enough: 'am I/if/I am he/ hero/hurt/there and/here and/here/and/there'. But such a paraphrase underestimates what concrete poetry can do, for in Morgan's hands even individual isolated letters, and especially the spaces (or absences) between them, become an eloquent expressive force in their own right. As printed on the page, the effect is to convey a remarkably powerful sense of hesitation and even deep self–doubt:

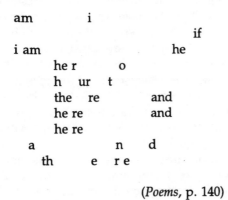

(*Poems*, p. 140)

Such doubt is all the more poignant when we come to recognise that the speaker is Christ, and that the last line of the poem (and the template for all preceding lines), is an otherwise jubilant and com-

manding line from the gospel of St John, namely: 'I am the resurrection and the life.'

The medium subverts the message with an element of expressive
and even interpretative uncertainty. Thus the words 'here' and
'there' are each repeated twice in the above passage, and yet they
are configured in a different way each time. Other lines are genuinely difficult to decipher, and open to more than one construction.
The following, for example, is quite obscure at first glance:

> am   e   res   ect
> am   e   res   ection

This can be decoded as 'a mere sect' and 'a mere section' (the next
lines give us 'of the life of men'). But the first line could equally
well – and more forcefully – be taken to read 'am ere sect', imply-
ing that the truth of Christ is always prior to sectarian dispute. Yet
such truth is not easy – conceptually or expressively. In conceptual
terms the poem's gospel message seems conventional enough, yet
the single line ('I am the resurrection and the life'), repeated and
deconstructed as it is, sustains rival texts embedded within it. Thus
Christ's familiar words also contain 'i am the surd', not to mention
'i am thoth/i am ra/i am the sun', and 'i am the erect one'.

Morgan's structural resurrection is a strenuous process. The act
of faith, and even Christ's faith in himself, is questioned by a poem
which has to drag itself into coherence with much resistance each
time we attempt to read it on the page. The same resistance is the
operating principle behind the 'Emergent Poems' which Morgan
published in 1967, each of which is developed in similar fashion
from a single line taken from some other source – Dante's *Inferno*,
for example, or the *Communist Manifesto*. The process is used again
in 'Seven Headlines' in *The Second Life*; while 'Levi-Strauss at the
Lie-Detector' and 'Wittgenstein on Egdon Heath', from *The New
Divan* (1977), *start* with the key line only to proceed towards an
ironic subversion of it by the end.

Morgan is fascinated by such 'messages' and by the act of their
transmission, and in his world communication is frequently liable
to syntactic interruption, structural decay, accidental mutation and
interference. A few examples will suffice: 'Archives' reverses the
slow build up of 'Message Clear', by reprinting the phrase 'generation upon' again and again down the page, in a column that slowly
'decays', as first the vowels and then most of the consonants drop

out. Time passes and records are lost, or they become fragile and unclear. The very word 'generation' degenerates before our eyes, and the visual effect is like a long, narrow banner frayed and tattered at the end. 'Space Sonnet and Polyfilla', from *The New Divan*, offers two 14-line poems, the first of which has gaps in its text which the second one ('Polyfilla') supplies. This is done in such a way that if one were to lay the second on top of the first the gaps would be filled. The completed whole speaks of delirium on the surface of Mars, but with each poem standing on its own the effect is once again of a fragmented or static-ridden message.

'Unscrambling the Waves at Goonhilly' uses a 'printout' format to run through a scrambled set of morphemes to do with fish and stars. (The receiving dish at Goonhilly Down picked up the first satellite TV broadcast across the Atlantic in 1962.) Constructions such as 'telfish' 'sarphin' and 'doldine' gradually rearrange themselves until the poem concludes and confirms itself with 'dogfish' and 'telstar'. 'The Computer's First Christmas Card' runs through combined pairs of two syllable morphemes in similar fashion, all of them formed around 'happy', 'merry', 'jolly', 'berry', etc. But the machine falls at the last fence, for just as clarity seems about to be triumphantly achieved – it wishes us a 'M E R R Y C H R Y S A N T H E M U M'. In similar fashion, 'Spacepoem 3: Off Course' offers a series of adjectival phrases to do with free-fall conditions in a space capsule ('the golden flood'; 'the weightless seat'; 'the orbit wisecrack'; 'the hot spacesuit', etc.), and then permutates them into increasingly surreal or 'off-course' combinations. 'The Tower of Pisa' offers a more evolutionary approach to mutation by setting a complete line, and then following it with a structural and phonetic echo of itself for as long as the process can be sustained without losing some sort of semantic sequence: 'this is the cold base cut/this cold base is no cult/this is the cold old rock/this is the culled rock face...'

Mutation and permutation are the operating principles behind these and most of Morgan's 'concrete' or 'sound' poems, from *Gnomes* (1968) and *The Horseman's Word* (1970), to pieces such as 'The Hanging Gardens of Babylon' in *Themes on a Variation* (1988). Morgan particularly likes to use repeating lines (each one slightly changed from the one before) in order to liberate phrases, words, morphemes, and ultimately phonemes from their conventional semantic sequences. 'Opening the Cage' might even be taken to be an ironic comment on the freedoms offered by such (de)composition, for it consists of 14 different permutations of the 14 words in John Cage's line 'I have nothing to say and I am saying it and that is poetry'. The sheer 'literariness' of such a point of view would satisfy the most stringent Formalist.

Morgan's eye for accidental visual-semantic effects led him to write a sequence of nine poems called 'Interferences' in which key words suddenly suffer an unexpected deviation – as if altered by a typesetter's 'literal'. Yet the change is curiously effective, with a power of its own:

> and she took his hand
> placed it on her womb
> 'I am your virgian bride'
> with a smile worlds away

The poet found similar inspiration in two actual misprints in poems by Norman MacCaig. 'A Jar Revisited' is a highly intertextual poem which meditates on what 'fictitious spaec' might be (taken from a literal in MacCaig's poem 'Painting – The Blue Jar' which is itself an echo of Wallace Stevens); while 'Little Blue Blue' is a surreal exploration of 'blueness' prompted by the misprinted title of another MacCaig piece which should have been called 'Little Boy Blue'.

Morgan took this interest in 'found' material a stage further in his 'Newspoems (1965–1971)', subsequently published in *Themes on a Variation*. In these he set out to look for eye-catching phrases or graphic shapes embedded in the daily ephemera of newspapers or advertisements, constructing his lines by extracting irregularly shaped patches from the page. The ensuing cut-outs were photocopied and enlarged to give a set of 50 poems some of which are offered as 'Found Concrete' poems, or 'Unpublished Poems by Creeley'. Morgan recognises that such work springs from the concrete movement of the late 1950s, going back to Italian Futurism and Russian Constructivism in the first two decades of the century. In America Brion Gysin and William Burroughs also worked with 'found' material, but their use of fold-in and cut-up techniques was consciously random, whereas Morgan's method has been much more creatively selective. His aim is to 'dis-cover' alternative 'Newspoems' from within their original texts in much the same way as another kind of message ('i am thoth/i am ra') was found to be embedded in Christian scripture.

It is tempting to connect this fascination with buried, subverted or encoded messages with Morgan's sexuality, for his fine love poetry has contained veiled references to his own homosexuality for years, although he has not spoken about it in public until a recently published interview with Christopher Whyte.[7] In an interview with Robert Crawford from the same year (1988), Morgan responded with enthusiasm to the suggestion that episodes from his own life were indeed 'embedded' in his poetry, most notably in the long and difficult sequence 'The New Divan'.[8] He went on to say that after all 'poetry *is* a man's life' and not just a matter of linguistic metaphysics or readerly experience as certain critics would have it. Nevertheless, I would still point out that there are broader forces at work here, for structural destabilisation in the shape of change, fluidity and simultaneity has been central to modern experience after all, and to the modernist art which most appeals to Morgan. Having said that, it still may be no coincidence that gay writers such as Whitman, Hart Crane, Lorca and Genet have had so much of value to say about the instability of our times by way of celebration, turbulence, transmutation or subversion.

A more active engagement with metamorphosis is used for comic effect in 'The First Men on Mercury'. In this poem a newly landed Earthman addresses a Mercurian with the traditional banalities: 'We come in peace from the third planet./Would you take us to your leader?' The Mercurian replies in its own tongue '— Bawrr stretter! Bawr. Bawr. Stretterhawl?' But things start to mutate and to interpenetrate as the dialogue develops. By the end of the poem it is the Earthman who is speaking gibberish, while the Mercurian can now be read in clear, advising the humans to return, observing that 'nothing is ever the same', and promising that 'You'll remember Mercury'. (As a chemical element Mercury is notably fluid, of course; and as Hermes, messenger to the gods, he is equally quick, playful, ingenious and even unstrustworthy.)[9]

The same gradual linguistic interpenetration – a slow invasion of meaning – characterises a later poem, 'Shaker Shaken' from *The New Divan*. In this case the opening stanza is taken from a Shaker[10] sound poem of 1847. The poem reproduces this stanza no less than five times, but in each repetition Morgan gradually replaces the original nonsense phonemes with structurally matched English phrases and images of his own. The effect is as if the poem were slowly developing, like a clouded photographic print, into clarity and 'sense'. But the final 'message' is itself a surreal poem, full of languorous and haunting images: 'we mixed with the waters, the wily waters/till the tiger swam with us and loved us up' (*Poems*, p. 353).

'Shaker Shaken' demonstrates a unique development from nonsense straight into trans-sense, with a memorably musical effect when read aloud. It is one of Morgan's most successful achievements in the mixture of structural ('concrete') and aural ('sound') genres which he has made his own. In this respect the poet has acknowledged an affinity with Vladimir Mayakovsky and *his* relationship with the Russian Formalists and the poetic experimentalists of the 1920s. Mayakovsky's friend Alexei Kruchonykh advocated *zaum*, for example, as a 'transrational' sound poetry constructed from an imaginary language and hence universally 'intelligible'. Morgan has written about this movement and about these effects in the introduction to his own translation (into Scots) of Mayakovsky's poems.[11]

In both theory and practice, it is the Russian early modernists who have had most to say to Morgan about the nature and the role of metamorphosis in modern life and literature. Morgan acknowledged this in an essay called 'Heraclitus in Gorky Street: The Theme of Metamorphosis in the Poetry of Andrei Voznesensky', which first appeared in 1968, the same year as *The Second Life*. He has valuable insights to offer on Voznesensky, but it is clear that the essay tells us just as much about his own creative wellsprings. Thus it is the artist's 'desire', he observes, 'to "take over" and "make over" nature in metaphor or metamorphosis.'

> Yet we too are being taken over and made over. Values invade us as we them. A poet may have to bury and hide himself like a bulb, for anything to grow. Distraction is continuous, enormous, fascinating and frightening. Roles are adopted and discarded. The self shrinks, shudders, makes covert decisions, asks terrible questions. A poetry which wants meaningfully to interlock with this age must be prepared to be vulnerable, fluid, various, adventurous and searching.[12]

He goes on to discuss Voznesensky's 'Sketch of a Long Poem' from a 1966 collection. The passage he quotes begins with two lines which echo Heraclitus: 'Everything flows. Everything changes./ One thing passes into another'. Morgan comments:

Voznesensky's concern with the theme of metamorphosis...has three aspects. It reflects the quite real blurring, overlap, interchange, and evolution of forms which fast travel, cinema and television, modern art and newspaper and advertising techniques have made a familiar part of experience... it tries to resurrect the creative imagination through a development of that linguistic *ostranenie* ('dislodgement', 'alienation', 'making strange') which the Russian formalist critics of the 1920s saw as central to poetic vigour. In the poem, instability and paradox are shown as features of modern life that are at least as unavoidable (if one is open to the signs of change) as dogma and explanation.[13]

When Morgan talks of being 'taken over and made over', of 'instability and paradox', with 'blurring, overlap, interchange and evolution of forms' via 'fast travel...television...and advertising techniques', he is unmistakably describing the world of his own poems. From *The Second Life* onwards, he has found fruitful topics, structures and metaphors in the fields of space travel, television, newsprint and video technology – all the aspects of contemporary life, in fact, which 'cultured' people and literary pundits in the British tradition are prone to despise. This is indeed a world of contemporary surfaces, and Morgan's engagement with it does sometimes run the danger of being no more than superficial. But at its best, his work has explored the unstable, seductive and shocking face of the new – simultaneously shallow and vertiginous – more fully than any other poet writing in English today.[14]

The ambiguous beauty and terror of the world's face are recognised in 'The Unspoken' in which Morgan remembers feelings of exaltation and shame at significant moments in his life – from the courage and camaraderie to be found even in the brutality of war (he served with the RAMC in the North African campaign), to the cost of technological hubris, to his own homosexuality, which certainly was 'unspoken' at the time. Indeed, I think Morgan's sexuality may well be relevant to the sense of risk which he associates with what I have called the 'vertiginous seduction' of the new. He has also acknowledged that considerable creative power can be gained from the kind of undeclared or redirected personal feeling which is what 'The Unspoken' is in part about:[15]

When the television newscaster said
the second sputnik was up, not empty

but with a small dog on board,
a half-ton treasury of life orbiting a thousand miles above the thin
    television masts and mists of November,
in clear space, heard, observed,
the faint far heartbeat sending back its message
steady and delicate,
and I was stirred by a deep confusion of feelings,
got up, stood with my back to the wall and my palms pressed hard
    against it, my arms held wide
as if I could spring from this earth –
not loath myself to go out that very day where Laika had shown
    man,
felt my cheeks burning with old Promethean warmth
rekindled – ready –
covered my face with my hands, seeing only an animal
strapped in a doomed capsule, but the future
was still there, cool and whole like the moon,
waiting to be taken, smiling even
as the dog's bones and the elaborate casket of aluminium
glow white and fuse in the arc of re-entry,
and I knew what I felt was history,
its thrilling brilliance came down,
came down,
comes down on us all, bringing pride and pity,
but it is not like that.

(From 'The Unspoken', Poems, pp. 164–5)

In these strangely tense lines the romance of the moment is simultaneously acknowledged and denied ('a doomed capsule' and 'but
it is not like that'), while the poet experiences an almost erotic
surrender to history descending on him, like Jove in a shower of
gold, or indeed like the small shooting star made by space capsule
and dog as they burn on returning to the atmosphere of our world.
This is not 'science fiction' poetry in any trivial sense; it is an
expression of complex feeling experienced and encoded by way
of what our technology sends to us.

Even Morgan's most overtly futuristic science fiction poems
contain shards of contemporary experience and pain – most notably 'From the Domain of Arnheim' and 'In Sobieski's Shield'. The
latter poem in particular develops his fascination with messages

and interferences as he postulates a kind of matter transmitter which will 'broadcast' humans across space to a distant galaxy ('Sobieski's Shield') and there reconstruct them like the corporeal equivalent of a television picture. But this molecular reassembly turns into a resurrection of a different kind, with unpredictable results. The narrator's wife has arrived with red hair, his son has only one nipple, and he himself has four digits on one hand and a strange heart-shaped sign, like a birthmark, on his arm. Once again the message has been slightly scrambled, as the narrator begins to experience anachronistic memories that are not his own. Indeed, the poem itself is slightly scrambled by being written entirely without punctuation for, as Morgan has the narrator say, 'I laugh to think they thought they could divide the indivisible':

is that a lake of mercury I can't quite see
through the smoke of the fumarole it's lifting now
but there's something puzzling even when I
my memory of mercury seems to be confused with
what is it blood no no mercury's not like blood
what then what is it I'm remembering or nearly
remembering look dad mercury he says and so it
must be but I see a shell-hole filled with rain-water
red in the sinking sun I know that landscape too
one of the wars far back twentieth century I think the
great war was it called France Flanders fields I remember
reading these craters waterlogged with rain mud blood
I can see a stark hand brandishing nothing through placid scum
in a lull of the guns what horror that the livid water
is not shaken by the pity of the tattoo on the dead arm
a heart still held above the despair of the mud
my god the heart on my arm my second birth mark
the rematerialization has picked up these fragments I have
a graft of war and ancient agony forgive
me my dead helper

(From 'In Sobieski's Shield', *Poems*, p. 182)

Here 'message' and 'transformation' have become the same 'indivisible' thing. In this context Morgan's comment on one of Voznesensky's poems relates directly to 'In Sobieski's Shield', and to the theme of transformation in his own work as a whole:

Man transforms both himself and his world, and what charac-
terizes Voznesensky is the joy he takes in envisaging the transformations; but there is nothing vapidly optimistic about the joy.
Wherever he goes and whatever he does, man takes with him his
handful of earth, his handful of pain, of history and remembrance.[16]

Of course the 'sea-change' of art has never had to depend on
technology or 'matter transmitters'. Prospero just called it his
'rough magic'. But Morgan's poetry is particularly drawn to the
instability and fluidity to be found among the surfaces of the
modern world, and not least to the curious marriage that
we make between our emotional lives and the technology around
us which does so much to reflect, transmit, distort and generate
new images of ourselves. In this respect – like Voznesensky – he
is almost always optimistic. Thus it is that the imaginative
kaleidoscope of his long poem 'London' ends with a moment's
peace and beauty as he imagines the detritus of everyday human
life, beating like messages indeed, against the aerials and receiving
dishes at the top of the GPO tower – a futuristic spike and the
centre of electronic communication among the old rooftops of
London:

> But still of life
> not in clean waves and airs
> the messages most heard
> come to the tower
> from asphalt and smoke
> and break in rings
> of strange accident
> and mortal change
> on the rain wet
> silver bars.
> It is its own
> telegrams,
> what mounts, what sighs,
> what says it is
> unaccountable
> as feelings moved
> by hair blown over
> an arm in the wind.

In its acts
it rests there.

('London. iii. The Post Office Tower', *Poems*, p. 242)

'London' transforms the usual cityscape. By defamiliarising or by 'dislodging' it from its everyday aspect, Morgan gives the world back to us as a message of 'strange accident and mortal change', and part of that 'mortality' has to do with sexual ambivalence. Life may not come in 'clean waves and airs', but it is always present, 'unaccountable' and worthy of tenderness. This insight was at the heart of his poem 'Glasgow Green' from *The Second Life*, also of 'Christmas Eve' in *From Glasgow to Saturn*, and it is the subject again, with darker shadows, of a much later piece called 'Dear man, my love goes out in waves' from *Themes on a Variation*.

The poet's most sustained engagement with the contemporary world of accident and mortal change is to be found in his 'Instamatic' poems and the later 'Video Box' pieces. At first sight the principle of the Instamatic poems would seem to be to *resist* transformation, and to offer instead the bleakest and most unmediated vision of what the front pages of our newspapers have to tell us about ourselves. Thus the Instamatic pieces are written as if they were descriptions of instant 'snapshots' taken to illustrate some event in the news. Curtly named by location and date alone, these imaginary pictures of real events adopt a deliberate detachment, reminiscent of the documentary tone to be found in other poems such as 'In the Snack-bar', 'Stobhill' and 'At Central Station'. The subject–matter is often grim, and the measured 'blankness' of Morgan's style mirrors our initial sense of shock perhaps, or our incomprehension as we struggle to make moral or emotional sense of what he is 'showing' us.

FALLIN STIRLINGSHIRE OCTOBER 1970

A man has thrown his collie into the dustbin
outside his house. The dog
has been struck by a car.
He glances briefly into the bin
before he bangs down the lid:
the animal is whimpering and scuffling, already
it has half sunk into the ashes.

> In the background the man's wife
> looks coldly from the window, approving.[17]

Some of the Instamatic pieces describe moments of splendour or beauty such as Stravinsky's funeral in 'VENICE APRIL 1971', or the mysterious peace of swans on a millpond in 'ELLINGHAM SUFFOLK JANUARY 1972'. But for the most part they respond to moments of bizarre violence or shock, or they reflect human pain and folly with a gleefully black irony. There is the businessman, for example, who committed suicide by using an electric drill on his head ('SHREWSBURY FEBRUARY 1971'), or the block of frozen urine, ejected from an airliner, that landed in someone's garden ('ADDLESTONE SURREY OCTOBER 1971').

At first sight the deliberately matter-of-fact delivery of these messages from the media seems to offer little hope for imaginative transformation. But Morgan's eye is not the disinterested camera that it pretends to be, and his snapshots soon develop a creative metamorphosis of their own. (In the last analysis, of course, language can never be separated from tone, and even in a strictly lexical sense it will always contain the seeds of figurative or symbolic reference. Nor is photography a neutral act, however 'objective' the lens itself might be said to be.) Sea-change is everywhere, and the documentary pretence of these poems only serves to reinforce its presence.

In 'BELFAST 5 MARCH 1971', for example, Morgan sets an archetypally Romantic image, a 'flag of flame', against the 'classic frieze' of a phalanx of soldiers and the 'classic silhouette' of a sniper shooting at them. Here the icons of official and unofficial coercion are paradoxically married. Caught in ritual conflict, they are both equally 'Classic' – frozen by the camera in just the way that Roman or Greek warriors have been frozen by the sculptor's art. Yet the cause and the light they fight under is one of Romantic disorder, for their 'flag of flame' is made by a burning bus, hanging 'big and full above the Falls Road.' With a 'thin moon squeezed into the top left corner' of this device, there is little room for gentler illumination, nor for mutability, nor a feminine presence, nor the virgin fierceness of Diana – however one chooses to interpret the moon in such a context. Instead, we are given the Classical discipline of warring men under the chaotic thrill of Romantic revolt. The result is chill stasis (for Morgan plays on three meanings of the word 'frieze') and burning rage:

BELFAST 5 MARCH 1971

A bus burns, its flag of flame
hangs big and full above the Falls Road.
A thin moon is squeezed into the top left corner.
In the mid-foreground you would think camp-fires
had been started: milk-bottle petrol-bombs
with their fierce brief scattered lights.
Light flickers on the vizors of a frieze
of charging soldiers, and on their rifles.
On a roof behind the burning bus
one sniper kneels in silhouette.
Your eye travels in rage from the classic frieze
to the classic silhouette.

(*Instamatic Poems*, p. 9)

The burning bus and the milk-bottles filled with petrol are plain facts. But they are equally effective symbols of a breakdown in public life and human sustenance. Morgan uses these, along with the would-be scholarly detachment of 'mid-foreground' and those conflicting images of Romanticism and Classicism, to make a moving comment on the political situation in Northern Ireland, not to mention the anguished paralysis felt both by those involved and those who can only stand and watch.

Despite its ostensible status as an unmediated documentary text, a typical front-page 'message' from the modern media has been powerfully transformed in 'BELFAST 5 MARCH 1971'. Other examples can be found in 'VENICE APRIL 1971' and especially in 'TRUK LAGOON UNDATED REPORTED FEBRUARY 1972' in which a literal sea-change has taken place as an American diver photographs human remains in a Japanese submarine, undisturbed since it sank at the end of the war:

> ... Bones shine
> half out
> of the silt, or
> from a glove of coral, or
> lie crossed like cuneiform
> too hard to decipher on tablets of sand.
> Nothing wavers, the Pacific
> is at peace...

(*Instamatic Poems*, p. 37)

A sailor's hand has grown 'a glove of coral', but the richness and strangeness of *this* scene is deceptive. Whatever it means is 'written' on tablets of 'sand' rather than stone, and even then it is 'too hard to decipher'. Except, perhaps, for a 'flake of rust' in the closing lines of the poem – symbol of time and decay – which hangs for a moment 'perfectly suspended/in the tomb of the victor's strobe.'

Fourteen years after the Instamatic poems, Morgan published *From the Video Box* (1986), a set of 27 poems subsequently collected in *Themes on a Variation*. The video box pieces explore another aspect of contemporary communication technology by purporting to describe short videotapes made by members of the public in an open booth – the 'video box'. Such facilities were indeed set up in Glasgow and other cities as a 'right to reply' which would enable viewers to comment for themselves on what they saw on television.

Here the dispassionate description of fixed 'Instamatic' images has been replaced by free verse monologues of a more dynamic and dramatic sort. This has allowed Morgan to explore the fears and failings of people whose loneliness is all too poignantly implied by their need to talk *to* television *about* television. There is comedy, too, with an appeal for a lost cat, a sexual bet and an impromptu political broadcast. More than this, however, the imaginary programmes described in these poems make their own comment on the utterly surreal nature of video reality, especially when satellite dishes can bring a *mélange* of all conceivable subjects and cultures to our screens. There is a 'world jigsaw final' which is won by a man who can assemble a picture of the mid-Atlantic 'photographed from a plane', and there's the broadcast which included a subliminal image of the creation of the universe, embedded in the middle of a costume drama about the Borgias.

Morgan's interest in the concept of 'interference' lies at the heart of many of these poems, for phrases from other sources keep invading both the programmes and the viewers' comments. These include lines from Shakespeare, Hogg's *Confessions of a Justified Sinner* and Shelley:

> ...I need a total mobile wraparound,
> a dome of many-coloured glass, in fact,
> that will not only stain the white radiance
> of any enternity there may be but
> oh, oh,

> positively dance round the
> threescore, fivescore wedded, embedded
> screens of talk, tale, trail and trial.[18]

There are other kinds of interference in the video box where we live – less intertextual and more disturbing. A mother thinks that she catches a glimpse of her long-drowned sailor son in a documentary programme: 'a blizzard of images,/a speeded mosaic of change/in the Americas'. She thought his body was buried in Gourock, but now she cannot be sure. The conceit allows Morgan to create a memorable metaphor:

> ... oh images, images,
> corners of the world seen
> out of the corner of an eye –
> subversive, subliminal –
> where have you taken my son
> into your terrible machine
> and why have you peeled off
> my grief like a decal
> and left me a nobody
> staring out to sea?

> ('17', *Themes*, pp. 128–9)

Another viewer is haunted by a vision of blue, like a glimpse of the sky, or 'the slow opening of an eye', which appeared to swirl out of a dirty grey screen ('... switching through a score of channels/in that disgruntled and half-idle mood I'm sure you know'), before being lost again. It is a curious reflection on the nature of many lives that his imagination has been caught by a video representation of the sky, or by a screen that seems to have been returning his own gaze. In either case he speaks his loneliness to the video box alone:

> Wherever I go I see that patch of blue.
> Did anyone else watch it? Is there happiness?
> Hope in things that come and go?
> Why should we not know?

> ('7', *Themes*, p. 120)

The physical principles of magnetic recording are explored in several 'scratch video' poems in which lines are repeated to imitate the aural back-tracking of dub and rap artists using vinyl records, or perhaps the visual mistracking of videotape. The result certainly serves to estrange the linear nature of language, and yet the technical trick itself – in another medium, of course – is familiar enough:

> ... but I want to be authentic
> on the black the black chesterfield just as the sun
> went down reddish outside and I could switch
> from the set to the sky and back sky and back
> and back back there was a squeezed sunset
> on the set between gables and a helicopter cut
> through the reddish screen like a black tin-opener
> while suddenly a crow flew suddenly a crow
> a crow flew through the real red outside what we
> call the real red and tore it silently it silently
> a scratch in air never to be solved scratch
> in air ...
>
> ('6', *Themes*, p. 119)

That 'scratch in air' is as vulnerable and fluid as ever Keats's name was when 'writ in water'. Such textual instability, and the halting expressive force of it, has everything to do with Morgan's interest in embedded meaning and 'blurring, overlap, interchange and evolution of forms'. In this poem he manages a dislodged and searching beauty which Voznesensky might well envy.

'It is grand and fine', Morgan writes in video box poem '23', 'to think/how the satellites in their places/are waiting to receive and give/it all. What shall we live to see?/White dish, listening eye:/if objects can be poetry,/you are.' Faced with the prospect of multiple channels of rubbish on our airwaves it is easy to call Morgan's optimism no more than naive. He recognises this in the poem, of course, but I am still not sure that he has fully addressed himself in a political sense to the disparities in our culture by which we expend so much intellectual power and incomparable technical skill on the dissemination of trivia – as if we built the great cathedrals only to sell souvenirs from them. On the other hand, Morgan has had the courage to confront and to affirm the 'shock of the new', and to incorporate specific aspects of it in the subject matter and the structure of his poetry. This has been relatively rare in twentieth-century verse, not least among modernists such as Eliot and Pound. Apart from MacDiarmid, I can think of few other poets writing in English this century who could stand with Morgan to justify Wordsworth's prophecy that:

> The remotest discoveries of the chemist, the botanist or the mineralogist will be as proper objects of the poet's art as any upon which it can be employed, if the time should ever come when these things shall be familiar... and palpably material to us as enjoying and suffering beings.[19]

In fact Morgan published an essay on just this issue in 1963.[20]

The world of electronic media is as 'new' to us as chemistry was to Wordsworth, and it is in this world that Morgan has found a particularly rich vein of poetic metaphor and expressive structure. In every collection since *The Second Life*, in poems which have been playful or dark, experimental or lyrical, Edwin Morgan has explored a most fruitful fascination with changing messages and messages of change. Here, too, he has found memorable codes for a poignant sense of his own emotional life as something half-hidden and half-spoken, embedded in the surface sensationalism of an everyday world which is so very packed with information, and just occasionally, if we are lucky, with private communication.

Notes

1. S. Andrews, 'Interview with Edwin Morgan', Stirling University student newspaper, *Brig*, October 1977.
2. Joan Eardley (1921–63), Scottish painter well known for her powerful seascapes and her studies of Glasgow slum children. Morgan owns the painting he describes.
3. See 'The Second Life', 'The Sheaf', 'The Unspoken', 'The Witness', 'Glasgow Green'.
4. Eardley's paintings in this vein reflect the work of Glasgow photographer Oscar Marzaroli who took many studies of people and street scenes in the Gorbals.
5. See Morgan's comment on 'randomness' in an interview with R. Crawford in C. Whyte (ed.), *Edwin Morgan. Nothing Not Giving Messages* (Edinburgh: Polygon, 1990), p. 135.

6. F. Morgan, *Poems of Thirty Years* (Manchester: Carcanet, 1982), p. 263. Hereafter referred to in the text as *Poems* with the page reference.
7. Interview with C. Whyte, 'Power from things not declared', in Whyte (ed.), op. cit., especially pp. 183–7.
8. See 'Nothing is not giving messages', ibid., pp. 132, 143. See also Morgan's comments to C. Whyte, ibid., pp. 147–8.
9. Compare Morgan's comments to Crawford on 'mercurial' qualities, ibid., pp. 127–8.
10. The Shakers were an American fundamentalist religious sect given to 'speaking in tongues'.
11. E. Morgan, 'Introduction to *Wi the haill Voice*', *Essays* (Manchester: Carcanet, 1974), pp. 62–4. See also his comments on Gomringer's hopes for concrete verse as 'a universal common language', in 'Into the Constellation: Some Thoughts on the Origin and Nature of Concrete Poetry', ibid., pp. 27–34.
12. *Scottish International*, Vol. 1, January 1968; *Essays*, op. cit., pp. 71–2. Note that there are recurring images of hidden identity and buried growth among many of the poems in *The Second Life*.
13. *Essays*, op. cit., p. 73.
14. Compare his comment that 'my own main interest as a poet is bound to centre on Scotland, and from there it will veer towards Voznesensky or Weores or Creeley or Gomringer just as often as to any poet living in the south of England.' E. Morgan, 'The State of Poetry – A Symposium', *The Review*, Vol. 29–30, Spring–Summer 1972, p. 54.
15. See interview with C. Whyte, 'Power from things not declared', in Whyte (ed.), *Nothing*, op. cit., pp. 160–2. Consider also the extraordinary leap into a sermon-like style at the end of 'Glasgow Green'.
16. 'Heraclitus in Gorky Street', *Essays*, op. cit., pp. 76–7.
17. E. Morgan, *Instamatic Poems* (London: Ian McKelvie, 1972), p. 21. Hereafter referred to in the text as *Instamatic Poems* with the page reference.
18. E. Morgan, '20', *Themes on a Variation* (Manchester: Carcanet, 1988), p. 131. Hereafter referred to as *Themes* with the page reference.
19. W. Wordsworth, Preface to the second edition of *Lyrical Ballads* (1800–02).
20. E. Morgan, 'A Glimpse of Petavius', *Essays*, op. cit., pp. 3–15.

11

'Half of My Seeing':
the English Poetry of
Iain Crichton Smith

Colin Milton

Born in Glasgow in 1928 but brought up on the largely Gaelic-speaking island of Lewis in the Outer Hebrides, Iain Crichton Smith belongs to an ancient and distinctive indigenous culture which has attracted surprisingly little attention from the custodians of the mainstream, purportedly 'British' cultural tradition. He himself has commented wryly on how selective even the current enthusiasm for 'minorities' and 'multi-cultural perspectives' is:

> In an age where women are seen as a race different from men, when children too are enfranchised, the inhabitants of parts of this island are not seen at all, as if they did not exist...[1]

Much of Smith's English poetry is concerned with making his own culture and its values and traditions visible to the non-Gael. Reading it we become more aware of the cultural diversity of these islands, and of the importance of maintaining it against the forces of uniformity and standardisation which sometimes seem irresistible. As Smith says, 'a Britain that is without the Welsh and Gaelic communities... would be, at the very least, less interesting than it is at the moment' (TH, pp. 58–9). We become conscious too, through the contact his work allows us with one of our oldest native traditions, of the irony involved when defenders of 'our' way of life invoke an allegedly unitary national culture, menaced by imported alien traditions and in need of defence against them. It was the ideological forebears of such people, Scots as well as English, who attempted, often successfully, to reduce linguistic and cultural diversity in these islands.

The circumstances in which Smith grew up and which shaped his values and his art are radically different from those which have formed most of us. Products of what we are encouraged to think of as a more developed, more sophisticated and in every sense richer kind of society, we might suppose that what he has to say is marginal – or irrelevant – to our lives and concerns. But it is precisely because Smith arrived in our modern urban, technological society from a different kind of community that he can see its character more clearly than we can and, through his poetry, help *us* to see it clearly. Till he left the island at the age of 17 to go to university in Aberdeen, Smith lived in a scattered rural community which depended largely on fishing and crofting, which lacked many of the material comforts which we take for granted and which was, by urban and mainland standards, poor – Smith has described the life as 'hard' but 'not bitter'. It was the kind of community which we are inclined to see as archaic, as belonging to a past stage of social and economic development now left behind. Smith challenges that assumption in the long reflective, autobiographical piece which gives its title to his recent collection of essays, *Towards the Human*, emphasising that the community he grew up in was not 'a dull, peasant-like society but rather...a highly intelligent one which sees quite clearly what is going on around it' (*TH*, p. 45). The point has to be stressed because we tend to assume that when two cultural traditions clash, it is the weaker, the less developed, which is defeated and marginalised.

'It is the Old' (*CP*, p. 53), from Smith's 1965 volume *The Law and the Grace*, is an ironic comment on this belief; the poem uses the family relationships between younger and older generations as a metaphor for the relations between indigenous populations and invaders who establish themselves as a social and political elite, turning the 'natives' into a menial class. The poem starts with an unexpected reversal of the roles we expect to be played by members of different generations belonging to the same household:

It is the old
who get up in the night to build the fires for the young.
Their gods, they imagine, are disposed
in a leisurely lazy heaven and prolong
a Norman sleep against the cold
and bitter frost.

In this household, 'It is the old/who get up in the night' to serve the young, who remain lazily in bed. We are struck, shocked even, by this idea, but it quickly becomes clear that we are not meant to take it literally: the relationships involved are political rather than domestic. The relationship between the older and the younger generations in the poem implies that it is not necessarily the 'mature' culture which is the dominant one. The 'young' are in charge here; but while youthfulness is associated with vigour and energy, it also has connotations of immaturity and ignorance. The poem challenges that unexamined social Darwinism which, even in this post-imperial era, tends to lead us to assume that political dominance is proof of a higher degree of civilisation. Through his use of the terms 'Saxon' and 'Norman', Smith invokes the Norman Conquest – the most familiar instance in English history of a foreign aristocracy assuming control by force of arms and reducing the native population to a subordinate role. The instance is deliberately chosen to remind English-speaking readers that *their* forebears were once a subordinate population in their own native country (a reminder which is reinforced by the reference to the Romans in the final section of the poem). Smith's aim is to help members of the dominant culture to understand the feelings of those like the Scottish Gaels and the Welsh in a culture dominated by English-speakers.

But the relationship between the two traditions as it is presented through that of two generations is more complex than we might expect. The 'old', for example, do not feel resentful at serving the 'young'. If they feel their power, they also feel 'idolatry of their poise'. The new elite, on the other hand, who might be expected to feel secure, feel in their dreams 'dread' of the abyss of unformed darkness, which the fire 'steadily' lights. Troubled by subconscious doubts about their ability to maintain control, they long in sleep for even more powerful figures whom *they* could serve, so lightening their responsibilities. The final image of the poem is difficult to interpret, but seems to suggest that habits of mutual dependence evolve in such circumstances which are hard to shake off. The Norman 'young' cannot face the world until it has been ordered, organised in a way symbolised by the lighting of the fire; the Saxon 'old', in their turn, idolise the 'poise' of the sleepers, not guessing at the insecurity which troubles their sleep.

This admiration of the 'old' for the 'young' is the result of what Smith calls, in relation to the Gaels, 'interior colonisation'; more

dangerous than enforced obedience, it involves an *inner* acceptance
of the 'superiority' of the ruling culture, and a desire to serve it. It is
this that made the Highlander 'proud of being a soldier', and still
leads many people in the Highlands 'to believe that the English
world must be presumed to be more important than [their] own
since it deals with "real" issues' (*TH*, p. 38). Using the terms
'Saxon' and 'Norman' associates the situation with the distant
past, but the poem is also relevant to the present relationship
between Highland culture and the mainstream culture of the British Isles, and serves as a reminder that 'colonisation' is something
that has happened in the recent as well as the remote past, and at
home as well as abroad. And it is a reminder that though we think
of the colonial era in British history as over, colonialism of a kind
decisively shaped the history of parts of this country, with effects
which continue to be felt.

Smith's account of growing up on Lewis makes it clear that if the
community was less complex socially and less developed techno-
logically than that on the mainland, it was nevertheless more
advanced in human terms (Smith has said that two of the things
he remembers best about coming to the Scottish mainland are
seeing his first train and his first beggar). As the human deficien-
cies of our own society become more apparent, we may come to see
Gaelic culture in a new way – 'it is possible that far from the world
of the islands being archaic it is a model of a world which might
return, though not exactly in the same form' (*TH*, p. 34). We may
need to learn from island society because the social structures
typical of developed, industrialised societies largely fail to offer
us the sense of community which we need, leaving us to bear a
burden of 'alienation and abstraction' which is the main (though
not the only) cause of the problems endemic in the modern city:

> Deeper than any disease that society suffers from is the sense of
> the lost home, the ugliness of the new one, the destruction of
> community. And when we see the policemen advancing in Brix-
> ton with their shields, is it not against those who have not found
> a home to replace the one which they have lost?
>
> (*TH*, pp. 54–5)

It was because he came from a different kind of community that
the juxtaposition of train and beggar made such a powerful impression on Smith, and he returns again and again in his poetry to

the contradictions created by modern social conditions. In our individualistic, materialistic society, 'contradictions must always abound... and associated with these contradictions are innumerable guilts' (*TH*, p. 48). These 'innumerable guilts' are the subject of many of Smith's poems. Sometimes, as in 'For My Mother' (Fulton, p. 4), the guilt is personal. The speaker is angered by the fact that, in our society, those who do hard, unpleasant work are usually less well rewarded than those whose lives are more comfortable:

> You have so little and that I have more
> (money, I mean) angers me. As well,
> I had four years at University where
> I sipped good learning under a proud bell.
>
> You on the other hand were gutting herring
> (at seventeen) on a hard Lowestoft quay
> with glassy hands...

He contrasts his own relative prosperity with his mother's poverty, remembering particularly how he 'sipped good learning' at university – an image suggesting gentlemanly ease and enjoyment – while his mother was far from home 'on a hard Lowestoft quay', gutting herring in the dark and cold before the dawn. The image of sipping wine is ironically echoed in the picture of his mother's 'glassy hands to which dark blood would cling' ('glassy' points back to 'sipping' and suggests the pallor and brittle sensation produced by extreme cold). Here anger at the unfairness of society, the lack of any just relation between human worth or need and reward, and guilt at belonging to the privileged minority is intensified by the personal connection between the people involved. In an effort to assuage it, the speaker links his mother's work with his own:

> The herring in my hand,
> bloody and gutted, would be far more solid
> than this more slippery verse...

The implication is that, despite appearances, it is the poet's work which is more difficult – therefore he deserves his superior social position – and society is not, after all, as unjust as it appears. But, as Smith remarks in connection with this particular poem in 'Towards the Human', 'Metaphor can sometimes be used to conceal insoluble contradictions in life... In the end society lives and works outside the metaphor.' Here the metaphorical 'resolution' does not banish the injustice (or the guilt), and the poem ends with a melancholy epiphany which is a recognition rather than an evasion of the truth: instead of Joyce's dove-like girl on the sea-shore we see 'the lonely figure in the doubtful light/with the bloody knife beside the murmuring sea/waiting for the morning to come right.' The hardship and impoverishment of the mother's life is condensed into a single, powerful image, which captures an entire life arrested eternally at the moment before any kind of fulfilment even begins to be possible. Much of the poignancy of the image comes from the fact that the woman is clearly aware of her situation, but cannot do anything to change it – any more than she can make the dawn come more quickly.

In 'To My Mother', which centres on personal guilt, the emphasis is on a single unfortunate individual; in 'In Your Long Skirts' (Fulton, p. 168) the mother is just one figure among many in a photograph of a large group of fisher-girls found after her death among her effects. The emphasis here is on just how many people were (and are) denied the chance to live fully in an unequal, class-based society. The second stanza presents the years from the beginning of the century till now as dominated by deaths: of the girls in the picture, of the victims of two world wars, of the fish in the sea:

> The girls are all dead and you are dead.
> Two wars have happened since and many fish
> have bred and died in the cold North Sea.

Girls, wars and shoals of fish are linked in order to suggest the way in which ordinary people have often been treated as if they are not fully human and individual, but as a 'work-force' or as cannon-fodder. So, in the last stanza, the speaker – who has already noticed the evidence of a life of hardship and sacrifice in the girl's 'severe lips' – sees from the photograph the toll exacted by their hard lives on the whole group. And they are gazing at a sun which is somewhere off the edge of the photograph, emblem of a joy which can only be longed for and felt bitterly as out of reach:

> In that brown picture you all look very old
> for twenty-year-old girls and you're all gazing
> to a sun that's off the edge and is made of salt.

By drawing attention to the way in which metaphor can seem to offer a resolution for a painful contrast, 'To My Mother' makes us suspicious of what Smith calls 'the glitteringly aesthetic' (*TH*, p. 48). Ironically, the warning comes from a writer who, in his early work, is perhaps the most fertile coiner of striking images among contemporary Scottish poets, a master of the 'glitteringly aesthetic' – of those 'sweet and random strains/which leaped obliquely from the vast unknown/concordances and mirrors'. The description comes from Smith's 1974 sequence, 'Orpheus' (*CP*, pp. 165–70), which uses the story of the Greek musician's visit to the underworld to explore the way in which his own poetry has changed and the reasons for that change. In his encounter with the god, Orpheus refers to the difficulty the poet faces in creating art amid the contradictions and injustices of contemporary society (with 'the beggar seated in alternate gloom/and negligent neon'). In the last section of the poem, Orpheus returns reluctantly to the upper world as the god has commanded, and finds himself among the city slums, far away from the 'changing grace' of the natural world he had celebrated before. The people of the slums are unglamorous, but they have, nevertheless, a kind of generosity and nobility which Orpheus comes to see as a human equivalent of the natural beauties he has responded to before:

> the sordid
> stout valiant women so unkempt, sublime,
> laughed gaily in the morning without hatred.
>
> So that beyond the shade he saw the human
> invincible spirit playing, as one goes
> through utter darkness and sees water gleaming
> and all the way one walks through resonant meadows

In the final lines, the poet's work has changed and his distance from 'ordinary people' has diminished; like them he is involved in the struggle to live creatively in difficult circumstances. Both are described as if they were soldiers in the trenches of some bitter war:

> What he had lost was the secret and random strains
> which leaped obliquely from the vast unknown
> concordances and mirrors but the gains,
> though seeming sparer, were more dearly won

> as less in mobile warfare than in trench
> one sees the fates closer as they loom
> in their thorny helmets whether German, French,
> or some quite other nation; and they seem
> so like his own – the cheeks, the teeth, the chins –
> that he must love them not as in a dream
> but on this smoky field of green and orange.

The image is a reminder of the situation of the poets of the Great War who, like Orpheus, found the language and conventions they had inherited inadequate to the realities they were experiencing and, like him, had to sound a 'graver, heavier tone' in order to express them.

If contemporary society, class-divided, unequal, competitive and materialistic, is a 'war' for many of those who live in it, the appeal of the kind of secure and supportive Highland community Smith grew up in is easy to understand. But though it might offer clues as to how we could live together more successfully, that community already belongs to the past and cannot be recreated. And anyhow, despite its virtues, the society of the islands was 'never an Eden from which we were thrust by the sword of economics' (*TH*, p. 18) – the islands ceased to be isolated and self-sufficient and began to be drawn into the economic and political life of the larger society a long time ago. 'Of the Uncomplicated Dairy Girl' (*CP*, pp. 136–7) captures the moment in the history of the island when its relationship to the larger society brought benefits without compromising its cultural integrity. The poem begins with a vivid picture of the dairy girl:

> in gown that's striped in blue and red
> feeding the hens in a windy spring
> by the green wooden shed
> where shade after quick shade
> endlessly shuttles ...

In contrast to the austere picture often presented of Lewis and its people in Smith's poems, this is lively and colourful – the girl's gown 'striped in blue and red' is seen against the green of the shed, 'against the blue,/against the stone'. It is also a surprising picture – we do not expect a girl at work in an isolated rural community to be wearing a 'gown' in fashionable stripes. The dress is in fact an import, its bold colours contrasting with the subdued tones and patterns of local cloth which are derived from the colours of the island landscape. The dress is a fashionable, urban creation, brought home 'from the fishing' like the other exotic imports which the girl has brought back in the 'large yellow chest' – the confectionery, the 'hats,/silken things and coats'. Single, without responsibilities, the girl can afford to buy the things she likes, and she has obviously not yet succumbed to the pervasive puritanism of the island. Wearing the gown to feed the hens suggests that she has put it on not to make an impression on anyone, but just for the sheer pleasure of it. But the things brought back from the fishing are a reminder that, remote though it is, the island has direct (and growing) links with the wider world. The relationship with that world suggested by the chest full of novelties and luxuries is a positive one, and it is at this point that the speaker would like to 'freeze' the relationship between island and mainland, just before the islanders are drawn into the violence and destruction which are also a feature of that wider world. He asks the girl to 'stay there...for a moment' at the point 'just before your straight-backed brother/marched off to save the King'. Elites, rulers are 'saved', maintained in power by ordinary men. And the brother's departure is the first step in an involvement which has lead in this century to the creation of a NATO base at Stornaway and the stationing of nuclear submarines in the Holy Loch. The birthplace of Scottish Gaelic culture has become, as Smith records bitterly in 'Light to Light' (Fulton, pp. 103–5), a site for weapons of mass destruction designed to defend the society which has nearly destroyed that culture, truly a situation, as he says, of 'multiple ironies'.

The contrasts between island values as Smith remembers them and the priorities of the mainland shed light on the nature and origins of those 'contradictions' which show the unfairness and injustice of contemporary society. One important element is class; Smith remarks that while mainland society is 'concerned with class to a great extent...the community in which I grew up was a classless one.' Distinctions were made between people of course, but standards of worth were intrinsic, not extrinsic:

> The criterion in such a society always was, not what class does such or such a man belong to, but can he do the things that are necessary? is he a good fisherman, is he a good teacher...?
>
> (TH, p. 44)

And on the island it was not the most materially successful who
were most respected:

> It was not the richest individual that the islanders always looked
> up to, rather they looked up to the schoolmaster and the minis-
> ter, whose success is not to be measured in money.
>
> (*TH*, p. 19)

True to this tradition, Smith rejects class or money as a way of
judging people. We are all unique and therefore uniquely valuable
individuals, a conviction most firmly and straightforwardly expressed in 'None is the Same as Another' (*CP*, pp. 219–20) which
uses the traditional image of humanity as a group of pilgrims. It is
a poem with none of the complexity, indirectness or irony of
Smith's early manner; in its use of repetition and apostrophe, and
its looseness of form, it resembles some of Lawrence's later poems.
Since the poem is an affirmation of kinship – as well as a recognition of differences – its accessibility is entirely appropriate. The
poem begins with an assertion – 'None is the same as another/O
none is the same'. The emphasis is necessary because we live in a
complex society in which people are nearly always thought of as
belonging to a group or a class. The uniqueness of every human
being is a matter for both sorrow and joy: sorrow is mentioned first
since life is short and death final and 'never again will you see/that
one, once gone'. But human uniqueness also means that if we can
see beyond the superficial resemblances ('many will look the
same/but all are different') life is a series of encounters with the
new and surprising. However, the endless variety of human individuality is not the only source of new experience: the poem
suggests that the individual himself (or herself) has no stable,
consistent, predictable identity:

> ...many will look the same
> but all are different
> and their ideas fly to them
> on accidental winds
> perching awhile in their minds
> from different valleys.

Ideas have an autonomy of their own, and come and go as they
will; the self is not a single, coherent, evolving entity, but a succes-

sion of temporary 'identities' whose constitution at any particular moment is determined by forces operating outside the control of the individual. In those circumstances we cannot hope to 'understand' the other – but we can touch in another way:

> Stranger, I take your hand,
> O changing stranger.

It is the class divisions in contemporary society, combined with its prevailing individualism and materialism, which are responsible for the injustices described in 'To My Mother', 'In Your Long Skirts', the final sections of 'Orpheus' and many other poems. Social circumstances force many people into narrow and unsatisfying lives and prevent them from developing fully. Smith's anger at this is increased by his rejection of the idea of an afterlife in which the injustices of this life will be redressed. In an early poem, 'Dying Is Not Setting Out' (*CP*, p. 22), he rejects the idea that dying is a journey to our real home – it is an end, not a new beginning. The poem draws its imagery from the powerful (and in the Highlands all-too-familiar) longing of the exile for home, and links going to heaven with going home to the islands. The connection suggests why certain kinds of religious belief, with their promise of eternal life, have appealed so strongly in the Highlands:

> Dying is not like sailing
> by the shores of Mull or
> Tiree. Sheet's less willing
> and twists in thick air.

In reality 'We sail into the grave/of the more than dead' because death itself is only the beginning of a process of change which returns us to the elements of which we are made. Identity is not preserved beyond death – the fundamental fact of death, as of life, is change, process, a fact very movingly communicated in the opening of one of Smith's finest long poems, his elegy on the schoolmaster, and Gaelic and Classical scholar, John Maclean (*CP*, pp. 120–4). Described by Ian Alexander as a 'noble elegy',[2] this poem has, in both senses of the phrase, a grave eloquence. But, like many elegies, it reflects on death in the interests of living.

The opening section celebrates the rightness of the rhythms of nature, moving through the sequence of growth, blooming and fading; the metre is largely regular, the rhymes perfect, form reflecting sense. Natural life moves to its 'own unwilled and accurate funeral/without interrogation.' The implicit contrast is with human beings who are not compelled to follow nature's patterns, but who have free will and who can (and characteristically do) 'interrogate' things. The opening lines suggest that our choice is whether to follow, albeit consciously and deliberately, the natural sequence of growth, flowering and death or not; much of the vocabulary here, although used at this point in relation to things in the natural world, points forward to the scholarly virtues which the dead man exemplified: the roses fall 'perfectly', the woods appear 'exact' and 'married to the fact', their 'funeral' is 'accurate'. Such 'exactitude' is achieved in the natural world without effort; in human life it is a difficult accomplishment – achieved through 'interrogation' (the word is chosen deliberately to suggest a strenuous, prolonged questioning). The answer to the question in the second line ('How shall we live?') is hinted at here in the suggestion that we need to find some human equivalent of the unforced 'rightness' or natural things, but that for us, the life in which we express our natures to the fullest is not one in which we simply follow our impulses; 'fruition' for human beings implies an examined rather than an unexamined life. It reminds us too of the much older question which would have been central to the tradition in which Smith grew up – 'What must we do to be saved?' That question sees this life as the prelude to and probation for a 'real' life which is to come – what we do here and now is (only) a means to an end. The poem challenges this belief, opening with a question which suggests that this life is an end in itself: an end because it comes to an end, with nothing beyond. Leaving the graveyard, the mourners leave the body:

> It remains,
> the body in the casket, and begins
> its simple mineral weathering.

The neuter pronoun emphasises that the dead are only physical entities, weathered through time like features of the landscape to barer, simpler forms. The living, in contrast, return 'to [their] complex human burning', the verb suggesting both life-as-process in which we are consumed, used up, and also the pain of sentient existence, filled as it is with loss and mourning. But what we mourn is now a thing, no longer human or personal, which 'changes as we mourn it', but changes in a different way from our human changing. The irrationality (in one sense) of mourning is suggested here, but also its inevitability. Our rituals, customs ring round the flux of our 'burning', imparting shape and structure; in an image reminiscent of that at the end of Larkin's 'Churchgoing', Smith gives rituals like the funeral a human rather than a supernatural significance – 'routines/wed and enring us as we move and burn'.

The poem concludes, in its seventh section, with the wish that this death be accepted as a proper end to a productive existence and not seen as an 'abdication'. Here the fertility of autumn is emphasised in a way reminiscent of Keats's great ode – sweetness and fading are bound inextricably together, one cannot happen without the other. The shape of the coffin and the shape of the cells in the honeycomb are the same:

> ... let the humming of the latest bee
> bear its last honey home. Beneath this sky
>
> the hexagonal coffin crowned with flowers restores
> your body to the earth from which we came
> to build our shaking ladders.

We come from and return to the earth, from dust to dust, but not in the sense of the burial service: here the view of man is an evolutionary one – we have developed, precariously, over millions of years from the simple elements of the natural world and return to them in death. But the shaking ladder, an appropriately rickety image for even the most durable cultures man has created and a recurrent one in Smith's poetry, is transmuted, in a fine tribute to Maclean, becoming a deep-rooted tree, its leaves the scholarly volumes 'that burn and glow,/the foliage of your autumn'. The image picks up earlier references to the flame-like colours of autumn leaves, but also serves as a kind of metaphorical realisation of the speaker's wish to accord the dead man an appropriately Roman funeral – his volumes constitute a kind of permanent, unconsumable pyre, a lasting memorial – and though the man is dead, his body subject to the 'simple mineral weathering', his books have the attributes of the living: they 'burn and glow'.

Apart from celebrating scholarly integrity, love of literature and committed teaching, the poem also celebrates a man who, while firmly rooted in his own culture, indeed *because* firmly rooted there, was a scholar and interpreter of another one distant in time and space. The final image brings the reflections in the sequence full circle, suggesting that here at least was a man whose being did reflect, even in death, the rightness of the natural cycle.

Smith writes movingly about Maclean and what he represented not only because he admired him as an individual, but because he grew up in a society where the teacher and the minister were the most respected men in the community. In their work both men were concerned with non-material values and both served the community as a whole. Both have 'cliù', an untranslatable concept roughly equivalent to 'reputation' but with no exact English equivalent – a fact which underlines the intimate connections between language and cultural patterns and also the radical differences in ethos which can exist in geographically adjacent cultures.

Having grown up with this idea of what achievement means, Smith is magnificently scathing about the way in which mainstream society celebrates ephemeral reputations: 'What's your success to me who read the great dead...?' he asks contemptuously of the citizens of bourgeois land. This poem, like 'The Law and The Grace' (*CP*, pp. 72–3), is an indignantly eloquent response to a sense of being judged and found wanting. Here the pressure comes from the marginal place of the serious writer in contemporary society and the low esteem in which serious literary talent is held, while in the earlier poem it came from a religious tradition hostile to the arts. But the situation in both poems is essentially the same: Smith has escaped from a restrictive religious ethos only to find that contemporary society offers not limitless freedom and opportunity, but different kinds of limitations. However, the speaker of each poem does not so much claim success as deny the relevance of the criteria which have been used to define his 'failure' – the committed artist is his own sternest critic, judging his unfinished work against his inspiration, and against the achievements of his great predecessors. He does not, Smith says, 'need a democracy to judge it'.[3] The poem ends with an audacious image drawn from modern technology: the great poets of the past are seen as satellites in stationary orbit over the speaker, constantly observing him:

> What are your chains to me,
> your baubles and your rings? That scrutiny

turns on me always. Over terraced houses
these satellites rotate and in deep spaces

the hammered poetry of Dante turns
light as a wristwatch, bright as a thousand suns.

Conventional rewards are no more than baubles and rings, even
if in a materialistic society they are often pursued with a ruthless
disregard for others. In 'Dear Hamlet' (CP, pp. 109–10) the speaker
sympathises with the prince, victim of Claudius's ambitions, com-
forting him by describing his uncle as 'the small and simple man'.
The description is sharply at odds with our usual notion of Claudius as a devious, powerful and ruthless schemer and, as if antici-
pating our surprise, the speaker assures us he means what he says
– 'yes he was simple' – and goes on to explain this challenging
assertion. Claudius was 'small and simple' because he was satisfied
with the most banal material and social rewards:

So little sufficed him, just a queen, a kingdom,
salutes from guards, dinners with dinner-jackets,
bow-ties and crowns, the glitter of cut glass,
the colour of poison.

If the island community offers support and validation, it is also a
place where most of the life of the individual is visible to everyone
around in a way that it is not in more complex social structures;
concealment, disguise, role-playing, if not impossible are more
difficult here, where the self is 'reflected back from the others by
plain mirror and not by the exaggerating or attenuating mirrors
that one sees in fairs' (TH, p. 14). This makes living in the island
community a real challenge; if it is supportive, the community, a
plain mirror for the self, is also candid. In some ways (though not
in others), 'It is far more difficult to live in a small community than
to live in a city':

The community is the ultimate critic, not easily taken in, with its
own system of checks and balances. To be part of the community
is in a sense to belong to everyone, to be open, vulnerable, to be
willing to abide by its judgement.

(TH, p. 24)

For some, this is too difficult to face; leaving the community, becoming an exile, is often an economic necessity, but it is also the resort of those who 'wished to avoid facing up to the responsibilities of the island world' (*TH*, p. 24). And the human advantages of the traditional community have also to be balanced against the constraints it places on individual development. It tends to be 'conservative and hostile to change' with 'a dislike of the person who individualises himself too much, who tries to succeed for his own purposes' (*TH*, p. 26). The free exploration of the possibilities of the self is not possible in such an environment, where change and development are frowned on. Smith recollects how when he left to go to university he felt 'paradoxically free since I could walk down Union Street without anyone knowing who I was. Invisibility became important to me ... To leave the community was to emerge into one's individuality, into a future which seemed free and unjudged, though of course it was not' (*TH*, p. 27). The contemporary, urban society which Smith entered at that moment is a place which allows, and even encourages, the individual to experiment with different identities; in it, people are constantly acting parts and playing roles, and the playhouse, the circus, the fair with its exaggerating and attenuating mirrors, are recurrent images for the contemporary urban world in Smith's poetry. In the society outside the island, where people are often judged by the social class they belong to, or by purely material standards of success, we are surrounded by distorting mirrors, like Hamlet in Smith's poem of that name (*CP*, pp. 66–7). The prince sees 'distorted images/of himself in court dress, with big bulbous eyes'. In this 'place of mirrors', where 'Images bounce madly against reason/as, in a spoon, wide pictures, fat and jolly', the tragic prince sees himself reflected back as a comic figure. The poem is essentially an image of contemporary life rather than a comment on Shakespeare's play, and the identification of the central figure with Shakespeare's hero is wry comment on the individualism of modern society and the position of the artist or intellectual in it.

The image of the fairground Hall of Mirrors recurs in 'The Notebooks of Robinson Crusoe' (Fulton, pp. 207–12), a fine reflective sequence combining verse and prose. Like Hamlet (and Orpheus), Crusoe is an isolated figure, but as a castaway he is *physically* separated from his society as well, suggesting a more fundamental rejection of it. The sequence traces a process of self-examination and struggle through which Crusoe (like Orpheus) is

finally reconciled to returning to a society which he sees as false
and corrupt:

When they rescue me I shall return to the perfumed vaudevilles
and machinery, to the music halls of the fat sopranos...I shall
see the advertisements which illuminate the sky...I shall leave
my bare island, simple as poison, to enter the equally poisonous
world of Tiberius, where there are echoes and reflections, a Hall of
Mirrors in which my face like all faces swells like a jester's in
a world without sense.

In an earlier section Crusoe had prayed to be saved from his
arrogance, and he has clearly made some progress. If he still sees
his society as a grotesque and tawdry spectacle – as one kind of
'poison', the equivalent of the Capri of Tiberius, the degenerate end
of an empire – he has come to recognise that the 'island' of his
aloof isolation from that society is also a kind of poison; it is the
home of the snake, of solipsism and of fruitless questionings.

Ironically, the two most respected figures in the kind of community Smith grew up in, the teacher and the minister, also represent
institutions and forces which have often been distorting and destructive. When a national system of education was created in
Scotland in 1872, Gaelic was ignored altogether, and though its
position had improved by the time Smith went to school in the
1930s, English was the medium of most of his schooling and his
early literary education was largely in English literature. The area
he grew up in was a Gaelic-speaking one, but the emphasis in
school was on the English language and English culture, not on
the language and culture native to the region. Smith himself experienced the 'interior colonisation' he refers to in connection with
the history of the Highlands, developing a youthful contempt for
his own tradition and a conviction that 'foreign writing [was] more
serious, more interesting, more advanced'.

Smith describes the effect of this anglicising education in telling
images: the school is 'the castle which by its language dominates
the surrounding countryside' (*TH*, p. 42). The kind of cultural
domination it represents is an even more serious threat to the
indigenous tradition than military occupation. Gaelic speakers
may come to feel their own language and culture as inferior, or at
least less important, because English is so central to their educational success and their prospects in the wider, post-school world.

Consequently, the very survival of Gaelic is threatened and if the language were to be lost, a whole way of looking at the world and a distinctive system of values would vanish. In Smith's memorable phrase, if Gaelic dies the islander will 'live in a disappearing landscape' (*TH*, p. 20). The dominance of English and the vulnerability of his own language means that for the the Gaelic-speaking writer 'To write in English becomes a form of treachery and this is so because Gaelic does not have the strength to allow explorations into language beyond itself' (*TH*, p. 21).

But the writer who also has the English language and literary tradition available to him is aware of the greater scope for the individual expression they offer him, just as the wider society outside the island offers greater (if still limited) scope for other forms of individual expression. The island community puts limits on individual expression in art, just as it does in other ways. The poetry which appeals in such a community, for instance, will not be the expression of a unique individual consciousness, but will 'emerge from that society itself and will incorporate its values' (*TH*, p. 46). In both creative and performing arts, the emphasis will be on sincerity and accessibility rather than on virtuosity and complexity; in fact 'such a society is not interested in the aesthetic in any real sense', but in 'genuine feeling related to [its] own concerns' (*TH*, p. 45).

'Poem of Lewis' (*CP*, p. 2), which has often been seen as describing 'the people's disregard for poetry',[4] illustrates this. The opening of the poem is often taken to imply that the islanders reject all poetry; in fact it says, rather, that they only 'have time for' one particular kind. The poem begins with a conditional:

> Here they have no time for the fine graces
> of poetry, unless it freely grows
> in deep compulsion, like water in the well,
> woven into the texture of the soil
> in a strong pattern.

In a hard-working community like this, people literally 'have no time' for complex forms of art, since they lack the leisure needed to appreciate them; they also have no time for such art in the metaphorical sense – they are contemptuous of it, since they cannot see its point or purpose. So the disregard is for certain kinds of poetry – as 'unless' in the second line suggests, what *is* accepted is a poetry which is intimately linked with, and grows immediately out of, the landscape itself. Here Smith is thinking of the importance of the depiction and celebration of place in Gaelic poetry (as in the work of Duncan Ban McIntyre – the subject of a fine celebratory poem) and the use of poetry to record and comment on the life of the community. This is the poetry which, in an image derived from tweed and tartan (themselves expressions of communal creativity), is 'woven into the texture of the soil in a strong pattern'. The metaphor continues and develops, taking the process a stage beyond the weaving which describes the Gaelic tradition; the 'material' (Smith plays on literal and literary senses) could be (but in this society is not) 'tailored' – the thought could be shaped and finished off using rhyme, something which is not employed in Gaelic poetry. The result would be an intellectual, reflective kind of poem like Smith's. Such poems demand for their creation and appreciation both a greater sense of an independent self than is found, or would be tolerated, in the traditional community and an individual intellectual life instead of an accepted, inherited framework of beliefs.

'A Young Highland Girl Studying Poetry' (*CP*, pp. 30–1) describes the kind of encounter between these contrasting cultures which a compulsory anglicised education creates. The poem opens with a dramatic image: the frown of concentration on the girl's brow as she tries to understand the poem is described in terms of a plough cutting into the earth. It is an image natural to a rural community – and one which establishes that the girl belongs to such a community – but if also conveys a discomfort which is rooted in lack of aptitude for this kind of activity. In some ways the poem qualifies the confident affirmation of the value of poetry made in 'Poem of Lewis'. There poetry was linked with grace, and the islanders' indifference to it, or to its more intellectual forms, seen as a failing. Here, in contrast, the suggestion is that many ordinary, unliterary people have no aptitude for, or spontaneous interest in, complex literature: it is something imposed on them by modern schooling, and takes no account of their own interests, aptitudes or traditions. The second stanza suggests that traditional skills and knowledge, passed down through the community rather than through schooling, are more important than studying literature. Women's tasks in traditional communities were concerned with vital things like healing and bringing to birth. Living from the earth, they did not become 'soulful'; native roses themselves, they had no need of the 'foreign rose', which is not, as John Blackburn suggests, Calvinism[5] – it would be difficult to think of a less appropriate symbol for that creed – but the 'rose' of high art. It is 'foreign' not because it comes, like Calvin's ideas, from another country, but in the metaphorical sense that it is alien to the lives and sensibilities of people like this. Those who belong to a rooted community, in harmony with the rhythms of nature, have no need of intellectual poetry, which, it is implied, is compensatory, created out of some sort of unease, some disharmony with circumstances. It is a 'complex solace' created by (and for) troubled minds and dealing in 'abstractions of the grave' (rather than the concrete life-centred practicalities of the traditional culture).

But Edwin Morgan is wrong to suggest that the poem implies that ordinary members of traditional communities 'have no access to the world of art'.[6] They may have no need for the complex literary solace of poetry, 'Yet they were dancers', the poem tells us – that is, creators of and participants in a strongly physical form of artistic expression. The poem also contrasts previous generations of women and girls, who had at most a brief formal schooling, with the present generation, who have to stay at school much longer. However, the contrast is not between the uneducated and the educated, but between two kinds of education – one a matter of custom and tradition, centering on the concerns of the community, the other established by the state to produce a citizenry and workforce for the modern world. In 'Towards the Human', Smith mentions the way in which, in Derick Thomson's poetry, 'wisdom is contrasted with the knowledge derived from books, for this kind of wisdom is that which is reflected back from the character of the community'; 'Books on the other hand are the works of individuals produced for individuals' (*TH*, p. 33). In formal education, traditional knowledge and skills are largely ignored and personal interests and aptitudes subordinated to a curriculum designed by politicians and educationists.

The poem celebrates the traditional knowledge and skills of the women of the community, suggesting that they are more central to human experience than poetry could ever be. It suggests too that their acquisition, and the harmony with life that they bring, is actually threatened by modern education. Using the image of a growing plant again, the speaker suggests that those like the girl should be allowed to 'grow along' the valleys bearing the fruit of 'bright children'. The imagery links such people, who are the majority but not therefore any less valuable, with the earth itself:

they 'walk' on it rather than 'fly' above it like the poet; they are rooted in it (but are not earth-bound); they blossom (though as the native rather than the foreign rose) and bear fruit. A few individuals, on the other hand, fly above the earth, experiencing the 'bitter winds' and learning from them 'a kind' (but not the only kind) of 'praise'.

The conflict between Gaelic and English is a serious enough one for Smith to contend with, but the religious tradition he was brought up in created an even more fundamental tension in his work. Smith grew up in a strongly Calvinist atmosphere, in which art was regarded with suspicion. John Blackburn reports Smith recalling 'how once his mother found him making little wooden hens in the shed behind the house. She asked him, "Why do you make wooden hens when the Lord has made real ones?"'[7] The implication is that the artist is both usurping God's creative role *and* mocking his creation. Art is merely an inferior (and useless) copy of the real. And in doing something 'useless', the artist is ignoring his God-given duty to work productively. Smith rejected Free Presbyterian theology while still a young man, but his inner struggle with this powerful system of beliefs is one of the major sources of energy in his work:

> On the island I had felt religion as a restrictive force, but the fact that I have wrestled so much with a particular kind of religion in my poetry suggests that I do not have the ease to discuss it freely. Religion has been internalised in my personality whether I like it or not and its dilemmas will always be with me.
>
> (*TH*, p. 27)

In the circumstances it is hardly surprising that much of Smith's poetry, among it some of his most difficult and interesting work, should be devoted to exploring the origins, processes and purposes of art with a scepticism which grows out of his religious background. Even in the early part of his career, when his virtuosity as a creator of images is most evident (and the image most central to his poetic effects), he expresses doubts about figurative expression. 'To My Mother' demystifies one of the central devices of poetry – the assertion that apparently dissimilar things are 'really' similar – by showing how it can be a strategy for evading intellectual or emotional difficulties. Metaphor (and its relatives) can be consolatory, false solutions on the imaginative level for problems which are painful or intractable in real life, rather than – as traditionally claimed – ways of communicating 'deeper' harmonies and interrelations which underlie 'apparent' contradictions. In his comments on 'To My Mother' in 'Towards the Human', Smith emphasises how common this strategy is in poetry: faced with painful personal, social or political situations, the poet finds (and offers) spurious comfort through a purely metaphorical resolution of the problem. The consequence is that we turn away from the difficult business of confronting and resolving the conflicts, contradictions and injustices around us.

Smith's suspicion of figurative language is not confined to its use in poems which deal with social issues, nor is it a consequence of his own increasing commitment as a poet to exploring such issues. One of the most ambitious of his early works is a long meditative poem in 15 sections entitled 'Deer on the High Hills', which appeared in 1961 (the same year as his third collection, *Thistles and Roses*). The problem of representation in poetry, and in art in general, is at the centre of this subtle, complex and difficult work. Early in the poem, in Section IV (*CP*, p. 37), Smith tells us what sort of poem *not* to expect: 'Forget... these poems/that solved all or took all for myth'. This poem will be of a different kind, tentative and exploratory – a characteristic which leads Morgan to describe it (mistakenly) as 'somewhat confused'.[8] The poem explores – and exemplifies – the way in which human beings appropriate the natural world intellectually as well as exploiting it materially. We project our personalities, our needs, interests and desires, out onto the world around us, so that what we call 'nature' is largely a reflection of our own being, rather than a separate world with its own alien life and laws, the 'wild systems' which, in section VII, the deer are said to inhabit. But, through its references to Gaelic culture and traditions, the poem also reminds us that different societies have looked at nature in very different ways – that the dominant Anglo-Saxon tradition represents only *a* way of looking at the world and not *the* way. As the poem develops, Smith increasingly questions, and attempts to free himself from, the human-centred view he sees as characteristic of 'nature' poetry in the English tradition, and he struggles to forge a poetic language which grows out of his own native landscape ('You must build from the rain and stones') and which could serve as a medium for a poetry which would be as much at home there as a 'stylish deer on the high hills'.

Such a poetry already exists in the Gaelic tradition in the work of
poets like Duncan Ban McIntyre (section VI, *CP*, p. 38), whose
poems express the life of the deer, rather than imposing human
meanings on them: 'They evolved their own music which became/
his music'. 'Nevertheless he shot them also' because despite McIntyre's understanding of the life of the deer, or rather *because* of that
understanding, he did not sentimentalise them – he recognised
their separate, alien mode of being and did not attribute human
feelings to them or to the rest of the natural world. So the stricken
deer did not 'kneel in a pool of tears. . . /And the rocks did not
weep with sentiment./They were simply there: the deer were simply there'. In the opening sections of Smith's poem, however, the
deer, driven down from the hills to the roadside by the harsh
weather, are certainly not 'simply there'. In fact they are described
entirely in human terms: they look and move like French aristocrats dispossessed by the Revolution; in approaching human hab-
itation they 'beg like fallen nobles for their bread'.

Here, the patterns of human history are projected onto the natural world – but ironically man is the 'peasant' and the deer the
'aristocrats.' In breaking free from the control of their instincts and
separating themselves from the natural order, human beings have
set up a new tyranny in which they claim the right to exploit the
natural world for their own ends – for food, for emotional sustenance, or for images and symbols. At the same time they have
become divided against themselves and lost the 'aristocratic'
wholeness of being possessed by other living things. It is not only
the deer which are humanised; the whole cycle of life and the
seasons is used as a metaphor for social and political conditions –
rigid, hierarchical societies are 'frozen' until a political 'spring'
brings a 'thaw'. We might expect Smith to sympathise with the
peasant rather than the aristocrat, but the final lines of II (*CP*, p. 36)
present men very much from the viewpoint of the deer, as clumsy,
crude and destructive beings, 'tyrants who cannot dance but throw
stones/tyrants who can crack the finest bones:/tyrants who do not
wear but break most ancient crowns'. In the section which follows
it is even clearer that the speaker identifies with the deer, aloof and
fastidious, rather than with his fellow 'peasants', but the kinship he
claims has less to do with an understanding of deer than with a
familiar kind of flattering self-image which artists and intellectuals
have often adopted since the Romantic period to make their marginalisation seem like a privilege.

The two final sections of the poem raise the possibility that we may be trapped in an anthropomorphic world, unable to break free from our human-centred perspective and establish contact with any other form of being. Section XIII (*CP*, pp. 44–5), with its references to the conventional meanings given to things belonging to the natural world in the literary tradition, reminds us of how much that tradition, and indeed the language itself which we have inherited, carries a heavy and largely unnoticed figurative freight:

> Do colours cry? Does 'black' weep for the dead?
> Is green so bridal, and is red the flag
> and eloquent elegy of a martial sleep?

The penultimate stanza alludes slyly to one of the greatest of MacDiarmid's vernacular lyrics, asking 'And are rainbows the/ wistful smiles upon a dying face?'[9]

If our way of seeing and talking about the world inevitably expresses our own self-absorption as human beings and our human sense of being central to the natural world, then the deer are forever beyond our understanding with a 'language' and therefore a world of their own. The possibility leaves the poet frustrated and despairing, with 'desolate lips', feeling that he cannot draw on the traditional symbols in his poetry without distorting the natural world he wants to describe. However, the tone of the final section is different, expressing a stoical determination to face what is, for the poet, the most challenging fact about the world – that nothing is (or is even *like*) anything else and so – a bleak realisation for the poet – 'There is no metaphor'. The only legitimate way of describing things is to use the adjective derived from their names:

> The rain is rainy and the sun is sunny.
> The flower is flowery and the sea is salty.
> My friend himself, himself my enemy.

This is all that can be said. In one sense this is trivial and empty, in another it is the expression of an important truth which literary language (and language in general) often obscures – that everything is absolutely unique and imcomparable.

The poem goes on to suggest that we unconsciously humanise the things around us to relieve our isolation ('being lonely I would speak with any/stone or tree or river'). Losing that sense of contact with nature seems as desperate as drowning – 'This distance deadly! God or goddess throw me/a rope to landscape'. The reference to 'the wine of Italy' which follows indicates that Smith is thinking of those classical gods and goddesses who represent personified natural forces. But the poem ends with two memorable stanzas which affirm the need to hold to the insights which have been so strenuously worked for:

> The deer step out in isolated air.
> Forgive the distance, let the transient journey
> on delicate ice not tragical appear
>
> for stars are starry and the rain is rainy,
> the stone is stony, and the sun is sunny,
> the deer step out in isolated air.

The problems raised in 'Deer in the High Hills' are central to Smith's thinking about poetry – and have continued to preoccupy him. Their implications go beyond poetry however, beyond literature and even beyond natural language in general; they extend to any of the 'languages' used in representating the world. 'Sketch', from his 1975 collection *The Notebooks of Robinson Crusoe* (Fulton, p. 203), is about the way in which, in painting, the artist's inner conflicts are often projected onto his subject. Looking at a Van Gogh landscape, the speaker reflects on the way in which the things portrayed in the painting serve as vehicles for the expression of the painter's inner torment; they are not allowed to be themselves, but are twisted and distorted by his inner turmoil. The 'failed missionary' paints his failure in the 'squashed church' of the opening line, which 'leans out of the thunderstorm' in an oddly human way. His disappointment in love has also made him suffer intensely (he 'burns in his studio' so that the paints 'reek' of him) and his suffering inevitably shapes the world he sees and paints.

The poem conveys the disturbing power of Van Gogh's work very well, but at the same time criticises it by implication, because in it things are not allowed 'to be themselves'. The relation between the artist and the world he/she portrays is a constant preoccupation in Smith's work; he returns again and again to the question of whether every representation is coloured by human concerns and feelings or whether the artist can apprehend and convey the otherness, even alienness of the world around. The poem expresses a hope that a time will come when the things around us are not appropriated for human use ('When shall the flowers be allowed to be themselves, when shall the vase/again contain them?'). It suggests too that the projection of human frustration and torment onto the world around which characterises Van Gogh's work is not just an idiosyncrasy of this particular artist but is perhaps characteristic of modern art and reflects the conditions of modern society. There is also the possibility of a different kind of art, one which would, in Conrad's phrase, 'render the highest kind of justice to the visible world' – but that could only come into being if we were to create a society in which Van Gogh's torments, sexual and religious, no longer afflicted people.

Smith comes closest to describing such an art, and the kind of artist who could create it, in some of his poems about the Gaelic tradition; in 'Duncan Ban McIntyre' (Fulton, pp. 89–90), for instance, where the Gaelic poet's love 'for a small corrie' expresses itself as a kind of inexhaustible loving attention to even the smallest thing in it – 'Patiently he numbered every blade of grass'. The poem begins by emphasising the apparent insignificance of the place McIntyre celebrated – it is only a small corrie, not some large or obviously impressive place; but the interest and importance of a place (or a person) does not depend on outward impressiveness but on the quality of attention we bring to it (or him or her). McIntyre is part of a long and distinctive tradition, the heir of the 'Celtic monk carving a Celtic cross/with such an intent delicacy, such precision'. The implicit contrast is with the English Romantic tradition in which the poet's personality is projected outward onto the natural world.

The contrast continues in the description of the poet himself, who is nothing like the conventional Romantic or Modernist conception of the artist as an outsider, tormented and driven, at odds with society and himself. This man was the antithesis of these things – 'gentle happy tranquil and a careful/meticulous poet who loved every stone/and every slope, and who was always cheerful'. The impression is of a man wholly at one with himself and with his environment. The last stanza challenges another idea about the artist in our Romantic individualist tradition; earlier McIntyre had been described as a genius, but the final emphasis is different. It was something outside rather than inside him which 'made him a poet':

All poetry's made by love and his life shows it.
An ordinary man unable to read or write,
this corrie in Argyllshire made him a poet.
Whatever it was that made that glen all light
worked in his heart till speech was necessary.
Natural as a lark he sang his song
and patient too as a scientist who would marry
music to fact, research to a musical tongue.

The final lines emphasise again the difference between Gaelic culture and our modern urban and technological society – in the poetry of Duncan Ban MccIntyre two things are combined which we tend to think of as incompatible or even opposed; his work is both lyrical *and* scientific, uniting the song of the lark with the patience of the researcher. It is a conclusion which inevitably brings to mind Smith's comments on MacDiarmid's change of poetic direction.[10] Smith felt that in turning his back on his early lyric impulse and attempting to create a poetry of fact and science, MacDiarmid had denied his own deepest poetic energies; this poem suggests that the two impulses need not be separate, but also suggests that their unification is perhaps only possible in a particular kind of linguistic and cultural environment.

In 'Duncan Ban McIntyre', Smith celebrates a synthesis of the lyrical and the objective, of individuality and rootedness which is perhaps not now possible in either Gaelic or English-language culture. But, not surprisingly in view of his divided situation, the idea of synthesis, of integration, is of central importance to Smith. He has said that poetry 'is not simply a personal gift. It cannot arise from the divided man'.[11] His own work suggests, however, that the presence of inner conflicts – between two languages and cultures, between the impulse to create art and a religious tradition inimical to it – is a powerful stimulus to creativity. At the end of 'For Poets Writing in English Over in Ireland', from Smith's recent collection *Exiles* (CP, pp. 238–40), the speaker reflects on his own linguistically and culturally divided state. He repeats and adds to some lines written by an Irish poet on the death of his wife which he has been reading in translation, adapting the expression of sorrow at personal loss to his own situation, in which choosing to work in one language and tradition means the rejection of another, equally loved. The elegiac quality of the poem's conclusion conveys very movingly Smith's sadness at having to choose. However, the final lines are a kind of synthesis as well, bringing together English and Gaelic traditions in the borrowing of lines translated from Irish to conclude the poem. They are a reminder that Smith's work in English owes much of its distinctiveness and power to the influence of his Gaelic inheritance:

'Half of my side you were, half of my seeing,
half of my walking you were, half of my hearing.'
Half of this world I am, half of this dancing.

Notes

The author is grateful to Carcanet Press for permission to quote from *Iain Crichton Smith: Collected Poems* (Manchester, 1992), referred to in the text as *CP* with page references. Poems not included in that volume are from Robin Fulton's *Iain Crichton Smith: Selected Poems 1955–1980* (Loanhead, 1981), referred to in the text as Fulton with page references. Grant F. Wilson's *A Bibliography of Iain Crichton Smith* (Aberdeen, 1990) provides a complete listing of Smith's work up to 1988.

1. Iain Crichton Smith, 'Towards the Human', in *Towards the Human: Selected Essays* (Loanhead, 1986), pp. 13–70 (p. 66), hereafter referred to as *TH* with page references.
2. J.H. Alexander, 'Ian Crichton Smith's English Poetry', in D.S. Hewitt and M.R.G. Spiller (eds), *Literature of the North* (Aberdeen, 1983), pp. 189–203 (p. 199).
3. Crichton Smith, 'A Poet in Scotland', in *Towards the Human*, op. cit., pp. 84–6 (p. 85).
4. John Blackburn, 'Iain Crichton Smith', in John Blackburn (ed.), *Hardy to Heaney* (Edinburgh, 1986), pp. 171–88 (p. 175).
5. Ibid., p. 186.
6. Edwin Morgan, 'The Raging and the Grace', *Essays* (Cheadle, 1974), pp. 222–31 (p. 223).
7. Blackburn, op. cit., p. 175.
8. Morgan, op. cit., p. 224.
9. Hugh MacDiarmid, 'The Watergaw', in M. Grieve and W. R. Aitken (eds), *Hugh MacDiarmid: Complete Poems 1920–1976* (London, 1978), p. 17.
10. Crichton Smith, 'The Golden Lyric: An Essay on the Poetry of Hugh MacDiarmid', in *Towards the Human*, op. cit., pp. 176–91.
11. Crichton Smith, 'Poetic Energy, Language and Nationhood', ibid., pp. 87–93 (p. 93).

12

Vernon Watkins and R. S. Thomas

Dennis Brown

Vernon Watkins (1906–1967) and R. S. Thomas (1915–) have both expressed preoccupations of Anglo-Welsh verse in the latter half of this century. Special numbers of *Poetry Wales*,[1] in particular, have considered their work in this light, and the nature of their contributions to a sense of Welsh cultural identity remains of critical interest. Nevertheless, both poets have written specifically in English and out of a largely English tradition – in each case with particular debts to mainstream Metaphysical and Romantic poetry. And while each poet, in ways, seems somewhat at the margins of recent poetic trends, each appears, at times, to be influenced by well-known contemporary writers – Watkins by his friend Dylan Thomas and R. S. Thomas by the later Ted Hughes. Both are essentially religious poets working within a predominantly secular culture: Watkins's stance is that of neo-Platonic rapture; Thomas's is that of *via negativa* scepticism. Both are particularly concerned with the relation between time and eternity. At the same time, both Watkins and Thomas conform to the twentieth-century norm of expressing themselves through collections of short poems rather than aspiring to quasi-epic structure: Watkins's lyrics are typically conventional in form; Thomas's mature poems, though scarcely experimental in the modernist sense, are somewhat free and formless verse-mediations. Hence, for all the similarities between these two Anglo-Welsh writers, the differences between their characteristic productions are quite marked.

Vernon Watkins's early poetry establishes the short, sometimes occasional, lyric as his major vehicle. 'Sycamore',[2] for instance, gives a voice to the tree itself and asserts a lyrical counterpoint (which will become familiar) between living beauty and mortality. However, in the first two volumes especially – *Ballad of the Mari*

Lwyd (1941) and *The Lamp and the Veil* (1945) – there are somewhat
longer poems of a different kind: 'Ballad of the Mari Lwyd', for
instance, constitutes a remarkable verse-drama, 'Yeats in Dublin' is
a somewhat literalistic autobiographical piece replete with versified conversation and 'Sea-Music For My Sister Travelling' is a
rhapsodic (and rather expressionistic) evocation of ocean-voyaging.
Although 'Ballad' and 'Sea-Music' are exciting in their own ways,
there is little in these poems to suggest any ongoing alternative to
the poet's commitment to the short lyric. In a later collection, *The
Death Bell* (1954), there are several rather mannered ballads. But
Watkins's main mode of expression is the intense lyric focused on
some subject – bird, shell, tree, rock, fountain, etc. – which lights up
into brief epiphany.

In *The Lady and the Unicorn* (1948), 'Swallows Over the Weser'
offers a typically heightened moment:

> ...Here to lie, here to dream on the Summersoft meadow
> Watching their wings in the sunlight, their wings that transfix
>   the bright aether,
> Diamondly flying, is lovely.

(114)

Watkins is adept at creating leisurely, musical lines which flow
naturally into each other: he is also skilful in the placement of
short, line-length sentences ('Darkness divines great light' or 'All
that I touch is truthful, and is fair')[3] which are similar to the
contemporaneous, early style of Theodore Roethke. Watkins is
from the beginning an essentially musical poet and his early passion for Shelley, in particular, shows even in his maturer work. His
debt to Yeats has been studied by fellow Welsh poet Roland
Mathias:[4] at times this shows a little too clearly as borrowed idiosyncrasy – 'Prophetic Owen knew' or 'What Sandro Botticelli
found...'.[5] But in his most characteristic lyrics Watkins lacks the
oratorical rhetoric of Yeats's grand manner: he is best when he is
most relaxed and limpid:

> Many a bird; then hounds, with deer in flight:
> Light is her element; her tapestry is light.

(150)

There is little manifest development in Watkins's lyrical style: the early and later poems seem much of a piece and his ecstatic vision – autobiographically rooted in an early 'peak experience'[6] – appears constant. After *The Death Bell, Cypress and Arcadia* appeared in 1959: this was followed by *Affinities* (1962) and four posthumous volumes – *Fidelities* (1968), *Uncollected Poems* (1969), *The Ballad of the Outer Dark* (1979) and *The Breaking of the Wave* (1979). These have all been brought together by Ruth Pryor who edited the definitive *Collected Poems* (1986). With the partial exception of the longer experiments mentioned above, the whole volume attests the essential unity of Watkins's work and the continuity of his lyrical method. He is concerned, above all, to speak of eternity and the infinite. Despite a few contemporary references (to the Second World War, for instance), many of the poems appear oddly detached from their time: they could well have been written in the previous century – which creates a critical issue I shall return to.

Four characteristic poems will be discussed to demonstrate the nature of Watkins's contribution. The first, 'Spring Song' (pp. 29–30), comes from his first published collection. The immediate impression is of a fluid, lyrical style skilfully working out of a long tradition of such lyrics: 'Now the green leaves are singing,/Now the white snows are gone'. The verse bounds forward in a flowing present tense (judiciously sprung with present participles), making use of rhetorical questions in the fourth verse before switching to the past tense. The surprising 'darkness' at the end of the first verse introduces a contrastive autumnal note which connects up with the sombre spring described in the last verse. This spring involves an initiation and acquaintanceship with some vague figure (perhaps the Muse or even God) who introduces the poet to death. So spring is evoked in ambivalent terms: it points backward as well as forward and through migratory swallows becomes reminiscent of autumn and 'despair'. This last term, together with the notion of 'cold' sorrow, signals a slightly facile use of abstraction and personification sometimes characteristic of Watkins's verse (cf. 'A prey to hungry time', p. 165). Nevertheless, the overall fluency of the verse, the exactness of the description and the deployment of bold primary colouring (typically working as both description and symbol) helps the poem register its effects. One wonders whether the declaration about personal fasting and thirsting is much more than neo-Yeatsian rhetoric, but it leads to the final placement of the persona as artist finally outside the realm of nature, knowing the 'words' which birds are ignorant of. In the poetic realm 'new light' connects with 'first light', as autumn with spring and the grave with the swallows' return. Although rooted in a world of natural process, the poem alludes to a realm of correspondences which the Symbolist poets had made a type of norm.

'Music of Colours: White Blossom' (pp. 101–2) from *The Lady and the Unicorn* makes the reader confront such neo-Platonic correspondences (and paradoxes) quite directly. The poem is far denser than 'Spring Song' – more *symboliste*, intellectual and 'difficult'. It starts vigorously, bouncing forward with insistent reiteration of the word 'white' (eight uses in the first six lines and 20 uses of forms of the word in the whole poem). Most of the verses vary between five and seven lines in length but after the first two a triple-rhymed verse of three lines acts as a pivot of the whole poetic movement. I take the key line to be: 'White must die black, to be born white again'. Towards the end of the poem the poet confesses he lacks 'original white'. Taken together, these utterances anchor the metaphysical meaning of the whole. Rather as Shelley's 'white radiance of Eternity'[8] becomes diffused, on earth, into multiple colours so Watkins's missing primal light is intimated here only as approximations – blossoms, shell, spray, star, etc. – or prismatic alterations into the 'lived' rainbow. The assertions of a radical Absence, complexly related to a teeming variety of presences, is central to this poem, as to companion poems such as 'Prime Colours', 'Music of Colours: The Blossom Scattered' or 'Blossom Colours: Dragonfoil and the Furnace of Colours', and, indeed, it is a key to the vision which underlines the whole Watkins canon. In Post-structuralist terms, one might say that Watkins consciously works at time-honoured binary oppositions in order to probe the Reality beyond 'trace'. Such a procedure is remarkable in this poem by the way a rich range of personal perception and public allusion is wrought into a complex private mythology. A synaesthesia of colours and sounds is orchestrated in the diverse manifestations of spring (that 'green conspiracy') and related (under cosmic stars) to figures such as Noah, Jupiter, Venus, Solomon, Christ and 'Marlowe's queen'. A single resonant realm is created where the absolute and the contingent, death and resurrection, past and present are all symbolically conjoined. The poem is Metaphysical in the manner of Donne, ceremonious in the style of Yeats and supremely fictive in the vein of Wallace Stevens. It ends with a bold stroke: 'I know you, black swan'. How far the poem can bring its contemporary readers to so confident an avowal seems doubtful: but the attempt is resonantly affective.

'The Dead Shag' (pp. 174–5), from *The Death Bell*, appears at face value to operate at a far more realistic level – and in this lies much of its power. The evocations of the living bird's characteristics and behaviour are superb: 'shot/With every silk of the rock'; 'eye of jade', 'a questioning head/Buoyed up between crest and crest'. However, such descriptions are called forth by the poet's surprise encounter with the 'mummified bird' in a sea-pool. The sadly inert and bedraggled corpse is deftly contrasted with the 'jet-winged' activity of the live shags the poet is used to watching. The more philosophical implication is sprung from this contrast: for the specific (dead) bird is juxtaposed with the timeless Idea of such birds as embodied in dynamic images. This is typical of Watkins's mode of meditation. As Dora Polk has remarked of another of his poems:

> It is [the] notion of the perpetuity of life implicit in the transient existence of the particular creature which constitutes the sense of pastness (and futurity) that Watkins clearly possesses.[9]

She proceeds to suggest that:

> The quality of the generic continuity may be seized, perhaps, as a sort of Idealism mediating Plato and Aristotle.

In the poem, overall, the more hermetic aspects of Watkins's thinking are expressed as the familiar juxtaposition of light and darkness, motion and stasis, life and death. The poem resolves as an affirmation of 'the light of day' through acceptance of 'that dark'. We appear to have moved some way from the specific corpse of the bird: the concrete encounter has become transmogrified into a larger principle inherent in Watkins's imaginative world.

'Cornfields' (p. 360), in *Fidelities*, represents a final example of the poet's succinct power. The form is the quatrain – perhaps the most characteristic vehicle of Watkins's vision. The poem's lightness and liquidity again remind us of Shelley:

> Joy weighing at dusk
> The scales, heavy and light,
> The balance of ear and husk,
> Daybreak dreaming of night?

The poem celebrates Heraclitean flux yet typically recuperates this as neo-Platonic recapitulation and pattern. Moving ears of corn, the pregnant mare and the nesting bird are brought together to exemplify the familiar themes of resurrectional pattern, the 'dream' of process, the final unification of oppositions and the beauty and eternity of the Real. Yet the specific Romanticism of the verse lies in its poignant celebration of transience rather than in a triumphant assertion of the eternal. 'A sigh moving in air' exactly describes the constituency of the poem itself. The rhymes are typically exact ('rise' – 'sighs'; 'fall' – 'stall'), the rhythm regular yet natural, the imagery specific and concrete: however, it is the indefinably plangent tone which marks it as a typical Watkins's piece. Published in the 1968 collection, 'Cornfields' is a 'classic' lyric which might well have been published in the 1820s: in this lies both its quality and its oddity as a production of the postmodern era.

Altogether, the main case for Watkins's poetry lies in its lyrical quality and its metaphysical depth. Its neo-Platonic insistence may be extrapolated, in terms of contemporary literary theory, with reference to, say, C.G. Jung's 'Collective Unconscious',[9] Mikhail Bakhtin's 'Great Time'[10] or Paul Ricoeur's *kerygmatic* 'interpreting tradition'.[11] Watkins reads twentieth-century Nature as one harmonious, ecological and interconnected whole which manifests an aesthetic teleology itself in 'natural' relation to a 'timeless' collective culture. Although the metaphysic is explicitly Christian, there seems little of the Fall in Watkins's world. The vision is idealising and Edenic. In Heideggerian parlance, one may say that the poetry consistently constitutes a mode of 'uncovering' or 'lighting'.[12] the world is a plentitude which reveals its Being in specific forms and colours:

> Calm is the landscape when the storm has passed.
> Brighter the fields and fresh with fallen rain.
> Where gales beat out new colours from the hills
> Rivers fly faster, and upon their banks
> Birds preen their wings, and irises revive.

('Peace in the Welsh Hills', p. 229)

It is a largely pastoral world and Watkins has little time for the 'cities burnt alive with fire/Of man's destruction' (p. 229). Herein lies the essential Romanticism of the stance. The Metaphysical poets, for instance, could include urban affairs and mechanical invention in their mystical vision: Watkins takes his stand with Blake and Yeats, in particular, to privilege the natural realm and largely ignore modern civilisation. This makes its own point in the era of Green politics; yet it also implies a kind of Manichean division (or binary opposition) between Nature and actual Culture which rather contradicts Watkins's own sense of holism and eternal recurrence. And in Christian terms, themselves, Watkins's metaphysic seems gnostic rather than truly incarnational. The vision is beautiful – but it leaves out most of the realities of modern life.

The apparent limitations of Watkins's philosophy show themselves on the level of language itself. For the timeless quality of his lyricism is effected by essentially traditional language. In 'Affinities' tradition is set against 'fashion' and the true 'smith' (itself a dated term) is related to the 'ancient poets'. This is a rewrite of Eliot's 'Tradition and the Individual Talent' that leaves little place for 'the new (the really new) work'[13] – which itself comes out of the search for 'next year's words'.[14] Eliot is said to have admired Watkins's talent and in 'Ode: to T.S. Eliot' Watkins commends the master for having 'pruned' the English language. Yet Eliot's achievement was also to *update* poetic diction, imagery and rhythm – a feat continued in different ways by such writers as Auden, Dylan Thomas, Larkin and Heaney, Watkins scarcely attempts this – less so even than the Yeats of 'The Second Coming' or 'Nineteen Hundred and Nineteen'. Some forty years after the Imagist project he could publish a line like: 'The sun's hands with the Winter's death are bloody'.[15] This is rather exceptional, yet a comparison with such like-minded poets as Theodore Roethke, H.D. or Robert Duncan makes Watkins's style appear oddly anachronistic. Kathleen Raine has commended his language as that of 'sacred analogy'[16] – as 'defending ancient springs' (Watkins's own phrase). But *Four Quartets* demonstrates how new and old words can 'dance' together – sacredly at that. Hence one's final doubt about Watkins's overall contribution has less to do with his philosophy, as such, than with his aesthetic and style. Can a postmodern readership accept a post-Second World War Romantic verse which appears to have learnt nothing from high Modernism?

R.S. Thomas has slowly won a deserved reputation as a kind of verse Samuel Beckett – an intensely self-honest sifter of ultimate truths. Where Watkins is a highly musical poet, Thomas is a poet of terse, meditative speech. His work succeeds through stark simplicity:

>   ... One thing I have asked
>   Of the disposer of the issues
>   Of life: that truth should defer
>   To beauty. It was not granted.[17]

Thomas's poetry itself – especially the later work – is always more characterised by truth than beauty. It works away at key terms – 'God', 'machine', 'absence', 'prayer', 'darkness', 'language', 'equation' – springing Pascalian surprises out of a dark Kierkegaardian commitment. It can also astonish with its imagery – 'blowing/On the small soul in my/Keeping'; 'The machine ... / ... singing to itself/Of money'.[18] Many of the later collection titles indicate the subjects of Thomas's mature preoccupation – *H'm* (Him, hymn, hum, ahem, home, om, etc.), *Laboratories of the Spirit*, *Frequencies* or *Experimenting with an Amen*. Like Watkins, Thomas expresses himself almost entirely through the short poem, focusing on a specific situation or thought: vivid insights shine out like stars from an intensely sceptical darkness. 'Via Negativa' is one title-poem which encapsulates the poet's approach – an Areopagite (yet also pastoral) enquiry into the meaning of reality, especially modern reality. Where Watkins celebrates the radiant 'lighting' of Being, Thomas broods on a darkness that can occasionally 'dazzle'.[19] He has succeeded in creating authoritative religious expression for an age of general unbelief.

There is considerably more sense of a development in Thomas's career than in that of Watkins. This comprises a gradual tightening of style and narrowing of focus to develop a profound metaphysical preoccupation. His early poetry appears comparatively local, rural and Welsh. In his first main publication, *Song at the Year's Turning* (1955),[20] we are introduced to the rugged Welsh landscape and its somewhat uncouth inhabitants, such as Iago Prytherch. The language, here, varies between starkness and lyricism rather in the manner of the early Wordsworth. *Poetry For Supper* (1958) and *Tares* (1961) develop such characteristics and, in particular, build up a dour picture of rural Wales in that era. Thomas's attitude to Wales and Welshness itself appears ambivalent but in his next three collections, *The Bread of Truth* (1963), *Pietà* (1966) and *Not That He Brought Flowers* (1968), there is evident a geographical broadening of his subject matter as well as a metaphysical deepening. His 1952 BBC dialogue, 'The Minister',[21] had parodied Thomas's personal situation as a young pastor preaching a universal and transhistorical *kerygma* in a very particular time and place: Thomas's career might be characterised as a gradual extrapolation of his experience from the particular here and now to space-time in general. *H'm* (1972) is the collection where the transition is most marked – especially in the powerful 'Genesis' myth-poems in which he attempts to rewrite the meaning of the human struggle from scratch. In *Later Poems* (1972–1982)[22] Thomas drastically cut contributions from the two collections – *Young and Old* (1972) and *What is a Welshman* (1974) but *Laboratories of the Spirit* (1975), *Frequencies* (1978) and the more diffuse *Between Here and Now* (1981) are well-represented and indicate Thomas's own sense of his main direction. This might be described as a progression away from the objectivising gaze at Welsh rural life toward a subjective wrestling with the meaning of time, space and human life in general. This emphasis is confirmed in different ways by his most recent collections – *Experimenting with an Amen* (1986)[23] and *The Echoes Return Slow* (1988).[24] In the four poems examined below I have concentrated on what I take to be Thomas's main developing interest – the meaning of Being in itself, and for God.

'Song at the Year's Turning'[25] might almost have been written as a partial disclaimer of Watkins's particular stance and style. It begins: 'Shelley dreamed it. Now the dream decays/The props crumble.' At the centre of the poem is 'despair', 'the world's wood' and 'this tortured place'. Thomas, whose understanding of the 'crucified God' seems close to that of Jurgen Moltmann,[26] tends to ground his verse in suffering rather than the visionary gleam. However, although history is 'sterile' and winter 'rots', light has its 'cold splendour' and purgation is promised in the last line. The poem is short and tersely coherent – three verses composed of three couplets each, frequently deploying short pointed sentences, sometimes in the form of brusque rhetorical questions (e.g. 'Is there blessing?'). Like much of Thomas's work, the verse expresses a dour mood of rough disenchantment. If we take the poem as something of a manifesto, then the overt refutation of Shelleyan Romanticism signals a commitment to the angst of Existentialism and an acceptance of human guilt ('a mortal sinned') which places the poet well the other side of T.E. Hulme's denunciation of Romanticism as 'spilt religion' and acquiescence in the myth of perfectibility.[27]

There may be hints of an Eliotic influence here – decay, dust, wind, rot and purgatorial flame – but the voice is unique and the poem can shock with raw, original imagery – 'You cannot stanch the bright menstrual blood'. For all its finally metaphysical interest the verse goes in fear of abstractions and articulates its vision through concrete specifics: trampled 'tears', 'naked boughs' or 'new grass'. The 'strange marriage' hinted at does not appear to find any consummation in the poem itself; the choice is between rotting and purgation. It is a solid and disturbing production. In so far as it is a 'Song', the poem constitutes a lyric suitable, say, to the kind of musical treatment given to some of Wilfred Owen's verse in Benjamin Britten's *War Requiem*. Yet the poem also constitutes a personal argument, balancing contrasts – 'dust'/'lust', 'grace'/ 'place', 'blame'/'flame'. The last question is: 'who is there to blame?' It will take the poet the rest of his career to tease out possible answers to this.

'Once' is the first poem of the *H'm* collection, in *Later Poems* (p. 11), where a distinctive new poetic direction is announced. It seems to me (and to others)[28] that the influence of Hughes's *Crow* is evident here: there is the same use of blunt, paratactical accumulation, brash, incisive narration, rapid (almost cartoon-like) metamorphosis and bold primal mythologising. In 'Once' such qualities reinforce Thomas's usual terseness to rework and personalise the Adam and Eve story:

> God spoke. I hid myself in the side
> Of the mountain.
> As though born again
> I stepped out into the cool dew,
> Trying to remember the fire sermon...

The poem energises Being as Becoming: 'God looked at space and I appeared'; 'forms hungry for birth'; 'You, rising towards me out of the depths of myself'. Teleology, here, is worked out against a neo-Darwinian scaffolding. Yet Thomas, like Teilhard de Chardin, looks less back down the evolutionary ladder than forward towards human self-reckoning: in this case, not to the 'Omega Point'[29] but to 'the Machine'. It is toward this phenomenon that Adam and Eve walk at the end of the poem – the 'mingled chorus' of geological and biological process behind them. They hold hands as 'confederates', confronting the future as a mode of nemesis. The

'Machine' will stand as a key metaphor for the world of sophisticated scientific technology which Thomas's later poetry will scru-
tinise, *sub specie aeternitatis*, with appalled fascination. But contrary
to the companionship 'Once' seems to promise, that scrutiny will
be undertaken in a mood of abandonment and isolation.

'The Absence', from *Frequencies* (*Later Poems*, p. 123), is one of a
great number of Thomas's poems which seek to probe, as directly
as possible, the mystery of divine Being. What the poem appears to
sponsor might be termed 'proximity' rather than presence or even
immanence. God's absence is itself 'like a presence' – a room just
vacated or about to be entered. The poem uses plain, contemporary
words to tease out something both complex and timeless. As the
poet says: 'I modernise the anachronism/Of my language'. As in
most of the later poems metre and rhyme are eschewed – perhaps
as distractive ornamentation. Indeed, Thomas systematically uses
enjambement across the four–line verse form so that a kind of
formal deconstruction characterises the whole. The effect is of a
persistent searching across the normal boundaries of thought and
expression:

> Genes and molecules
> have no more power to call
> him up than the incense of the Hebrews
>
> at their altars...

As often in such verse, there seems to be no compelling reason why
the line-endings are exactly where they are placed. Hence the overall effect tends to devalue the integrity of the line itself in the
interests of truth-telling: transcendence is attempted precisely
through rending the veil of aesthetic convention. Yet the final
breakthrough occurs on the existential plane: the 'emptiness' the
poet feels without God is posited as a 'vacuum' which the divine
'may not abhor'. Thus though 'words' and 'equations' have failed,
the poem has not – it leaves us on the verge of apotheosis.

'This One' is a key poem in Thomas's 1986 collection, *Experimenting with an Amen* (p. 58). The protagonist appears to be the poet
himself, although the 'journey' seems to be universal and Dantesque – the leopard, lion and wolf of the *Inferno* here turned into
'gargoyles', while the speeding 'vehicles' place the quest in proximity to a specifically modern highway. The protagonist is a spiri-

tual seeker, caught between darkness and light and unassured of the 'verdict'. However, the poem moves firmly toward affirmation, brusquely spurning the laughing world of 'Others' with slightly neo-modernist *hauteur*. The 'one' is 'still', having 'withdrawn' to achieve inner balance as 'love' – 'the bridge between/thought and time'. In contrast to the 'consumers', the pilgrim is a spiritual dowser with his 'green/twig': what he 'divines' with this is the fine balance of life against death – 'the bottomless/water that is the soul's glass'. The lines are as broken by radical enjambement as elsewhere, inherently paratactic rather than given to clausal sub-ordinations and full of tricky rhetorical questions. The starkest of the latter is the disarming: 'Could/it be?' There is a Heideggerian dimension to this apparently *faux-naif* enquiry which resonates in so much of Thomas's verse. The poem mediates between 'there' and 'where' in a way that finally prioritises ontology over epistemology or linguistic relativism. The poem establishes the 'soul' as centre of the protagonist's experience and constitutes the poet as, intrinsically, a 'shepherd of Being'.[30] This journey is not 'without destination': nor, we can confidently affirm, has been Thomas's poetic pilgrimage overall.

Thomas's most recent collection, *The Echoes Return Slow*, consists of paired prose pieces and poems which articulate the general development of the poet's life and career. Although one hopes for yet more from this gravid bard, there is the strong sense of an ending about the volume: the 'echoes', indeed, 'return slow'. Some of the most directly moving of these pieces concern Thomas's work as a priest, and they remind us that, for all his intellectual scepticism about the possibility of divine 'appearance', his work has always taken for granted 'the contemporaneity of the Cross' (p. 83). His incarnational verse-theology depicts suffering and darkness as a fundamental ground for the interrogation of Being: as he puts it (paradoxically?) in an earlier poem: 'nailing his questions/ One by one to an untenanted cross'.[31] The reality of pain, which includes death too ('walking the bone's/plank over the dark waters': *The Echoes*, p. 95), is something the poetry addresses head on. The ultimately liberational aspect of his religious thinking in the verse is an insistence on choice as well as circumstance. As he puts it in 'The Unvanquished':[32]

But you
who are not free to choose

what you suffer can choose
your response.

At the same time, for all the dourness of his vision, there are moments when the dark is light enough. In 'Suddenly', for instance, God is depicted as even 'voluble', while the earlier 'The Bright Field' describes a moment of revelation which anticipates 'the eternity that awaits you'. What is extraordinary about Thomas's writing is the way a mode of doubting religious orthodoxy is given expression in terms of varied, felt experience: the ideas are specifically lived through. Thus while religious orthodoxy may appear, generally, as an anomaly within twentieth–century culture, both the existential depth of Thomas's verse and its cautious language-relativism render it authentically contemporary. His poetry shares a world with Francis Bacon's painting, Sylvia Plath's verse or Samuel Beckett's drama or prose. Thomas is the laureate of postmodernist pilgrimage.

His authenticity is particularly conveyed in terms of his choice of verse form and style – including the swift stylistic response to new poetic development in *H'm*. In particular, Thomas has evolved a voice of internal spiritual wrestling which picks its way across the dry bones of modern discourse. His poetry abounds in questions and, in an important sense, one might say that the whole Thomas canon is in the interrogative mode. Thus the poet questions himself, God and the reader about ultimate matters: e.g.

What power shall minister to us
at the closure of the century,
of the millennia?[35]

Such questions tend to be as simply worded as they are philosophically profound. Yet this does not mean that Thomas has any naively positivistic faith in 'plain language'. He knows that words are partial and essentially caught in 'the verbal hunger/for the thing in itself'.[36] Yet he also knows that he must use words when he speaks to us – the trick is in using them in carefully chosen ways which reactivate meaning. So he improvises, deconstructs, straddles sentence across line and detonates his sudden surprise images. In this he utters a species of prophecy fitting to the times we live in.

We see, then, that Vernon Watkins and R.S. Thomas are quite

contrastive poetic practitioners, for all that they have much in common. Philosophically, the difference lies between neo-Platonism and Existentialism; theologically, between Christianised natural Supernaturalism and Incarnationalism; in literary terms, between neo-Romanticism and personalised Postmodernism. Such a comparison inevitably favours Thomas to the degree that poetic thought and language should be specifically of an age as well as for all time. Watkins's verse has great lyrical merit – but it is rather of the kind we associate with, say, Shelley and Tennyson. In Thomas one perceives a sensibility which is of the age of Einstein, Wittgenstein, Bonhoeffer and even Derrida, and a language which is akin to that of Pound, Eliot, Auden and Ashbery. The work of both poets is exciting and enriching; but stylistically one looks backward and the other forward. Watkins's work remains to remind us of 'the light that never was, on sea or land';[37] Thomas's will endure to challenge our complex technological civilisation as it spins on, ever faster and often threatening to fly apart, into the double millennium and beyond. Yet what both poets insist on is that the material realm is not, in itself, enough: culture as Postmodernity will prove fatal, in the end, if the question of Being (and the Real) is not insistently and continually readdressed.

Notes

1. For example, *Poetry Wales*, special Vernon Watkins issue, No. 12, Summer 1977; *Poetry Wales*, special Thomas issue, No. 7, Spring 1972; *Poetry Wales*, special issue on Thomas's later poetry, No. 14, Spring 1979.
2. *The Collected Poems of Vernon Watkins* (Ipswich: Golgonooza Press, 1986), p. 12. All page references will be to this volume.
3. The first quotation from 'First Joy', ibid., p. 103; the second from 'The Listening Days', ibid., p. 142.
4. See Roland Mathias, *Vernon Watkins* (Cardiff: University of Wales Press, 1974), especially pp. 487–57.
5. The first quotation from 'The Broken Sea', *Collected Poems*, p. 92; the second from 'The Healing of the Leper', ibid., p. 136.
6. This is described in, for instance, Michael J. Collins's essay 'Vernon Watkins', in *British Poets 1914–1945*, the *Dictionary of Literary Biography*, Vol. 20, ed. Donald E. Stanford (Chicago: Bruccoli Clark, 1984), pp. 396–7. See also Gwen Watkins's account in *Vernon Watkins 1906–1967*, ed. Leslie Norris (London: Faber, 1970), p. 16. This 'road to Damascus' experience appears to have been a vision of eternity during a nervous breakdown.

7. From 'Testimony', *Collected Poems*, p. 165.
8. 'Life, like a dome of many-coloured glass,/Stains the white radiance of Eternity,/Until Death tramples it to fragments.' P. B. Shelley, 'Adonais', lines 462–5.
9. Dora Polk, *Vernon Watkins and the Spring of Vision* (Swansea: Christopher Davies, 1977), p. 145.
10. Where the 'chronotope' of many centuries finds specific articulation and 'every meaning' has its 'homecoming festival'. See M. M. Bakhtin, *Speech Genres and Other Late Essays*, trans. Vern W. McGee, eds Caryl Emerson and Michael Holquist (Austin: University of Texas Press, 1986), p. 170.
11. See the essay 'Structure and Hermeneutics', in Paul Ricoeur, *The Conflict of Interpretations*, ed. Don Ihde (Evanston, Ill.: Northwestern University Press, 1974), this essay translated by Kathleen McLaughlin, pp. 27–61: see especially p. 46.
12. See the essay 'The Origin of the Work of Art', in Martin Heidegger, *Basic Writings*, ed. David Farrell Krell (London: Routledge & Kegan Paul, 1978), this essay translated by Albert Hofstadter, pp. 149–87.
13. T. S. Eliot, *Selected Essays* (London: Faber, 1958), p. 15.
14. 'For last year's words belong to last year's language/And next year's words await another voice.' From 'Little Gidding', T. S. Eliot, *The Complete Poems and Plays* (London: Faber, 1969), p. 194.
15. From 'Niobe', *Collected Poems*, p. 169.
16. See Kathleen Raine, 'Vernon Watkins and the Bardic Tradition', in her *Defending Ancient Springs* (Oxford University Press, 1967), pp. 17–34.
17. From 'Petition', R. S. Thomas, *Later Poems* (London: Macmillan Papermac, 1984), p. 12.
18. The first quotation from 'Invitation', ibid., p. 15; the second from 'Other', ibid., p. 37.
19. Cf. Henry Vaughan, 'The Night': 'There is in God (some say)/A deep, but dazzling darkness.' Quoted as epigraph in Patrick Grant, *A Dazzling Darkness: An Anthology of Western Mysticism* (London: Collins, Fount Paperbacks, 1985).
20. All references to the selection from this volume in R. S. Thomas, *Selected Poems 1946–1968* (Newcastle upon Tyne: Bloodaxe Books, 1990). This selection also includes poems from *Poetry For Supper, Tares, The Bread of Truth, Pietà* and *Not that He Brought Flowers*.
21. See *Selected Poems*, pp. 19–33. The parody consists in the considerable distance created between the chapel Minister, Elias Morgan, and Thomas's own role as ordained priest of the Church of Wales.
22. *Later Poems* includes selections from *H'm, Young and Old, What is a Welshman, Laboratories of the Spirit, The Way of It, Frequencies, Between Here and Now* and *New Poems*.
23. R. S. Thomas, *Experimenting with an Amen* (London: Macmillan Papermac, 1986).
24. R. S. Thomas, *The Echoes Return Slow* (London: Macmillan, 1988). Granted that Thomas is still, happily, alive at the time of writing there is as yet no definitive *Collected Poems* as with Watkins.

25. *Selected Poems*, p. 36.
26. See Jurgen Moltmann, *The Crucified God* (Student Christian Movement, 1974).
27. See the essay 'Romanticism and Classicism' in T. E. Hulme, *Speculations: Essays on Humanism and the Philosophy of Art*, ed. Herbert Read (London: Routledge & Kegan Paul, 1965), pp. 111–40.
28. See, for instance, J. P. Ward, *The Poetry of R. S. Thomas* (Bridgend: Poetry Wales Press, 1987), p. 83.
29. See Pierre Teilhard de Chardin, *The Phenomenon of Man*, trans. Bernard Wall (London: Fontana Collins, 1969), pp. 283–6.
30. 'Man is the shepherd of Being', in 'Letter on Humanism', trans. Frank A. Capuzzi with J. Glenn Gray, Martin Heidegger, *Basic Writings*, p. 221. Since writing this essay, I have read D. Z. Phillips's study, *R. S. Thomas: Poet of the Hidden God* (London: Macmillan, 1986), which considers the philosophical implications of the poet's work at length.
31. From 'In Church', *Selected Poems*, p. 94.
32. In *Experimenting with an Amen*, p. 30.
33. In *Later Poems*, p. 201.
34. Ibid., p. 81.
35. From 'AD 2000', *Experimenting with an Amen*, p. 25.
36. From 'The Gap', *Later Poems*, p. 95.
37. Wordsworth's phrase in 'Elegiac Stanzas: Suggested by a Picture of Peele Castle, in a Storm, Painted by Sir George Beaumont'. See *Wordsworth: Poetical Works*, eds Thomas Hutchinson and Ernest de Selincourt (Oxford University Press, 1974), p. 452.

13

Anthologies of Women's Poetry:
Canon-Breakers; Canon-Makers

Jane Dowson

In her introduction to *Sixty Women Poets* (1993), Linda France alludes to a 'renaissance' in women's poetry; the proliferation of poetry collections and the number of anthologies of poetry by women certainly indicate the growth of literary and commercial interests in women's poetry over the last fifteen years. These anthologies also chronicle the discourses concerning women's relationship to the traditions of British poetry. The majority of anthologies and of feminist criticism of women's poetry have been published since 1980, significantly later than the equivalent recuperation of and attention to women's prose. The editors' introductions to these anthologies record developments in the exploration of a specific feminist poetics, from the questions of who are the women poets? and what is a woman poet? to an examination of the nature of women's poetry.

The number of gender-specific anthologies suggests an emergence of poetry written and published by women and would support the impression of a new vitality in women's poetry; 're-naissance' is perhaps misleading in that it assumes a previous life, but there is a sense that women have at last successfully intervened into the privileged sphere of literary activity. The implications of the anthology boom are not, however, that simple. With women particularly, publication is often delayed, and so an increase in publication does not necessarily register an increase in writing or of reputation. If women's writing is not published until the poet is elderly or dead, women cannot be perceived to be at the forefront of cultural change. Caution over major claims about the position of women is also due because anthologies have dual status and denote both achievement and limitation for the poets selected. There is an understanding that anthologies are consumed by the general reader more than by the specialist and, consequently, that anthologised poems are somehow marketable and that double-sided concept 'accessible' rather than demanding or innovative. It has to be conceded that anthologies can conceal the unevenness or narrowness of a poet's oeuvre, and, because anthologies tend to echo each other, they do not represent the range or development of the poet. This last point, however, is at the same time a statement about the influence of anthologies: one reason for the practice of anthologising the same poems is not just laziness or financial restriction on the part of the editor, but because preceding anthologies have created the popularity of certain poems through familiarising them. Anthologies also establish the canons of literature and can largely determine the perspective of poetry thereby represented, particularly where the organising principle is chronological, such as 'Twentieth Century' or 'Poetry of the Thirties'.

Women must, therefore, intervene into the anthology-formation of perceived developments of poetry. Anthologies of women's poetry, however, require a rationale which justifies a collection by gender; the dilemma for the editor is whether to present the collective poetry by women as defensive – a necessary antidote to exclusion from the male-edited equivalents – or as proactive texts which allow for new connections and definitions within the particular framework of reference. In other words, do the anthologies complement or contradict established versions of poetic activity? They do, of course, do both by unsettling attempts, past and present, to over-tidy literary histories. What is needed, however, is that the poetry is taken seriously and that there is discrimination in assessing the anthologies in the contexts of poetry activity as well as of the careers of the poets represented.

The bottom line is that anthologies of women's poetry force recognition of the existence of women poets. A trawl through anthologies of British or English verse quickly discovers the exclusion of women from the traditions of British poetry. Hence, retrospective volumes of poems by women have necessarily been directed at redressing the imbalance of representation. *The Penguin Book of Women Poets* (1978) spanned three and a half thousand years of world literature; *Poetry by English Women: Elizabethan to Victorian* (1990), *English Women Romantic Poets* (1992) and *Victorian Women Poets* (1994) specifically set women beside orthodox literary groups. Similarly, Catherine Reilly's *Scars Upon My Heart* (1981) and *Chaos of the Night* (1984) recover unknown poems by women in the First and Second World Wars.

The argument presented in these collections is that often the poets were respected in their day but have since been overlooked. Periodisation is frequently, albeit unwittingly, hostile to women because it is built upon publishing history, and, as already stated, publication of women's works is often delayed. Two of this century's major women poets, for example, Sylvia Townsend Warner (1893–1978) and Stevie Smith (1902–1971), are nearly wholly posthumous; Sylvia Townsend Warner's *Collected* and *Selected Poems* came out in 1982 and 1985 respectively; like Sylvia Townsend Warner's, the Stevie Smith collections which have appeared since her death, contain several previously uncollected poems.[1]

The Bloodaxe Book of Contemporary Women Poets (1985) marked a move away from the all-inclusive collection to one which was determinedly more selective in order that poetry by women should receive considered, rather than token, attention. To this end, Jeni Couzyn chose eleven women who were established as poets: Jeni Couzyn herself, Fleur Adcock, Ruth Fainlight, Elaine Feinstein, Elizabeth Jennings, Jenny Joseph, Sylvia Plath, Denise Levertov, Kathleen Raine, Stevie Smith and Anne Stevenson. The introduction addresses the phenomenon of women's exclusion from collections and critical surveys of poetry and takes the discussion further on to an examination of the nature of the woman poet. The individual profiles by or about each poet explain the connection between their poetry and lived experience: 'First and foremost, I wanted poems that were genuinely trying to make sense of experience' (Elaine Feinstein).[2] A recurring theme is that the choices available for women since the sexual revolution of the 1960s and 1970s indicate new freedoms but also create competing demands, especially between family life, and, more crucially, motherhood, and writing. Denise Levertov, the daughter of a Russian Jewish immigrant, and Ruth Fainlight discuss the political potential of poetry – 'A specifically female anger has been the impetus for many of my poems' (Ruth Fainlight)[3] – but there is little discussion of the aesthetics of their poetry. The selections and introductions reinforce the concept of the personal and private as the preoccupations of women poets. Diana Scott's *Bread and Roses, Women's Poetry of the 19th and 20th Centuries* (1982) had similarly represented women's relationships to oppression and emancipation. One of her aims was to encourage new readers to engage with and to derive inspiration from poetry. Interestingly, this volume has had little resonance in discussions of poetry, perhaps because most poets are only represented by a single poem. *Bread and Roses, Women's Poetry of the 19th and 20th Centuries* and *The Bloodaxe Book of Contemporary Women Poets* were produced in the wake of 1970s feminist criticism which essentialised female experience as restraint and repression. In *Shakespeare's Sisters: Feminist Essays on Women Poets* (1979) Gilbert and Gubar reread nineteenth-century poets such as Elizabeth Barrett Browning, Christina Rossetti and Emily Dickinson as women struggling to write out their indignations within the straitjackets of man-made forms and metres. Tillie Olsen's *Silences* (1980) was an influential study of the effects of suppression on women writers; for example, she lists the number of poets and novelists who attempted or committed suicide. Such 'victim feminism' can be disparaged because it reinforces the stereotype of the defeated authoress, but it was a necessary reaction against the wholesale prejudices towards women writers.

The title of *Ain't I a Woman! Poems by Black and White Women*, edited by Illona Linthwaite (1987), is both defensive and assertive. The poems are thematically arranged to correspond to the stages of evolution between childhood and age and to make connections across boundaries of race and colour. This combination of defensiveness and assertiveness is recorded by Adrienne Rich (b. 1929) in her accounts of her own development as a poet where she had to learn not to be apologetic as a woman writing poetry nor to be restricted to feminist protest. She recalls that her own impulses of liberation and confinement had been conditioned by both male pedagogic practices and by women's movements. She had been brought up on canonical male writers who had (de)formed her own identity by presenting female subjectivity as the projection of the male. Rich's emancipation began with the discovery and reassessment of poets like Elizabeth Barrett Browning and H.D., who had been dishonoured or concealed by academic traditionalism. An exact contemporary of Sylvia Plath (1932–1963), she has, for many women, herself been an important paradigm of a poet who integrated her professional and private lives. At a reading at the South Bank, London in 1994, she was cheered by a mass of women poets and her essays, such as 'Blood, Bread and Poetry: The Location of the Poet' (1984), have influenced women in the United States and Britain. Adrienne Rich's writings and her poetry set a new agenda for 'the dialogue between art and politics'.[4]

The debate is continued in publications such as *Women's Writing: A Challenge to Theory* (ed. Moira Monteith, 1986) in which Michelene Wandor discusses poetry as the mixture of private and public discourses; she charts her own evolution from 'protest' poetry to the freedom of experimentation with forms of the 'fictional voice' which solves 'the apparent conflict between the rationality of theory and political writing, and the wildness, the relative unpredictability of a poem ... I think I can date the change from about 1981.'[5] In *Stealing The Language: The Emergence of Women's Poetry in America* (1987), however, Alicia Ostriker advocated that women be more abrasive in order to counteract the 'fluttering poetess' stigma as inherited from the nineteenth century.[6]

In *Making for the Open: Post-Feminist Poetry* (1987) Carol Rumens, obviously keen to counteract the angry young woman image of the 1960s and 1970s, triumphed that 'excellence' had replaced 'feminism' in poetry. This denigration of the women's movement and Rumens's high moral tone inevitably alienated her sister poets and critics. The implication of this supposed victory took women back ten years to the place where women's experiences were assumed to be antithetical to art; the achievement of validating their lives through inscribing them received a bitter blow. The tactless title also suggested that women were freed from gender political agendas and were all the better for it. In the later *New Women Poets* (1990; 1993) Carol Rumens ostensibly rectified her previous insouciance and seemed to support the possibility that women's voices collectively mounted a cultural critique, although she was more impressed by the heterogeneity of the poetry.[7] In the second anthology, Carol Rumens aimed to select budding poets who had not yet published a collection, but who had achieved some reputation through gaining awards or prizes. (Incidentally, she approves of competition culture which keeps a check on quality.) The original goal of 15 became 25 poets, many of whom, like Linda France, Lavinia Greenlaw, Jackie Kay, Mimi Khalvati, Eva Salzman and Elizabeth Garrett, have since published their own collections. It is likely that *New Women Poets* was a step in the process.

Fleur Adcock's *The Faber Book of Twentieth Century Women's Poetry* (1987) is significant in opening up the ground for replacing women within the terrains of this century's poetry and positioning them firmly within the locus of contemporary poetry. It marks the axis where the feminist project is still committed to recovery but also to acknowledging the difficulty of identifying the specificity of poetry by women. Fleur Adcock also makes the point that the anthology should be the precursor to, not a substitute for, reading the poets' books. She draws the map of twentieth-century women's poetry from Charlotte Mew (1869–1928) to poets born in 1945, such as Eavan Boland, Wendy Cope and Selima Hill. The 64 poets cross several national boundaries – there is a predominance of North American, Australian and New Zealand, as well as British, writers – although there are not many black women: Gwendolyn Brooks and June Jordan are included, but not Maya Angelou or Alice Walker. Important neglected older poets like Frances Cornford, Elizabeth Daryush and E.J. Scovell are resurrected, but not Vita Sackville-West (unjustly dismissed as 'old-fashioned') or Anne Ridler who has mysteriously not been properly owned by women although she wrote a poem on menstruation as early as the 1930s. The disparity between the number of poems chosen can suggest the editor's private hierarchy in which Marianne Moore, Elizabeth Bishop, Sylvia Plath and Stevie Smith (notably the first three being American) are superior to Elizabeth Jennings or H.D. However, the overriding hand of the publisher and the prohibitive cost of per-mission fees may well have influenced the numerical decisions. At least this anthology stimulates the debate about 'who is in and who out' which draws attention to the poetry itself and raises questions about evaluation.

This question of value is addressed, although not solved, in the introduction. It is not for the overtly feminist commitment that the poems in *The Faber Book of Twentieth Century Women's Poetry* have been selected, but for their anti-sentimentality, anti-visionary or non-lyrical qualities, in favour of detachment, wit and originality – qualities which are gender neutral. For Fleur Adcock, the politics of the separatist collection is in demonstrating the variety of wo-men's poetry which draws attention to the corresponding variety throughout British poetry and which consequently counters a false sense of a homogeneous British tradition. The new mode of cele-brating range and difference is evident in other anthologies pro-duced around the turn of the decade like *The Rhythm of Our Days* (1991) where the editor, Veronica Green, proposes that 'there are as many voices as there are women'.[8]

At the same time, late 1980s feminist criticism was involved in investigating the opportunities and risks of promoting plurality and in theorising the relationship between subjectivity, language and culture. Jan Montefiore's *Feminism and Poetry: Language, Experi-*

ence, *Identity in Women's Writing* (1987) is a seminal, although not a large, work on the fine line between essentialism and universalism when discussing women's psycho-sexual relationship to language. Although contradictory in places where she tries to be conclusive, Jan Montefiore breaks ground in the discussions about poetry by women. *Feminism and Poetry* stimulated greater debate about the strategies of women poets and the implications for received ideas about tradition and authority in poetry. Liz Yorke, in *Impertinent Voices: Subversive Strategies in Contemporary Women's Poetry* (1991), draws upon French feminist theories to study the disruptive aspects of the ways in which women have articulated their experiences and how poetry particularly offers the chance to challenge the conventional logic of patriarchal linguistic formulations. Poetry practice and criticism in the 1990s continues to concentrate on the diversity of women writers. A poetics which forms an alliance with postmodern philosophies not only encourages women to advertise their differences but also to take advantage of the critical openness towards unfixing traditional subject positions through the manipulation of language codes.

The excitement of language, more than common experiences, is what connects Fleur Adcock, Gillian Clarke, Selima Hill, Liz Lochhead, Grace Nichols and Carol Rumens in *Six Women Poets* (1991). For Grace Nichols, especially, working in both Standard English and Creole is a means of reclaiming and exploring her language heritage.[9] The politics and also marketability of women together is further suggested by the publication of poems within frameworks of womanhood, nationality or region, such as *In the Gold of the Flesh: Poems of Birth and Motherhood* (1990),[10] *Naming the Waves: Contemporary Lesbian Poetry* (1988), *The Penguin Book of Australian Women Poets* (1986); *Fresh Oceans – An Anthology by Scottish Women* (1989), *Silent Voices: An anthology of contemporary Romanian women poets* (1986; 1989), *Five Women Poets* (from the North-West) (1994). The culmination of current anthologies is Linda France's *Sixty Women Poets* (1993); incidentally, the contribution of Bloodaxe to the spread of poetry by women should not go unnoticed.

Sixty Women Poets is something of a landmark. For a start, there is a significant number of poets, especially when the majority meet the original criterion for inclusion which was to have had at least two collections published – Linda France was commissioned to list 50 but found it too restricting. In a non-competitive way *Sixty Women Poets* is intended as a 'sister volume' to *The New Poetry*

(Bloodaxe, 1993) which contained 17 women out of 55 poets. Although not a tiny number, 17 does not do justice to the range of women's published poetry, largely because of its framework (no poet born before 1940), similar to the ageist grouping of *The New Generation Poets* (1994) which dismissed poets over 40. Linda France rejects the age-conscious arrangement of its big brother in favour of the alphabetical (and more user-friendly) ordering. The editor consulted the poets over the poems selected in order to prevent the overkill hazard of anthologies; there is the same number of poems by each poet and Linda France, unlike her more self-advertising male colleagues, did not include her own.

The starting point for selection was publication after the death of Stevie Smith in 1971. Not only does this date not overlap with other anthologies but it cuts off the more polemical poems of the 1960s. It also creates possibilities for detecting the influences of Stevie Smith upon women's poetry. Stevie Smith was ahead of her time in evading the simplistic assumption that the voice of the speaker is the voice of the author; her multivocal texts are often metalinguistic or subversively satirical. Her combination of irreverence and nostalgia for high culture and the imperceptible difference between parody and pastiche set her within the postmodern world and explain why she has been difficult to place within accounts of modern poetry. Stevie Smith is also a monument to the difficulties for women in being published, and more seriously, of being incorporated into the movements of British poetry. As Patricia Beer writes in 'In Memory of Stevie Smith':

> The Swimmer whose behaviour was so misinterpreted
> At last stopped both waving and drowning.
> . . .
>   She struck compassion
> In strange places: for ambassadors to hell, for smelly
> Unbalanced river gods, for know-all men.[11]

The conjunction of waving and drowning is a common motif in women's poetry; Stevie Smith's revision of myths and irreverence for, but obvious skill in, literary conventions are identifiable strategies of feminist poetry: she bravely overturns literary conventions in order to challenge convention itself. There are signs that contemporary women are enjoying the freedom of utterance and textual play exemplified by Stevie Smith; like her, current feminism is characterised by a relinquishment of the concern with history and representation in favour of a concentration on the machineries of history and representation.

Sixty Women Poets contains at least three generations of women and proves that age is not commensurate with outlook, contemporaneity or popularity. Among the senior citizens of women poets, born in the 1920s or before, stand Elizabeth Bartlett, Patricia Beer (whose *Collected Poems* (1988) established her as a first-rate poet and whose *Fire of Heraclitus* was shortlisted for the 1993 T.S. Eliot Poetry Prize), U.A. Fanthorpe, Elizabeth Jennings, Elma Mitchell, Ruth Pitter and E.J. Scovell (who has been enjoying a resurgence of interest since her *Collected Poems* (1988)). The mature and established poets include Fleur Adcock, usually described as 'accomplished', and those in *Contemporary Women Poets*, except for Kathleen Raine who normally refuses to be associated with women-only collections. Among the poets born during or after the Second World War are Gillian Allnutt, Wendy Cope, Vicky Feaver, Selima Hill, Michèle Roberts, Penelope Shuttle and Pauline Stainer. In the newer 1950s and 1960s generations are Alison Brackenbury, Carol Ann Duffy, Helen Dunmore, Linda France, Lavinia Greenlaw, Marion Lomax and Jo Shapcott.

Although its brief is 'poetry in Britain and Ireland' the biculturalism of many writers in *Sixty Women Poets* signifies the importance of resisting received associations of nationality as well as of age. Unified concepts of nationality, especially when allied to unified concepts of gender, tend to marginalise the feminine. Remembering that mobility prevents easy categorisation of regional and national traits, it is nevertheless instructive to indicate geographical groupings in order to demonstrate the heterogeneity of race and region and to reinforce the notion that contemporary poetry is decentred away from London and the South-East of England; poets, publishing and festivals are currently nationwide. Gillian Clarke is Welsh and Maura Dooley and Jean Earle are English but based in Wales; an impressive Scottish presence includes Carol Ann Duffy, Jackie Kay (an adopted black Glaswegian), Elma Mitchell, Katrina Porteus, Liz Lochhead and Kathleen Jamie; Southern Irish poets who are increasingly vociferous in writing, as well as writing about, poetry are Eavan Boland, Eiléan Ní Chuilleanáin, Rita Ann Higgins and Pauline Meeham; Nuala Archer and Julie O'Callaghan are American Irish and Nuala Ní Dhomhnaill is Anglo-Irish. Apart from Mebdh McGuckian, however, where are the Northern Irish women? No strangers at poetry events are Moniza Alvi from Pakistan, Lelen Bardwell from India, Sujata Bhatt who is Indian by birth, American by upbringing and European by residence, and Mimi Khalvati who was born in Tehran and educated in Europe; Anne Rouse and Eva Salzman from the United States have settled in Britain. Jean 'Binta' Breeze divides her time between Britain and the Caribbean and Grace Nichols, from Guyana, has lived in Britain since 1977. *Sixty Women Poets* does not distinguish between 'performance poets' (excluded from *The New Poetry*) and thereby helps to eradicate a term which has become pejorative. Now that many poets give readings (with varying degrees of willingness, but with consistent pressure from their publishers), when poetry is channelled through television and radio, and when the dramatic monologue is a favoured form, the distinction between performable and readerly texts seems fatuous.

The potential to dissolve conventional boundaries is where the politics of women collectively lie. It has to be said that the majority of poets are university educated, and so there is little range in terms of class; however, it is clear that in *Sixty Women Poets* grouping by gender draws attention to the intersection of age, culture and sexual orientation when considering female subjectivity. Although many poems are woman-centred, there is no possibility of conceiving of woman as a unitary subject. Not only is each individual capable of at least four identities – grandparent, mother, daughter, lover – but is also enabled to express the coexistence of, rather than the competition between, these identities: the new position, as presented by.Linda France, is that women are 'positive, creative and in control of their lives'. She concludes that the poets document a new confidence through the bold use of the first person singular, through the unashamed entrance into the wild zones of experience and through embracing the pleasure principle: several poems are erotic in a specifically sexual or in a wider sensual sense.

It is inevitable that terminology slips between the ideological and the aesthetic when assessing the poems; for women especially, language and experience are inextricably linked. There is, however, a risk of perpetuating the assumption that women are unconsciously adhering to the expressive mode rather than consciously negotiating with the processes of cultural formation, which of course includes gender formation. It is important to detect the mood of the poems, but not to assume that they operate simply as records of women's experiences. These negotiations with language and form need to be emphasised in order to stress the self-conscious preoccupation with the relationship between language and identity. Recognition of the formal awareness and intertextuality demonstrated by women poets leads to appreciation of their attempts to integrate with and to transform traditions. The range of tones – from the lyrical to the imitations of the male voice – not only defy the concept of woman as a unitary subject but also exhibit the ways in which it is the cultural codes themselves which are under scrutiny. The dual commitment of women is to the construction of an identity which is rooted in material conditions and is therefore guaranteed a place in history and also to the excitement afforded by poetry as 'metalanguage':

> Poetry is a privileged metalanguage in western patriarchal culture. Although other written forms of high culture – theology, philosophy, political theory, drama, prose fiction – are also, in part, language about language, in poetry, this introverted or doubled relation is thrust at us as the very reason-for-being of the genre. Perhaps because poetry seems, more than any other sort of imaginative writing, to imitate a closed linguistic system it is presented to us as invitingly accessible to our understanding once we have pushed past its formal difficulties. Oddly, we still seem to expect poetry to have universal meanings.
>
> (Cora Kaplan)[12]

The best poems not only negotiate the distance between realism and anti-humanism but are about that negotiation.

The current shift, then, in feminist criticism and in contemporary women's poetry is in foregrounding the processes of representation, rather than representation itself. Recurring strategies are the reversal of type; the revision of classical, historical and popular myths; the dramatic monologue, male and female; structural irony. Type is reversed through defamiliarisation of conventional gender behaviour, such as the pregnant woman's sexuality[13] or ageing – 'The first surprise. I like it' ('Getting Older', Elaine Feinstein),[14] and through reversing the subject/object position so that the woman is observing the male looking at her, most acutely in Carol Ann Duffy's 'Standing Female Nude'.[15] Relationships between women liberate women from the male gaze altogether: most wholly in the erotic lesbian love relationship such as Jackie Kay's 'Other Lovers'[16] or the slave girl's desire for her mistress in Carol Ann Duffy's 'Warming Her Pearls'.[17] Female relationships, whether mother and child, teacher and pupil or childhood friendships, are not, however, glamourised but explored. Poems about love are about finding new ways of expressing love which counteract received cultural codes. In keeping with postmodern emphasis on culture as the primary site of the formation of subjectivity (and language is of course instrumental in this process), it is the conditions and contexts of relationship which are examined. These frequently undermine the narratives of romantic love, like 'The Unsuccessful Wedding Night' (Selima Hill)[18] or Gillian Alnutt's 'Ode' which is a love song metaphorised as repairing a bicycle.[19] 'The Did-You-Come-Yet-of-the-Western-World' (Rita Ann Higgins) mimics masculine bravado and counteracts stereotyped feminine vocabulary:

> When he says to you
> You look so beautiful
> you smell so nice –
> how I've missed you –
> and did you come yet?
>
> It means nothing,
> and he is smaller,
> than a mouse's fart.[20]

Integral to the debunking of cultural codes is the mockery of powerful rhetoric, whether of the lover, the tabloid news editor, the scientist or the politician. The satire can operate on the level of personal relationships or as a strategy to expose institutional evils through imitating the grand discourses of Science, Education, Religion or Commerce. Hilary Davies describes the unspoken text of the eye-specialist enjoying the intimacy of the darkened room[21] and Lavinia Greenlaw rewrites the discovery of radium to show its devastating effects on the women workers.[22] As myth is one way of embedding cultural traditions, the revision of myth is now a common device for women and solves women's ambiguous relationship to history by conflating past and present tenses. Carol Ann Duffy's *The World's Wife* (1995)[23] is a collection of female monologues which simultaneously deflate canonised heroes such as Midas, Tiresias and Aesop and current myths of masculinity and femininity. Carol Ann Duffy is outstanding in her manipulation of language and her tightrope path between metapoetics and realism. It is the awareness that the speakers have themselves been linguistically structured, and by implication socially constructed, which accounts for the mixed responses to a disturbing male monologue like 'Psychopath'.[24] 'Poet for Our Times'[25] is one of many examples of her ability to 'popularise complex ideas about language, and its political role and meanings',[26] as is 'Translating the English, 1989... and much of the poetry, alas, is lost in translation...':

Welcome to my country! We have here Edwina Currie
and The Sun newspaper. Much excitement.
Also the weather has been most improving
even in February. Daffodils. (Wordsworth. Up North.) If you like
Shakespeare or even Opera we have too the Black Market.
For two hundred quids we are talking Les Miserables,
nods being as good as winks. Don't eat the eggs.
Wheel-clamp. Dogs. Vagrant. A tour of our wonderful
capital city is not to be missed. The Fergie,
The Princess Di and the football hooligan, truly you will
like it here, Squire.[27]

The number of frames of reference in the single poem, let alone within the still growing oeuvre is remarkable. The nearest to Carol Ann Duffy when it comes to combining a politics of transformation with self-contained discourse are Eavan Boland, Kathleen Jamie and Jo Shapcott.

Anthologies such as *Sixty Women Poets* are evidence that a separatist collection is not defensive but that it makes new links and definitions in poetry. To some extent it complements other activities but it also contradicts versions of literary activity which exclude or misrepresent women. It points to the possibility of a more democratic system of representation and of a more historically specific map of literary history which aims at inclusiveness and the celebration of difference. Although anthologies will always be divisive because they involve selection, they can be compiled in a spirit of collaboration rather than of competition. In charting the development in approaches to poetry, it is clear that women do not ignore traditions; they are conscious of the literary canon but have a new confidence in textual play and inventiveness. This is in accordance with the poetics of postmodernism which stresses plurality and dispersal – themselves symptoms of feminist activities of decentring – and a recognition of the intersections of sexual orientation and cultural formations in the construction of identities. It is no longer appropriate to seek for a 'woman's voice'; it is more enlightening to identify the strategies by which women revise the traditions. Variety and diversity should prevent a hardening orthodoxy about 'contemporary' poetry as the property of youth, for example. Diversity does not negate the question of value, but pushes towards a relative and context-driven system of value.

Notes

1. Sylvia Townsend Warner, *Collected Poems* and *Selected Poems*, ed. Clare Hairman (Manchester: Carcanet, 1982; 1985 respectively).
    Stevie Smith, *Collected Poems*, ed. James MacGibbon (London: Allen Lane, 1975), *Selected Poems*, ed. James McGibbon (London: Penguin, 1978), *Stevie Smith: A Selection*, ed. Hermione Lee (London: Faber, 1983) and *Me Again, Uncollected Writings of Stevie Smith* (London: Virago, 1981).
2. Elaine Feinstein, in Couzyn (1985), p. 114.
3. Ruth Fainlight, in Couzyn (1985), p. 130.
4. 'Blood, Bread and Poetry: The Location of the Poet' (1984), in Rich (1987), p. 174.
5. Michelene Wandor, 'Voices are Wild', Monteith (1986), p. 83.
6. Alicia Ostriker (1987), p. 12.
7. Rumens (1993), p. 12.
8. Green, 'Introduction' (1991).
9. Grace Nichols, 'The Poet's Introduction', in Kinsman (1992), p. 31.
10. *The Virago Book of Birth Poetry* (1993) has poems by men as well as women.
11. France (1993), p. 50.
12. Cora Kaplan, 'Language and Gender', in Deborah Cameron (ed.) (1990), p. 57.
13. 'White Asparagus', Sujata Bhatt, p. 62. This and subsequent page numbers refer to *Sixty Women Poets*, ed. France (1993).
14. 'Getting Older', Elaine Feinstein, p. 138.
15. 'Standing Female Nude', Carol Ann Duffy, p. 113.
16. 'Other Lovers', Jacky Kay, p. 183.
17. 'Warming Her Pearls', Carol Ann Duffy, p. 114.
18. 'The Unsuccessful Wedding Night', Selima Hill, pp. 156–7.
19. 'Ode', Gillian Alnutt, pp. 26–7.
20. 'The Did-You-Come-Yet-of-the-Western-World', Rita Ann Higgins, p. 151.
21. 'The Ophthalmologist', Hilary Davies, p. 96.
22. 'The Innocence of Radium', Lavinia Greenlaw, pp. 148–9.
23. See Carol Ann Duffy, *Selected Poems*, pp. 131–47.

24. 'Psychopath', ibid., p. 43.
25. 'Poet For Our Times', ibid., p. 80.
26. Hulse et al. (1993), p. 17.
27. 'Translating the English, 1989 ... and much of the poetry, alas, is lost in translation ...', Carol Ann Duffy, in *Sixty Women Poets*, ed. France (1993), p. 115. Extract courtesy of Anvil Press.

Bibliography

Anthologies and primary works

Adcock, Fleur (ed.), *The Faber Book of Twentieth Century Women's Poetry* (London: Faber, 1987).
Breen, Jennifer (ed.), *English Women Romantic Poets 1785–1832: An Anthology* (London: Dent, 1992).
Breen, Jennifer (ed.), *Victorian Women Poets* (London: Dent, 1994).
Cosman, Carol, Keefe, Joan and Weaver, Kathleen, (eds), *The Penguin Book of Women Poets* (London: Allen Lane, 1978; Penguin, 1979).
Couzyn, Jeni, (ed.), *The Bloodaxe Book of Contemporary Women's Poetry* (Newcastle upon Tyne: Bloodaxe Books, 1985).
Deletant, Andrea and Walker, Brenda (eds), *Silent Voices, An anthology of contemporary Romanian women poets* (London: Forest Books, 1986; 1989).
Duffy, Carol Ann, *Selected Poems* (London: Penguin/Anvil Press, 1994).
Duffy, Carol Ann, *The World's Wife* (London: Anvil Press, 1995).
France, Linda, *Sixty Women Poets* (Newcastle upon Tyne: Bloodaxe Books, 1993).
Green, Veronica (ed.), *Rhythm of Our Days: An anthology of women's poetry* (Cambridge: Cambridge University Press, 1991).
Hampton, S. and Llewelyn, K. (eds), *The Penguin Book of Australian Women Poets* (Harmondsworth: Penguin, 1986).
Hulse, Michael, Kennedy, David and Morely, David, *The New Poetry* (Newcastle upon Tyne: Bloodaxe, Books, 1993).
Kinsman, Judith (ed.), *Six Women Poets* (Oxford: Oxford University Press, 1992).
Linthwaite, Illona (ed.), *Ain't I a Woman! Poems by Black and White Women* (London: Virago, 1987).
McEwan, Christian (ed.), *Naming the Waves: Contemporary Lesbian Poetry* (London: Virago, 1988).
Otten, Charlotte, *The Virago Book of Birth Poetry* (London: Virago, 1993).
Palmeira, Rosemary (ed.), *In the Gold of the Flesh: Poems of Birth and Motherhood* (London: The Women's Press, 1990).
Pritchard, R.E. (ed.), *Poetry by English Women: Elizabethan to Victorian* (Manchester: Carcanet, 1990).
Ransford, T. (ed.), *Fresh Oceans – An Anthology of Poetry by Scottish Women* (Edinburgh: Stramullion, 1989).
Reilly, Catherine (ed.), *Scars Upon My Heart* (London: Virago, 1981).
Reilly, Catherine (ed.), *Chaos of the Night* (London: Virago, 1984).
Rumens, Carol (ed.), *Making for the Open: Post-feminist Poetry* (London: Chatto & Windus, 1987).

Rumens, Carol (ed.), *New Women Poets* (Newcastle upon Tyne: Bloodaxe Books, 1993).

Scott, Diana (ed.), *Bread and Roses: Women's Poetry of the 19th and 20th Centuries* (London: Virago, 1982).

Silgardo, M. and Beck, J. (eds), *Virago New Poets* (London: Virago 1993).

Various, *Five Women Poets* (Manchester: Crocus Books, 1994).

Secondary works

Gilbert, Sandra and Gubar, Susan (eds), *Shakespeare's Sisters: Feminist Essays On Women Poets* (Bloomington: Indiana University Press, 1979).

Kaplan, Cora, 'Language and Gender', in *A Feminist Critique of Language*, ed. Deborah Cameron (London: Routledge, 1990), pp. 57–76.

Montefiore, Jan, *Feminism and Poetry: Language, Experience, Identity in Women's Writing* (London: Pandora, 1987).

Olsen, Tillie, *Silences* (London: Virago, 1980).

Ostriker, Alicia, *Stealing the Language: The Emergence of Women's Poetry In America* (London: The Women's Press, 1987).

Rich, Adrienne, *Blood, Bread and Poetry: Selected Prose 1979–1985* (London: Virago, 1987).

Wandor, Michelene, 'Voices are Wild', in *Women's Writing: A Challenge to Theory*, ed. Moira Monteith (Sussex: Harvester, 1986), pp. 72–89.

Yorke, Liz, *Impertinent Voices: Subversive Strategies in Contemporary Women's Poetry* (London: Routledge, 1991).

14

Women Poets and 'Women's Poetry': Fleur Adcock, Gillian Clarke and Carol Rumens

Lyn Pykett

I regret the omission of women poets from this book. This is simply due to the fact that Britain in the last fifteen years has not produced a woman poet of real stature.[1]

The under-representation of women among writers of poetry, and the under-valuation of those women who succeeded in both writing and publishing poetry, has been briskly analysed by Fleur Adcock in her introduction to *The Faber Book of Twentieth Century Women's Poetry* (1987). The editors, publishers and critics of poetry, she notes, were (and, on the whole, still are) men.

> Men tend not to take women seriously. Women as a result tended not to take themselves seriously enough, and were in any case usually too busy, too oppressed or too under-educated to write... The Muse was female, the poet was male. There was a deep-seated conviction that women couldn't do it.[2]

As a consequence of the women's movement and the resulting heightened self-consciousness (although Adcock does not explicitly make this connection), the situation has completely changed. Even if male editors and critics retain their dismissive attitudes to poetry by women, 'women themselves want to read it, and there are not only women's presses but also general publishing houses which want to publish it.'[3]

Despite (or perhaps because of) the heightened profile of poetry by women and the gathering together of women poets in volumes devoted exclusively to women's work, the terms 'women's poetry' and 'woman poet' have become increasingly problematised. Many women writers, unless they write overtly and self-consciously as feminists, have been extremely reluctant to accept the label 'woman poet', and are often at pains to deny that they write women's poetry. Anne Stevenson's contribution to *Women Writing and Writing About Women* is a case in point. Stevenson describes in great detail the experiences of domestic entrapment that made her return to the writing of poetry in a difficult first marriage. She charts the genesis of a poem which she sees clearly as 'a woman's book' constructed of 'experiences I understood through having lived my life as a woman'.[4] Nevertheless, she determinedly distances herself from the role of 'woman writer', espousing instead the cause of a transcendent and hence genderless art. In order to fulfil her own and what she takes to be generally accepted notions of art, Stevenson feels that she must strive to be *more* than *merely* a woman poet. To write as a woman, whether 'old' or 'new', is to play a role which 'substitutes a public stance for particular perceptions' whereas 'a writer must leave herself free for particular perceptions.'[5]

A similar unease with the idea of the 'woman poet' is revealed in a symposium of female writers in a recent edition of *Poetry Wales*[6] in which the participants were asked whether they thought of themselves, or wished to be thought of, as 'women writers'. Most respondents refused the label, giving the standard, and in their way perfectly understandable, reasons: the fear of marginalisation and ghettoisation. Most of them share with Anne Stevenson a transcendent view of poetry as an expansion of human possibility and fear that writing as a woman (or being seen as a 'woman writer') would, at best, place unnecessary limitations on their art. At worst, if writing as a woman is understood as writing as a feminist, the result would be a diminished poetry of denial and exclusion.

Like Sheenagh Pugh, most of the respondents, I suspect in common with most mainstream poets whether male or female, would 'prefer to see poetry as universal and unifying rather than particular and divisive'.[7] Most of them wish to belong to (and be seen as belonging to) a central tradition of humane letters which they perceive to be gender-neutral. The ironies of the woman writer's affirmation of a literary tradition 'to which most women's poetry never officially belongs' and from which it has been more or less systematically excluded have been pointed out by Jan Montefiore[8] among others. The adherence of women writers to the idea of a gender-neutral tradition may perhaps be attributed in part to fear. For underlying the principled objections to the label and role of 'woman writer' is the old fear that the title is less a description than an accusation and a term of diminution and denigration. To be labelled as a 'woman poet' is to risk automatic relegation to the second rank. 'If there is such a thing as a poetry which is limited to part of humanity', writes Sheenagh Pugh, 'there is a simpler name for it than women's poetry, black poetry or whatever ... the word in question is mediocre.'[9] It is extremely ironic, and also indicative of a fundamental conceptual confusion, that a notion of poetry which, on the one hand, valorises particularity of perception, should, on the other hand, be so dismissive of a poetry that comes and speaks from a particular position or perspective.

Many, perhaps most, of the most prominent and widely published women poets, whose careers have no doubt been furthered by the current interest in women's writing, have been among the most assiduous in resisting the tag of 'woman poet'. They have also been concerned in their public (prose) utterances to distance themselves both from the idea of 'women's writing' and from feminism. Nevertheless, despite their unhappiness with the label and/or the women's movement, they have been profoundly influenced by feminism and have made a most important contribution to women's writing. Whatever their own views on, or relationship to, feminism their work has been shaped by the discourses of feminism and their resistances to them.

Fleur Adcock, who gives a very spirited account of the scandalous neglect of women writers and the failure to nurture women's writing, nevertheless warns of the dangers of 'separatism'. She sees separatism as 'an inevitable stage of the social revolution', but finds it 'hardly surprising' that it should prejudice and antagonise men (the ultimate court of appeal?) against 'even those women who, *like most real poets*' (my emphasis), address both men and women or an audience 'which is not defined in gender terms.'[10]

Carol Rumens has been much more polemical in her attempts to distance herself, and indeed everyone else, from feminism by proclaiming a 'post-feminist' era of poetry in her Chatto anthology. This is, to say the least, a curiously anachronistic designation given the period covered by the anthology – 1964 to 1984. As far as Britain is concerned 1964 looks distinctly pre- rather than post-feminist.

As a poet with a finely honed sense of particularities, Rumens is alert to the ironies of what she takes to be the situation of women's writing in 1985: 'The political orientation of much women's publishing (*without which, of course, it would not have come into being*) has sometimes, particularly in the case of poetry, led to the elevation of the message at the expense of the medium' (my emphasis). During the phase of feminist struggle (now, we are to understand, mercifully passed) *real* writers – those concerned with ' "the stern art of poetry" as an end in itself' – were 'swamped' by 'noisy amateurs proclaiming that women too have a voice'. I too find it difficult to read with either pleasure or instruction some of the poems collected in some self-consciously feminist anthologies from the feminist publishers. However, I find it hard to share Rumens's conviction that the fight is o'er, the battle won, and that the conviction that 'women have a voice, and the right to be heard goes without saying'. Like many of us Rumens is all too ready to take advantage of the political gains won by others, and to leave behind those for whom the struggle continues. The class assumptions of her definition of post-feminism are self-evident. She uses the term to designate the 'psychological condition' inaugurated by the radical social changes 'affecting many women (particularly those of the middle, i.e. writing classes)'.[11]

The trajectory of Rumens's own career to date provides an interesting example of the way in which much avowedly non-feminist poetry engages in a debate with and around the issues raised by the women's movement. Rumens's first collection, *A Strange Girl in Bright Colours* (1973), might be described as proto-feminist. It is minutely and often angrily focused on the particularities of the limitations of a young woman's initiation into domestic life: trapped, frustrated and burdened by her sense of responsibility for the lives of others. Many of these early poems constitute a record of alienation from marriage and domesticity, from former versions of the self; from the impoverished surroundings of the bleak housing estates of 'A Future' (p. 18) or the dingy flat of 'Houses By Day' (p. 17) where 'I have lived... an impenetrable year,/with only a mirror to smile at, and a hot-water system/for an echo. I can just remember/ . . . /an earlier daylight.' These poems are also a record of a struggle to get by – materially, emotionally and imaginatively – and of a desire to get out. One is reminded of Larkin's young housewives, pushed 'To the side of their own lives',[12] although Rumens is less detached and more angry than

Larkin. There is also momentary anger and sympathy for the awfulness of other women's lives, for example the girls from the council estate who 'with sober headscarves and great prams,/ shove for their lives' ('Distinctions', p. 23).

The largely self-focused anger of Rumens's first collection has, on the whole, disappeared from *Unplayed Music* (1981) and *Star Whisper* (1983). In both of these books Rumens begins to establish her distance from what Anne Stevenson has described as the 'sub-Plathian effortfulness' and 'inflated indignation'[13] which characterised much poetry by women in the early 1970s. However, although much of the proto-feminist anger of Rumens's first collection has been expunged from these two later volumes, they both contain a number of poems which offer ironic and reflective perspectives on women's lives and experiences. I am thinking of poems such as 'A Marriage' (p. 33), 'Double Bed' (p. 34), 'Gifts and Loans' (p. 36), 'The Strawberry Mark' (p. 37) and 'Rules for Beginners' (p. 40) in *Unplayed Music*, and 'The Carpet Sweeper' (p. 51), 'Double Exposure' (p. 52), 'The Most Difficult Door' (p. 67) and 'Lullaby for a First Child' (p. 55) in *Star Whisper*.

In *Star Whisper* we begin to see the development of that voice which emerges more fully in *Direct Dialling* (1985) which was published in the same year as the 'post-feminist' *Making for the Open*. Rumens's own collection, like her anthology, seems to aspire to a post-feminism which is defined as a movement away from a feminism which is alleged to have performed its work. There is still anger in *Direct Dialling*, but it is reserved for other causes than the cause of women. Rumens now strives for an impersonal (though not entirely genderless) voice with which to articulate broader (i.e. broader than the 'narrow' concerns of feminism) political, historical humanistic themes. In particular Rumens has become increasingly concerned with the past and present history and politics of Eastern and Mittel Europe.

These latter concerns persist in, even dominate, the concluding section of Rumens's *Selected Poems* (1987) and her latest collection *From Berlin to Heaven* (1989). However, a number of the later poems might also be described as 'post-feminist', not in the sense that Rumens uses that term in her Chatto anthology, but in the sense of having been marked by the agendas and perspectives of feminism. A number of the later poems cast a reflective, questioning and sometimes ironic eye on women's lives and on sexual politics. Familiar feminist isues are explored in 'Two Women' (p. 115), on

the uneasy coexistence of the confident capable working woman
who bears home 'the simple, cool-skinned apples/of a father's
loving objectivity' and the 'silent background face/that's always
flushed with work, or swallowed anger'. Some of these poems seem
to recapture something of the sharp edge of Rumens's earlier writing, but it is a more meditated anger. The awful ironies of the
captive power conferred on women by the ideologies of domestic
femininity are powerfully conveyed in 'A Woman of a Certain Age'
(p. 126) and 'In a Room' (pp. 102–3) which evoke the luxurious
confinement of the domestic woman.

> Valued as a princess,
> she has always been taught
> to brush out her hair, arrange
> her ankles, and wait.
> She is used to it all
>
> – the sensation of hunger
> – the need for patience.

The hollow emptiness of her daily existence and her powerless
power are artfully conveyed in the complex and self-undercutting
negatives of the final stanza: 'unchecked, unspent, she knows/how
terrible her power is,/how impossible not to use.'
    Thus despite her protestations, the evidence provided by Ru-
mens's work suggests that feminism and the women's movement
have been both enabling and liberating. Feminism has to some
extent provided her with both a voice and a subject. I would
suggest that this is also the case with a number of other non-
feminist writers who have both taken advantage of and made an
important contribution to the greater space for women's concerns
and issues in poetry, and the greater attentiveness to women's
voices that the women's movement has generated. Or, to put it
another way: despite their own ambivalent relationship to feminism these women writers have, neverthless, addressed its agendas.
    In particular a number of prominent women writers such as
Fleur Adcock, Gillian Clarke and Anne Stevenson (each of whom,
like Rumens, is uneasy about being labelled as a 'woman poet')
have all been involved in a minute and scrupulous celebration and
investigation of the domestic and familial which has been such an
important aspect of much recent poetry by both men and women.

Women writers have made a distinctive contribution to the development of this particular mode of contemporary poetry. I do not wish to suggest any simple causal relationship, but it does seem to me that the 'anger and celebration' which 'seem the warp and weft of contemporary poetry by women'[14] has been shaped by the women's movement's democratic emphasis on the value and importance of the everyday experience of 'ordinary' people, and, more particularly, its foregrounding of the domestic, as critique and/or celebration of women's domestic activities.

Feminist perspectives can be seen, for example, in the increased attentiveness of each of my selected poets to what Jenny Joseph has called the 'dailiness' of life.[15] A number of poems represent and explore the lives of 'ordinary' women. Fleur Adcock's 'The Soho Hospital for Women' (p. 80) is a notable example. Others include Jenny Joseph's own portrait of 'Women at Streatham Hill', burdened with shopping and life:

> Nobody asks what they have done all day
> For who asks trees or stones what they have done?
> They root, they gather moss, they spread, they are.
>
> It would seem more removal than volition
> If once they were not there when men came home.[16]

The questioning of sexual politics in this last line is, of course, an important aspect of many of the poems focusing on domestic and daily life. It is present too in a range of poems on sexual relationships. The sardonic wit of Fleur Adcock's erotic or anti-erotic poems has long been acknowledged. Again, it is difficult not to connect her irreverence about men and her wry interrogation of romantic love with feminism's sharp scrutiny of these matters. At first glance Adcock's 'Against Coupling' (p. 33) – a poem 'in praise of the solitary act' – would seem to make the radical separatist case with exemplary verve and grace (although, at second glance, perhaps, we might enjoy the joke but feel that the lady protests too much). The ironies and uncertainties of the pleasurable problems of sex are also wittily balanced in 'Double-Take' (*IB*, p. 44), on the residual attractions of a balding, paunchy ex-lover which leave the speaker 'cursing chemistry'.

Marriage too has come under close scrutiny. As I have already noted, some of Carol Rumens's early poems rail angrily at a young wife's sense of entrapment both within the domestic space and within marriage itself, for example in the nightmare vision of 'Houses By Day' (p. 17) in which 'The tight ring dragged on my thickening finger/ ... /The trauma of marriage swallowed me.' Elsewhere Rumens ponders the dishonesties and deceptions (both large and small) of married people and the frustrations, accommodations and consolations of the marriages they inhabit. These concerns produce some of the best poems in *Unplayed Music*: 'Double Bed' (p. 34), 'Gifts and Loans' (p. 36) and 'A Marriage' with its 'picture of marriage/as a whole small civilisation ... its religion, the love of children/whose anger it survived long ago'. It is a picture which the speaker of the poem admires but from which she is excluded, and which both threatens and is threatened by her own sexuality as she concludes that 'to look on him [the husband] as a woman/would turn me cold with shame.'

These women writers have not only written of women's experiences of marriage and participated in the re-examination of marriage and romantic love prompted by the women's movement. They have also engaged in a sometimes celebratory, sometimes angry, but almost always unsentimental scrutiny of women's experiences of family life. Each of my chosen writers has written with clarity, irony and affection of the pains, pleasures and frustrations of their own or women's roles as mother or daughter, as well as wife or lover, and of the experience of childbirth and of the rearing of children. I think of Adcock's 'Tadpoles' (*IB*, p. 7), a weaving meditation on generation and the generations addressed by a grandmother to her grandson, or 'On a Son Returned to New Zealand' (p. 29) which simultaneously affirms the mother's inseparable connection to her son and the child's inevitable separation from the mother: 'He is my green branch growing in a far plantation/He is my first invention ... He is my bright sea-bird on a rocky beach.' This poem is a very powerful evocation of the pain of separation and loss, not only the unavoidable separations and losses of the parent–child relation, but also the particular grief of a mother who lives (literally) in a different hemisphere from her child. This is felt sharply in the multiple ambiguities of the penultimate line's, 'He could go no further', which is at once a statement that the son has reached his destination, a sigh of relief that he has reached the limits of the physical distance which will separate them and a cry of grief that the distance is absolute (it is so great that the addition of extra miles could not make it greater).

The mother's gift of life to the child and the child's gifts to the mother are evoked in Carol Rumens's 'Lullaby for a First Child' (p. 55) and 'April in February' (p. 112). Gillian Clarke, on the other hand, explores the power and the complex tensions and struggles involved in the maternal feelings and in the relationships between mothers and children in 'Babysitting' (p. 11), 'Catrin' (p. 14), and 'Swinging!' (p. 18), each of which combines images of sensuous warmth with a barely submerged violence as the mother–child relation replays in various forms the first 'Fierce confrontation, the tight/Red rope of love which we both/Fought over' ('Catrin', p. 14).

The mother–daughter relationship, which has been freshly scrutinised by feminists, has also been explored by all of my selected poets, for example in the deceptively jaunty rhyming couplets of Fleur Adcock's 'The Chiffonier', in which the daughter sends a message of filial love and tries to come to terms with her feelings about her mother's illness and imminent death. Daughterhood and the links between women across the generations of families is also a prominent theme of Gillian Clarke and Anne Stevenson, most interestingly in 'Letter From a Far Country' and 'Correspondences' to which I shall return shortly.

Most of Carol Rumens's poems on daughterhood involve the father–daughter relationship, but in 'The Carpet-Sweeper' (p. 51) a chance meeting with an old Ewbank triggers childhood memories and serves as a point of reconnection with her mother. The carpet-sweeper becomes the focus of a newly sympathetic understanding of the mother's 'scolding face' and those moods when 'savagery and housework boiled in your heart'. The Ewbank also becomes a figure for the poet's new view of the domestic lives of women, as she makes it bear 'The sighs of all women/whose days are shaped by rooms.'

As I have already suggested, the frustrations of the domestic life are all too evident in a number of Rumens's early and late poems. On the whole my other writers tend to celebrate the domestic, as in Fleur Adcock's 'House-Talk' (p. 87) or in 'Saturday' (p. 29), her hymn to the sights, smells and sounds, and the physical and emotional fulfilment of ordinary domestic life. Gillian Clarke's 'Siege' (p. 77) is similarly, at least in part, a sensuous celebration of the domestic in its evocation of the tree-surrounded kitchen in which the speaker sorts out family photographs. One might argue, however, that this poem demonstrates and, perhaps, explores some of the ideological work performed by a particular version of the domestic. The speaker's kitchen is made the locus of memory and continuity in which, despite her sense of historical difference, her own sense of continuity with past generations is also confirmed. The kitchen is an island of stability which is nevertheless constantly in danger of being invaded by the violent disruptions of the world of public history which lies beyond its walls.

Each of the writers who form the main focus of this essay explores a variety of women's familial and social roles and experiences. Often, whether implicitly or explicitly, they expose and/or explore the tensions and contradictions involved in those roles and in the ways in which women are expected to combine them. They focus, too, on the complex relationships and conflicts between socially constructed roles and the ways in which those roles have to be lived by particular individuals in specific times and places. In this respect, as in other areas of their work already discussed, these 'non-feminist' writers intervene in the discourses of feminism, and appropriate feminist perspectives and debates as a means of addressing their own concerns. Moreover, when they write on women's concerns or of their own, specifically female experience, they do so with a confidence and authority borrowed from the women's movement.

The tensions, conflicts and contradictions of socially sanctioned 'feminine' roles have always been particularly acute for the woman who is also a writer. Anne Stevenson has written feelingly on the dilemmas of the woman who wishes to *be* a writer (rather than simply a woman who writes). Stevenson perhaps sees the problem in too sharply polarised a form as a choice between marriage, children and life as a 'writer with a handicap', and the real (if 'narrow' and 'selfish') independence of the spinster writers such as Emily Brontë, Stevie Smith, Elizabeth Bishop and Marianne Moore. Nevertheless, she is right to point out that one consequence of the woman writer's difficulties in combining her social, (hetero)-sexual and aesthetic desires has been a ready-made subject for poetry by women: the dilemma of the woman writer itself becomes the central subject of her poetry. Stevenson notes this tension between the woman writer and the domestic role in her own work: 'Though I have never considered myself to be a specifically feminist poet, many of my poems are about being trapped in domestic surroundings.'[17] This is clearly the route taken in a number of the poems I have discussed.

More ambitiously, perhaps, a number of women currently writing poetry have attempted to move away from the woman/writer
dilemma as the central subject of their poems and have aspired to a
broader vision of woman's experience and women's history. Stevenson's own *Correspondences: A Family History in Letters* (OUP,
1974) and Gillian Clarke's 'Letter From a Far Country' both share
this project. Both poems are broadly speaking epistolary in form.
Correspondences consists of a series of letters which circulate within
and between different generations of the same family. Clarke's
poem is a single 'letter home from the future/my bottle in the sea
which might/take a generation to arrive' (p. 52). Both poems focus
minutely on women's lives, and privilege the woman's voice. Both
explore the correspondences, disruptions and transformations between generations, by charting history through the female line.
Both are 'women's poems' in the sense that their images and
perceptions seem to grow (to paraphrase Anne Stevenson) from
experiences understood through having lived life as a woman.

Indeed 'Letter From a Far Country' seems self-consciously to
strive for a woman's language, in this case a language which is
essentially domestic. A shared domestic experience serves both as a
link between the different generations of women and as a way of
perceiving and shaping the history which Clarke's 'Letter' constructs and retrieves. It is a poem woven from domestic images:

> The waves are folded meticulously
> perfectly white. They are tumbled
> and must come to be folded again...
> ... The sea's a sheet
> Bellying in the wind, snapping.

(p. 56)

Clarke's poem owes a great deal to the celebratory re-evaluation of
women's domestic work offered by some versions of feminism. She
writes lovingly of the 'ceremonials' (p. 57) performed by a female
priesthood in daily domestic life and foregrounds women's domestic capabilities. However, her poem also makes us powerfully
aware of the limitations as well as the richness of women's domestic lives; sometimes the simultaneity of the richness and the limitation are figured in a single image, such as 'Familiar days are stored
whole/in bottles' (p. 57). There is also, perhaps, a submerged

feminist anger in the poem's understanding of the simultaneous centrality and marginality of the women. They are central to the emotional life, and are the cement of the social structure of the communities whose evolution and decline the poem traces, and at the same time they are utterly marginal to the community's relations with a wider public world. The women, who are the emotional centres of their worlds, whose lives are measured in laundry lists, in achieved piles of neatly folded washing and filled larder shelves, are also the watchers and waiters, the nurturers of others who act on the public stage, and whose work is more publicly honoured and valued. This understanding of the female lot is figured in the girl who must wait and pass time while 'the minstrel boy to the war has gone', and the girl who longs to carry the tea to the men in the fields, who longs 'for the feminine privilege,/for the male right to the field' (p. 58).

Among the many other things it does Clarke's 'Letter' replays (admittedly in an oblique way) an important debate within feminism. A feminism which insists on the centrality and value of 'women's' experience may find itself inevitably insisting on the centrality and value of women's domestic role. There is clearly a danger of essentialism here, of a too ready acceptance of the view that women's biological and social destiny is that of the domestic maker and carer. The main difference between the feminist and the traditional patriarchal versions of domestic woman is that the former now foregrounds and valorises what patriarchy had marginalised and devalued. Clarke clearly risks this essentialism: women, she writes:

> ... are hawks trained to return
> to the lure from the circle's
> far circumference. Children sing
> that note that only we can hear.

(p. 63)

Nevertheless, she feels the tension in the 'taut silk cords' that bind her to her grandmothers and the domestic tradition. One is left wondering too about the force and significance of the letter's concluding three stanzas. These are typographically marked off from the rest of the poem as an italicised coda which poses a series of questions about the consequences for the family, and particularly for children, of women's questing abroad to 'wander over the sea' or to hunt 'along with the men' (p. 64). As many feminists have argued, to imagine a world in which women may 'put to sea and sail away' is to imagine a different social order, and in particular a different role for men. Clarke's concluding stanzas emerge from this version of the problematic, but she is only able to pose the problem in terms of questions. Are these questions meant to prod the reader into rethinking her/his views of traditional gender roles, or are they, rather, rhetorical questions intended to overwhelm the woman reader with the enormity of the problem and send her back to the safety and dry land?

In a way the poem returns us to Stevenson's woman/writer dilemma by another route. 'Letter From a Far Country' embodies and reworks one traditional solution to the intelligent and articulate woman's struggle to reconcile her own sense of desire and authenticity with socially sanctioned feminine roles: she becomes a writer, or engages in some other form of cultural work which can be carried out in the domestic space and in the imaginative space left over from what the Victorians called her 'womanly duties'. Clarke's poem is a form of time-travel: it travels back and forth in time in its attempt to embrace the history of the writer's family and community. It is also a means by which the writer may travel out of the limitations of her own (domestic) time and space and, in the absence of far-flung voyages, embark on an inner journey. It is in this respect, perhaps, that the letter-writer expresses both her most basic continuity with her grandmothers and her distance from them. She too waits in the margins of other people's lives, her journey is circumscribed by the length of the school day and the demands of domestic tasks. However, the poem subtly changes the definition of centre and margins: through the life of the imagination and the making of poetry, the woman poet becomes both the minstrel boy who goes to war *and* the girl who waits and passes time.

In this essay I have focused on the way in which a few widely published and widely read women poets make women's experience, particularly women's domestic experience, an important focus of their poetry. They use the domestic as a subject, as an area of linguistic resource and as the focus for exploration, celebration and/or critique. I might, instead, have chosen a different body of

266 *Lyn Pykett*

poetry by women (for example, some of the work of Elaine Feinstein, Jenny Joseph or Ruth Fainlight, among others) in order to examine a different way of articulating a distinctively feminine voice through a woman-focused revision and reworking of traditional mythology. As I have suggested, many, perhaps most, of the poets I have discussed would not regard themselves as feminist poets; some would be reluctant to be considered as 'women poets'. It is certainly not part of my case to produce these women poets *as* (covert) feminists. Neverthless, as I hope I have shown, important aspects of their work do seem to have been shaped by, and within, the discourses of feminism. Nor is it part of my case to invent a genre called 'women's poetry': a prescriptive category which is defined in terms of a female or feminine language and/or subject-matter. Rather I would wish to suggest that feminist critical practice offers a way of reading which enables us to listen to and understand on their own terms the distinctive ways in which women writers work within and rework existing genres.

Notes

Page references to poems are given in the text. They refer to the following volumes:

Fleur Adcock, *Selected Poems* (Oxford: OUP, 1983). All references to Adcock's poems which simply give a page number refer to this volume. References citing IB are from Adcock's *The Incident Book* (Oxford: OUP, 1986).
Gillian Clarke, *Selected Poems* (Manchester: Carcanet, 1985).
Carol Rumens, *Selected Poems* (London: Chatto & Windus, 1987).

1. Geoffrey Summerfield, *Worlds* (Harmondsworth: Penguin, 1974), p. 2.
2. Fleur Adcock, *The Faber Book of Twentieth Century Women's Poetry* (London: Faber, 1987), p. 1.
3. Adcock, op. cit., p. 2.
4. Anne Stevenson, 'Writing as a Woman', in Mary Jacobus (ed.), *Women Writing and Writing About Woman* (London: Croom Helm, 1979), p. 173.
5. Ibid., p. 175.
6. 'Is There a Women's Poetry?', *Poetry Wales*, Vol. 23, No. 1, 1987, pp. 30–57.
7. Ibid., p. 30.

8. Jan Montefiore, *Feminism and Poetry: Language, Experience, Identity in Women's Writing* (London: Pandora Press, 1987), p. 38.
9. *Poetry Wales*, op. cit., p. 31.
10. Adcock, op. cit., pp. 2–3.
11. Carol Rumens, *Making For the Open: The Chatto Book of Post-Feminist Poetry* (London: Chatto & Windus, 1985), pp. xv–xvi.
12. Philip Larkin, 'Afternoons', *The Whitsun Weddings* (London: Faber, 1964), p. 44.
13. Anne Stevenson, 'An Essay on the Poetry of Carol Rumens', *Poetry Nation Review*, 1987, 12: 2, pp. 49–50, p. 50.
14. Christine Evans, *Poetry Wales*, op. cit., p. 43.
15. Jenny Joseph, *The Bloodaxe Book of Contemporary Women's Poetry* (Newcastle upon Tyne: Bloodaxe, 1985), p. 169.
16. Ibid., p. 173.
17. Anne Stevenson, 'Writing as a Woman', op. cit., pp. 163 and 164.

15

They Say, They Say, They Say:
Some New Voices of the Nineties

Michael Faherty

Recently, a hostile reviewer dismissed [my poetry] like this:

'His poems are not confessional, but it helps to think of a Confessional – a little box with a screen separating two parties. Think
of that screen as the page. A voice seems to come from behind
the screen, but if you read the poems aloud the only voice you
hear is your own.'

I can live with that.

Michael Donaghy[1]

Traditionally, the relationship between the reader of a poem and its
writer has been a rather intimate one. The writer tells us extremely
personal things about his or her life while we politely pretend not
to listen. Or, as John Stuart Mill suggested in the nineteenth century, it is the writer who pretends that we cannot hear him or her.
His argument went that while eloquence 'supposes an audience'
and can be said to be heard, 'the peculiarity of poetry appears to us
to lie in its utter unconsciousness of a listener' and can therefore be
said to be overheard. Where eloquence openly acknowledges its
intercourse with the outside world, poetry acts as if it does not
exist:

All poetry is of the nature of soliloquy. It may be said that poetry
which is printed on hot-pressed paper and sold at a bookseller's
shop, is a soliloquy in full dress, and on the stage. It is so; but
there is nothing absurd in the idea of such a mode of soliloquiz-

ing. What we have said to ourselves, we may tell to others afterwards; what we have said or done in solitude, we may voluntarily reproduce when we know that other eyes are upon us. But no trace of consciousness that any eyes are upon us must be visible in the work itself. The actor knows that there is an audience present; but if he acts as though he knew it, he acts ill.[2]

If this is the way writers ought to behave, there seems to be little question that the new poets of the nineties are acting very ill indeed. Not only do these writers act very much as if other eyes are fixed upon them, they often seem to prefer saying other characters' lines to their own. What was once a fairly straightforward and private affair has suddenly become a somewhat confusing and public one. Perhaps we should not be surprised then that the writers this new generation says it was weaned on were precisely those poets who did the most to make what was once so private so incredibly public, who pushed the intimate relationship between reader and writer to its limit, filling their poems with the sort of things you would not tell your dearest friend, much less the entire world.

The influence of the confessional poets on the contemporary poetry scene became abundantly clear during a number of events organised by the Poetry Society, particularly the Poets On Poets lecture series that took place in the winter of 1993–94 and the New Generation promotion the following spring. To what seemed somewhat general surprise, when these young poets were given the opportunity to speak on the poets of their choice, or simply asked to name some significant influences, the Americans quickly outnumbered their British and European counterparts. Poets as diverse as Simon Armitage, Elizabeth Garrett, Lavinia Greenlaw, Michael Hofmann, Kathleen Jamie, Sarah Maguire, Jamie McKendrick, Nuala Ní Dhomnaill, Don Paterson, Jo Shapcott and Matthew Sweeney all cited one or more of the confessional poets as playing an important role in the development of their work, with Elizabeth Bishop – the figure behind so much American verse in the fifties and sixties – receiving the most bends of the knee[3] Sarah Maguire is perhaps typical of these young British poets in that while she openly embraces the work of Bishop and Plath, her poetry does not, at least on first reading, seem to resemble theirs. As Maguire herself says, 'Some of my poems might well start from autobiographical events, but the formal demands of poetry mean they can't ever be "confessional"...There's no "me" you can know from my poetry.'[4] However, as Eavan Boland has noted, this may be the one great lesson everyone has learned from the extreme lyricism of the confessionals, the odd fact that the more we know their poetry, the less we feel we know the poets themselves. Boland says the strange effect is that it does not become easier to picture the speaker in the mind's eye, but considerably more difficult: 'They pose questions as to whether the self in their poems is invented or created, and force the reader to ask how much of the material is manipulated by being mediated through such a self'.[5] Lowell himself seemed very aware of this problem, pointing out that the more he tried to get 'the *real* Robert Lowell' into his work, the more he had to play with the poems:

> They're not always factually true. There's a good deal of tinkering with fact. You leave out a lot, and emphasize this and not that. Your actual experience is a complete flux. I've invented facts and changed things, and the whole balance of the poem was something invented. So there's a lot of artistry, I hope, in the poems. Yet there's this thing: if a poem is autobiographical – and this is true of any kind of autobiographical writing and historical writing – you want the reader to say, this is true.[6]

Even Plath – who appropriately insisted that her *Ariel* poems be read aloud rather than to oneself in the privacy of the armchair – warned practising poets not to misconstrue what confessional poetry was up to:

> I think my poems come immediately out of the sensuous and emotional experiences I have, but I must say I cannot sympathise with these cries from the heart that are informed by nothing except a needle or a knife or whatever it is. I believe that one should be able to control and manipulate experiences, even the most terrifying – like madness, being tortured, this kind of experience – and one should be able to manipulate these experiences with an informed and intelligent mind.[7]

The irony of confessional poetry, of course, is that the more 'real' the poets wanted the self to appear in the poetry, the more they were forced to make it up, to shape their private experiences into something more relevant to their readers. There is an unusual feeling in this poetry that the writer is being asked to play both the actor on stage speaking the lines and the audience in their seats listening carefully to them, asking themselves whether they find this particular version of the self convincing or not, whether they can imagine themselves in that particular costume and those particular shoes.

This is the same feeling that we get from so much contemporary British verse, particularly the work of poets like Simon Armitage whose renown, to some extent, is the result of a rather demanding schedule of public readings. There is a strong sense here that the writer is playing both actor and audience, consciously speaking the lines aloud to someone, and that that someone is often none other than the poet himself. Peter Forbes has called this style of writing 'stand-up pieces', no doubt thinking of texts like Armitage's series of short poems in *Book of Matches* that relies on the party game in which you are required to tell the story of your life in the space of a single match.[8] While Mill may have argued that 'the peculiarity of poetry appears to us to lie in the poet's utter unconsciousness of a listener,' Armitage says his experience is quite the reverse:

> For me, poetry has become a private thing, a dialogue between one part of myself and another. One informs and the other translates ... But at the same time, through wanting to publish poetry, put it on general release and make it public property, the process of writing is always consciously overseen or overheard. It's conspiratorial, but by definition it will always lead to the gallows or the stocks. It's bugged, and the person listening in is once again the author.[9]

In some of his poems, Armitage makes it clear that this style of writing owes a lot to the confessionals, whom he would like to think trusted that their audience was in on the joke the whole time, that they knew the things told in the poems had perhaps more to do with the public performance of telling such things than they did with any particular personal experience of them. His poem 'I Say I Say I Say' makes this point by putting a pseudo-confession on stage in the manner of stand-up comedy, turning on the spotlight, and filling the room with a relatively receptive audience:

> Anyone here had a go at themselves
> for a laugh? Anyone opened their wrists

with a blade in the bath? Those in the dark
at the back, listen hard. Those at the front
in the know, those of us who have, hand up,
let's show that inch of lacerated skin
between the forearm and the fist. Let's tell it
like it is: strong drink, a crimson tidemark
round the tub, a yard of lint, white towels
washed a dozen times, still pink. Tough luck.
A passion then for watches, bangles, cuffs.
A likely story: you were lashed by brambles
picking berries from the woods. Come clean, come good,
repeat with me the punch line 'Just like blood'
when those at the back rush forward to say
how a little love goes a long long long way.[10]

While Armitage himself has said in preface to reading this poem
that he sees no reason why the subject-matter of the sixties should
not still fit comfortably on stage in the nineties, it is clear that the
polemics of this text have more to do with the sixties' habit of
confusing the person saying the lines on stage with that same
person off stage. In fact, as the style of the poem itself suggests,
the audience is meant to say these lines together with the speaker,
hearing their voices as well as, if not louder than, his. As Armitage
has said about his recent work, 'Writing has become a way of
taking part without having to participate, and a way of being alone
without being lonely or broken hearted.'

Two other voices of the nineties whose work seems to have a
mixture of private rehearsal and public performance about it are
Carol Ann Duffy and Glyn Maxwell. Like Armitage, they write
poems that are highly dramatic, poems in which some sort of
monologue or dialogue is taking place although, once again, that
dialogue often seems to be largely with the self. In order to achieve
this, they make frequent use of the second person pronoun, speaking to a 'you' that is identifiable both as the speaker and as someone other than, or slightly detached from, the speaker. It almost
seems at times that this is the sort of practical technique one would
use in rough draft in order to achieve an effect of distance, but that
that technique has not been deleted from the version made available to the public, drawing attention to the creative process of
poetry as Bishop so often did, openly instructing herself halfway
through a stanza to 'Write it!' The other effect of using the second

person, of course, is to draw the reader into the poem, as if the text is addressed to us and talking about things we also have experience of. Maxwell's poem 'Dream but a Door' is a good example of this, at least for his male readers:

> Dream but a door slams then.
> Your waking is in the past. The friend
> who left was the last to leave and that
> left you, calm as a man.
>
> Wash in a slip of soap belonging
> only a week ago to a girl but
> yours now and washed to a nothing.
> As you and she, friends and not.
>
> Eat to the end as toast,
> the loaf she decided on, only last
> Saturday last. The crust is what
> you said you'd have. So have.
>
> Stop by the calendar, though,
> and peel. The colour today
> is yellow, and you will never remember
> what that means – 'J'.
>
> Drink to the deep the coffee, down
> to the well of the dark blue cup.
> The oaf with the nose of steam is alive
> and well again. Look up.[11]

For a flat with a sudden air of loneliness and abandonment about it, there seems to be an awful lot of voices rattling round here. While there is a natural tendency to read the poem as if the 'you' is our forsaken hero grumbling to himself on this particularly unpleasant morning, taking things step by step simply to get on with life, there is also a sense that the voice which commands him to do these everyday things has an authority and awareness about it that our 'oaf' does not yet possess. We get this very same sense of self speaking to self in the opening stanzas of Duffy's poem 'Adultery', though this time the experience may be more readily identifiable for female readers:

> Wear dark glasses in the rain.
> Regard what was unhurt

as though through a bruise.
Guilt. A sick, green tint.

New gloves, money tucked in the palms,
the handshake crackles. Hands
can do many things. Phone.
Open the wine. Wash themselves. Now

you are naked under your clothes all day,
slim with deceit. Only the once
brings you alone to your knees,
miming, more, more, older and sadder,

creative. Suck a lie with a hole in it
on the way home from a lethal, thrilling night
up against a wall, faster. Language
unpeels to a lost cry. You're a bastard.[12]

The voice speaking here is even more difficult to pin down than it
is in Maxwell's poem, since the 'you' in this text is not only the
voice of experience at one remove from all this pain as well as the
voice of inexperience feeling it with such incredible intensity, but
also the voices of the many who account for this long catalogue of
experiences, on whatever side of an adulterous relationship. As
with Maxwell, there is also the feel here of the poem putting itself
together, that Duffy is using the second person to interrogate the
first and make it commit its confessions to paper:

So write the script – illness and debt,
a ring thrown away in a garden
no moon can heal, your own words
commuting to bile in your mouth, terror –

and all for the same thing twice. And all
for the same thing twice. You did it.
What. Didn't you. Fuck. Fuck. No. That was
the wrong verb. This is only an abstract noun.

When questioned as to whether her use of the second person in
such poems was a calculated strategy to speak directly to the
reader, Duffy answered that it frankly had more to do with the
simple mechanics of putting a poem together: 'Not at the time of
writing the poem, which at that stage . . . is more of a dialogue with

myself. The "you" being perhaps the me that haunts the poem being addressed, or re-created, by the me who is recollecting in tranquillity. Afterwards, yes, I can see that "you" could tend to draw the reader into the poem'.[13] The problem, of course, is that while such a technique may help the writer write the poem, it does not necessarily help the reader read the poem. Part of the initial process of 'naturalising' the poem, to use Jonathan Culler's term, is finding the voice that fits the lines, but with poems such as these that voice often remains incredibly elusive. Perhaps our only certainty is that the voice should not be the poet's own since, as Duffy herself has said, that is the last place we will actually find her: 'I don't feel vulnerable or exposed in my poetry as I would in my diaries or letters. They are validated because they are ordinary feelings, so they become everyone's property.'[14]

A contemporary writer who has done as much as anyone to explore the elasticity of the poetic voice in the nineties is Jo Shapcott, who is just as comfortable speaking as a withering lettuce in the salad crisper of some carnivore's filthy refrigerator as she is writing an entire series of poems from the perspective of a mad cow. She not only enjoys giving voice to things that have previously been denied them, but she seems to suggest that the poetic persona should ideally be as flexible as a character in a cartoon. As with so many other poets currently writing, Shapcott plays both actor and audience, trying out a new voice while simultaneously listening to it and finding fault with it. This is particularly evident in a poem like 'Tom and Jerry Visit England', a text in which she gives the cartoon cat Tom a voice for the first time:

> O boy, I thought. A chance
> to visit England and O boy here, out
> of nowhere, a voice to describe it. Reader,
> I dreamt of coming back to tell you how I marched
> round the Tower of London, in a beefeater suit,
> swished my axe at Jerry, belted after him
> into the Bloody Tower, my back legs
> circling like windmills in a gale
> while ravens flapped around our heads.
> You would hear it all: tea with the Queen
> at Buckingham Palace and me scattering
> the cucumber sandwiches at the sight

of Jerry by the silver salver. I couldn't wait
for the gorgeous tableau: Queenie with her mouth
in a little shocked screaming shape, her crown
gone crooked as she stood cringing on the throne
with her skirts up round her knees, and Jerry
down there laughing by the footstool.
I would be a concertina zig-zag by that time
with a bone china cup stuffed in my face
and a floral tea pot shoved on my head so hard
my brains would form a spout and a handle
when it cracked and dropped off.[15]

Unfortunately, the poem itself cannot live up to the promise of its
title and all the things that we would hear and would see remain
no more than desires. While she may admire the abandon with
which the confessional poets threw themselves into their verse,
performing whatever contortions it seemed to require of them,
Shapcott finds that she has more in common with a pre-confes-
sional poet like Bishop, the writer that Seamus Heaney has called
the Cordelia figure of postwar poetry.[16] As the speaker confesses in
the following stanza, she too is more comfortable observing from
behind the curtains than on centre stage:

I can't get this new voice to explain to you
the ecstasy in the body when you fling
yourself into such mayhem, open yourself
to any shape at all and able to throw out
stars of pain for everyone to see.

This is a poem that, like the others, has a sort of rough draft feel
about it in that the reader is let in on the manner in which it was
made, its stops as well as its starts. Even the frustration the speaker
feels in the attempt to assume Tom's voice remains an essential
part of the final poem, finishing on a note of hesitation and resignation:

'Where's the mouse?' I tripped
over commas and colons hard like diamonds, looking
for him. 'Where's the mouse?' I kept asking,
'Where's the mouse?' I banged full face into a query –
and ended up with my front shaped

like a question mark for hours. That was scary:
I usually pop right back into myself in seconds.
So I hesitated for once before flinging myself
down the bumpy staircase where all the lines ended.
I went on my rear and at the bottom you would have seen me,
end up, bristling with splinters, and nose down
snuffling for any trace of mouse smell.

If Mill would accuse many of the nineties poets of 'acting ill', he might also accuse Shapcott of some rather poor judgement in casting. She seems to have deliberately chosen an American voice here that fits her British persona rather badly. As she points out in the poem, 'Cats prefer to skulk and sulk/in the dark, we prefer mystery/and slinking.' Ironically, what this text becomes is a somewhat confessional poem about the speaker's inability to write in the open style of the confessionals, adopting a voice that challenges her to live up to its reputation for unabashed public performance while using her language, particularly her tenses, to hold it back and prevent it from actually fulfilling its role.

Despite the apparent failure of this poem, Shapcott has achieved here what so many of her contemporaries have also achieved in their work. While participating in what has become the increasingly public business of British poetry, they have managed to create texts that work well on stage while somehow allowing the poets to remain very much off that stage watching, as it were, from the wings. They have done this, largely, by trying on voices, some which bear some resemblance to their own and some which clearly do not, some which tell of things that they may well have experienced and some which tell of things they certainly have not. It was almost inevitable, however, that this plethora of voices and experiences would cause some confusion among readers, wondering which voice to adopt for this poem and which to adopt for that. This is even more problematic with single texts that seem to contain a profusion of voices, each adequate and yet each giving the poem a slightly different spin. Perhaps not surprisingly, Boland says she had similar frustration when she first encountered Bishop's poetry, not knowing how to construct a consistent world around that elusive voice of hers:

No poet enters the life of another, whatever the disruptions of time and distance, through words alone. Poets imagine one another. They think and think until their own sense of the narrow streets of Florence explains the light and passion of the *Paradiso*... They imagine the cattle train bringing Mandelstam to Smirsk, and the cold library in London in which Yeats found it difficult to replace the heavy volumes on the shelf. It is hardly a pure critical process. All the same, I feel sure it is in these fires of rapport that poets have found and loved one another for a millennium. For all that, I have the greatest difficulty in reconstructing Elizabeth Bishop's life.... Being unsure how to place her, I had to rely on illicit critical methods to understand her: on snatches of comparison, modes of rapport which involved me trawling through my experience to understand hers.[17]

The sort of critical methods that were considered 'illicit' in Boland's early days as a young reader and writer have become, by necessity and the significant influence of Bishop herself, common critical practice in the reading of contemporary British poetry. What you often find in these texts is not so much the poet's experience as your own, not so much his or her voice as yours. While Mill seemed to suggest that the listener could sit comfortably back in his cushy seat while the poet took the stage, contemporary readers often find themselves suddenly in the spotlight, saying the lines, while the poet is nowhere to be seen, hidden well back in the dark.

Notes

1. Michael Donaghy's comment can be found in *Poetry Review*, Vol. 84, No. 1, 1994, p. 62.
2. John Stuart Mill, 'Thoughts on Poetry and Its Varieties', *Autobiography and Literary Essays*, eds John Robson and Jack Stillinger (Toronto: Toronto UP, 1981), pp. 348–9.
3. See the special issues of *Poetry Review* in volumes 83 and 84 focusing on these events.
4. Sarah Maguire's comment can be found in *Poetry Review*, Vol. 84, No. 1, 1994, p. 68.
5. Eavan Boland, 'Time, Memory and Obsession', *PN Review*, Vol. 18, No. 2, 1991, p. 20.
6. Robert Lowell, interview, in *Modern Poets on Modern Poetry*, ed. James Scully (London: Fontana, 1966), pp. 249–50.
7. Sylvia Plath's comment can be found in A. Alvarez, 'Sylvia Plath', *The Modern Poet: Essays from the Review*, ed. Ian Hamilton (London: MacDonald, 1968), p. 80.

8. Peter Forbes, 'Why the New Popular Poetry Makes More Sense', *Poetry Review*, Vol. 85, No. 3, 1995, p. 46.
9. Simon Armitage's comment can be found in *Poetry Review*, Vol. 84, No. 1, 1994, p. 8.
10. Armitage, *The Dead Sea Poems* (London: Faber, 1995), p. 9.
11. Glyn Maxwell, *Out of the Rain* (Newcastle upon Tyne: Bloodaxe Books, 1992), p. 65.
12. Carol Ann Duffy, *Mean Time* (London: Anvil, 1993), pp. 38–9.
13. Duffy, interview in *Verse*, Vol. 8, No. 2, 1991, p. 127.
14. Kate Kellaway, 'When the moon is an onion and the tree sings minims', *The Observer*, 20 June 1993.
15. Jo Shapcott, *Phrase Book* (Oxford: Oxford UP, 1992), pp. 3–4.
16. Seamus Heaney, 'Counting to a Hundred', *The Redress of Poetry* (London: Faber, 1995), pp. 164–85.
17. Boland, op. cit.

Index

Achebe, Chinua 5
Adcock, Fleur 239, 241, 242, 243, 245, 253–67 *passim*
Adorno, Theodor 14
Aesthetic autonomy 18
Alexander, Ian 203
Allnutt, Gillian 245, 248
Althusser, Louis 10, 83
Alvarez, A. 2
Alvi, Moniza 246
Angelou, Maya 242
Antheil, P. 26
Anthologies, politics of 237–52 *passim*
Archer, Nuala 245
Arendt, Hannah 72
Armitage, Simon 269, 271
Arnold, Matthew 17
Art: and poetry 9; and significance 12; and ideology 18
Ashbery, John 234
Auden, W. H. 234

Bacon, Francis 233
Bardic Cycles 143, 148
Bakhtin, Mikhail 23, 141, 226
and carnival 122
Bardwell, Lelan 246
Barrett Browning, Elizabeth 240
Barry, Peter 3
Barthes, Roland 10, 113, 115
Bartlett, Elizabeth 245
Bartok, Bela 26
Baudelaire, Charles 96, 154, 157
Beatles, The 3
Beauvoir, Simone de 98
Beckett, Samuel 227, 233
Beer, Patricia 244, 245
Belsey, Catherine 10
Benjamin, Walter 15, 63, 69, 72, 78, 83, 85
Berry, James 4
Bettelheim, Bruno 83

Bhatt, Sujata 246
Bishop, Elizabeth 242, 262, 269, 277, 278
Blackburn, John 213
Blake, William 9, 87, 144, 227
Blamires, David 24
Blok, Aleksandr 153
Bolland, Eavan 242, 245, 249, 270, 277, 278
Bohm, David 87, 88
Bone, James 10
Bonhoeffer, D. 234
Booth, Martin 3
Brackenbury, Alison 245
Brecht, Bertolt 11
Breeze, Jean 246
Britten, Benjamin 230
Brodsky, Joseph 112
Bonner, Stephen Eric 13
Brontë, Emily 262
Brooks, Gwendolyn 242
Bunting, Basil 23–32 *passim*
Burroughs, William 178
Byron, Catherine 135

Caedmon 29
Cage, John 178
Caird, James 144
Calvin 212
Campbell-Hay, George 156, 158
Canon, the 15, 16
Catullus 155
Cavalcanti, Guido 153
Clapton, Eric 29
Class: 9, 15, 48–9, 200, 208, 246, 256 and education 15; working 49, 66, 111
Clerk, Gillian 243, 245, 253–67 *passim*
Clough, Arthur 56
Coleridge, Samuel Taylor 17–19, 139
Consumerism 9
Conquest, Robert 2

Cope, Wendy 242, 245
Cornford, Frances 242
Cornford, John 149
Couzyn, Jeni 239
Crane, Hart 179
Crawford, Robert 179
Crichton-Smith, Ian 146, 156, 193–220 *passim*
Criticism 12, 14–15; moral and aesthetic 16–19
Culler, Jonathan 275
Culture Industry 14

Dada 3
Dante 176
Daryush, Elizabeth 242
Davie, George 144, 145
Davies, Hilary 248
Defamiliarisation 171
Derrida, Jacques 10, 11, 234
Dickinson, Emily 240
Différance 174
Donaghy, Michael 268
Donne, John 144, 244
Dooley, Maura 245
Doolittle, Hilda (H.D.) 240, 242
Dramatic monologue 246–7
Duffy, Carol Ann 245, 247–9, 272–5
Duncan, Robert 227
Dunmore, Helen 245
Dunn, Douglas 111
Dylan, Bob 3

Earle, Jean 245
Easthope, Antony 10
Eco, Umberto 5
Einstein, A. 234
Eliot, T.S. 4, 7, 23, 59, 111, 144, 190, 227, 234, 245
Empiricism 38–9, 41–2
Empirical reality 136
Empson, William 12
Existentialism 229, 234

Fainlight, Ruth 239, 266
Fanthorpe, V. A. 245
Feaver, Vicky 245
Feinstein, Elaine 239, 247, 266

Finnegan, Ruth 29
Forbes, Peter 271
Form 33–4, 45
Foucault, Michel 3, 10
France, Linda 237, 241, 243–6
Freud, S. 37, 40

Gaelic 143–69 *passim*
Garrett, Elizabeth 241, 269
Genet, Jean 179
Gender 237–67 *passim*
Gilbert, Sandra 240
Graves, Robert 98
Gray, Thomas 56
Green, Veronica 242
Greenlaw, Lavinia 241, 245, 248, 269
Guattari, Felix 111
Gubbert, Susan 240
Gysin, Brion 178

Haffenden, John 49, 52–5
Hampson, Robert 3
Hardy, Thomas 38, 51
Harrison, Tony 48–56, 60, 111
Heaney, Seamus 9, 98, 103–17, 125, 227, 276
Hegemony 72, 209–10
Heidegger, Martin 12, 103, 106–9, 113–14
Heraclitus 180
Higgins, F. R. 124
Higgins, Rita Ann 245, 248
Hill, Geoffrey 78, 49
Hill, Selima 242, 234, 245, 248
Hitler, Adolf 84
Hofmann, Michael 269
Horace 154
Hughes, Ted 23, 97–100, 103, 106, 221, 230
Hulme, T. E. 229
Hulse, Michael 2, 4

Identity 4–5, 124, 131, 136, 140, 246–7; national versus regional 118–69, *passim*, 193–220 *passim*, 245–6
Imagination 18–19, 118, 126, 134

Irony 5
Italian Futurism 178

Jacobite rebellion 147
Jakobson, Roman 89
Jamie, Kathleen 249, 265
Jennings, Elizabeth 239, 242, 245
Johnson, Samuel 17
Jones, David 23–27, 30
Jordan, June 242
Joseph, Jenny 239, 266
Joyce, James 112
Jung, Carl 98, 226

Kafka, Franz 171
Kaplan, Cora 247
Kavanagh, P. 111
Kay, Jackie 241, 245, 247
Kearney, Richard 103, 107–8
Keats, J. 52, 190, 205
Kennedy, David 2, 4
Kenner, Hugh 30
Kermode, Frank 17
Khalvati, Mimi 241, 246
Kristeva, Julia 27
Kruchonykh, Alexei 180
Kwesi Johnson, Linton 4

Labour government, 1945 44
Lacan, Jacques 10, 140–1
Langland, R. 29
Larkin, Philip 33–47 passim, 49, 205, 227, 256–7
Lawrence, D. H. 49, 96
Leavis, F. R. 2, 5, 10, 17, 30
Lenin, V. 144
Leonard, Tom 4
Levertov, Denise 239
Lévi-Strauss, C. 66
Linthwaite, Ilona 240
Literature 5, 127; challenge of 6; and life 16
Literary criticism 7
Lochhead, Liz 243, 245
Lomax, Marion 245
Lorca, F. 179
Lowell, Robert 270
Lucie-Smith, Edward 27

MacDiarmid, Hugh 145, 153, 191, 216, 219
Maclean, John 144, 203, 205–6
MacNeice, Louis 124
Macpherson, James 143
Maguire, Sarah 269
Makin, Peter 30
Mao Tse-tung 66
Marsh, Edward 49
Marvell, Andrew 93–4
Mathias, Roland 222
Mayakovsky, Vladimir 180
Maxwell, Glynn 272–4
McGuckian, Medbh 118–42, 242
McIntyre, Duncan 215, 218–19
McKendrick, Jamie 269
Meeham, Pauline 245
Messiaen, Olivier 26
Mew, Charlotte 242
Mill, John Stuart 268, 271, 277–8
Milosz, Czeslaw 112
Milton, J. 15, 27
Mitchell, Elma 245
Modernism 1, 26–7, 30; neo-modernism 23–4
Moltmann, Jurgen 229
Montefiore, Jan 242, 254
Moore, Marianne 242–3, 262
Morgan, Edwin 170–92, 212
Morley, David 2, 4
Morrison, Blake 2, 3, 118
Mother–daughter relationship 261
Motion, Andrew 2–3, 34–5, 40, 118
Mottram, Eric 2
Movement, the 1–3
Muldoon, Paul 118–42

New Poetry, The 2
New Lines 2
Neumann, Eric 98
Nicholson, Colin 4
Nicholson, Norman 3
Nichols, Grace 243, 246
Ní Chuilleanáin, Eiléan 245
Ní Dhomhnaill, Nuala 245, 269

O'Callaghan, Julie 245
Oedipus complex, the 41
Olsen, Tilly 240

Ong, Walter 29
Orwell, G. 84
Ostranenie 90
Ostriker, Alicia 241
Ovid 171
Owen, Wilfred 230

Pater, Walter 17
Paterson, Don 269
Paulin, Tom 10, 48, 118–42
Personnel management 16
Petrarch 153, 155
Piccolo, Lucio 97
Pitter, Ruth 245
Plath, Sylvia 233, 239–40, 242, 269–70
Poetry: as anthropology 105–12; and art 9; and being 226–32 *passim*; as bricolage 66–7; as business 277; and canon 15, 16, 237–52; as challenge 120, 141; and change 170; and class 9, 5, 15, 48–9, 53, 66, 111, 200, 208, 246, 256; as confession 268–71; concrete 3, 174–5, 177, 180; and concreteness 6, 8, 9, 130, 136; and consumer society 4, 8; and criticism 3–4; and desire 122–3; as disciplinary discourse 8; and emotion 33–4; and empiricism 38–9, 41–2; as enactment 6; as escape 127; and experience 13, 163; as feminine 137–9, 242–3; as feminist 237–67 *passim*; and form 13, 18, 45, 133–4, 135; and history 62–9, 75, 77, 79–80, 84, 103–7, 127, 129–30, 215; and identity 4–5, 124, 131, 136, 140, 246–7; as interrogation 121; love 14, 147–55, 159–61, 248; as message 170–92 *passim*; Metaphysical 224; and nationality 118–42 *passim*; and nature 38, 40, 110, 204, 226–7; and oral culture 29–30; performance 2, 3, 246, 272; and philistinism 2; and place 5,

25–7, 29, 103–6, 108–9, 128, 157, 210–11, 228; and pleasure 17–18; and politics 1–20, *passim*, 246; and popular music 3; and postmodern culture 5, 30, 234, 248; and postmodern philosophy 243; and post-structuralism 30, 244; and provincialism 2; public and private 41; and regional identity 118–169, *passim*, 193–220, *passim*, 245–6; and religion 228–36 *passim*; and representation 247; and resistance 8, 134, 138; and ritual 205; and sensuousness 13; and sexual politics 257–60; and sincerity 5–6; and significance 3, 8, 11–13, 16; and social stability 17; as sound 28–30; and Standard English 4, 243; and subjectivity 113–16, 245–6; and theory 10; as timeless 223–7 *passim*; and transformation 170–92 *passim*; and uniqueness 13–14; and utopia 9; visual 3; and voice 273–78 *passim*
Polk, Dora 225
Porteus, Katrina 245
Potter, Dennis 6
Pound, Ezra 7, 23–4, 144, 153, 191, 234
Pryor, Ruth 223
Pugh, Sheenagh 254–5

Reading, Peter 56–72
Redgrove, Peter 87–102
Raine, Craig 89–90
Raine, Kathleen 227–39
Reilly, Catherine 288
Rich, Adrienne 242
Richards, I. A. 6, 9, 17
Ricoeur, Paul 226
Ridler, Anne 242
Rimbaud, A. 157
Roberts, Michelle 245

Roethke, Theodore   222, 227
Romanticism   229
Ronsard, P.   153, 155
Ross, William   153
Rouse, Anne   246
Rumens, Carol   241, 243, 253–67
Russian Constructivism   178;
    Formalism   171, 180–1

Sackville-West, Vita   242
Salzman, Eva   241, 246
Scott, Diana   239
Scottish Renaissance
    movement   145
Sexual politics   257–60
Shakespeare   52, 170–1, 188
Shapcott, Jo   245, 249, 269, 275–7
Shelley, P.   9, 144, 188, 222, 224,
    234
Shklovsky, V.   114
Shuttle, Penelope   245
Skovell, E. J.   242, 245
Smith, Stevie   239, 242, 244, 262
Social Darwinism   195
Social realism   172
Spanish Civil War   145
Stainer, Pauline   245
Stalin, J.   84
Stevens, Wallace   96–7
Stevenson, Anne   239, 254
Stravinsky, I.   26
Surrealism   3
Symbolism   38, 157, 224
Synaesthesia   157, 224
Sweeney, Matthew   269

Tennyson, A. L.   51, 234
Thatcher, M.   10
Theory   10; and art   11, 19; and
    beauty   10; and careerism   11;
    conservative nature of   11–12;
    and 'resistance'   11–12; and
    Thatcherism   11–12

Thomas, Dylan   221–7
Thomas, R. S.   221–36
Thomson, Derick   143, 212
Thomson, James   156
Tomlinson, Charles   97
Townsend-Warner, Sylvia   239
Tradition   1, 4, 8, 13–16, 19–20, 40,
    46, 48, 108, 157, 238, 242;
    Aristocratic Anglo-Irish   105;
    British   181, 193; English   214;
    Gaelic   193–200;
    Metaphysical   221;
    Modernist   1–3; Movement
    1–3; Romantic   218, 221;
    Welsh   193–220

Uccello, P.   78

Valery, Paul   12
Value   10, 12, 242, 250
Value judgement   9, 12
Van Gogh, V.   217–218
Varèse, Edgar   26
Vendler, Helen   110
Voznesensky, A.   180, 190
Villon, F.   25

Wandor, Michelene   241
Watkins, Vernon   221–236
Whitman, Walt   179
Whyte, Christopher   179
Williams, Patrick   135
Wittgenstein, L.   234
Women: and difficulties of
    writing   262–3; and domestic
    life   256–7; poets   254–67; and
    politics of publishing   237–67
Wordsworth, William   1, 7, 9, 23,
    51–2, 144, 191, 228

Yeats, W. B.   24, 38, 105, 111, 153,
    172, 222, 242, 227
Yorke, Liz   243